C0-GGF-871

The Heritage of New York

THE HERITAGE OF

Historic-Landmark Plaques of the
New York Community Trust

Preface by Whitney North Seymour

NEW YORK

Fordham University Press
New York / 1970

Ref.
F
128.7
H47

First Published 1970 by Fordham University Press

© Copyright 1970 by Community Funds, Incorporated

Library of Congress Catalog Card Number: 69-13762

ISBN 0-8232-0825-7

Printed in the United States of America by
the Halliday Lithograph Corporation
West Hanover, Massachusetts

426911

The Landmarks Preservation Commission gratefully acknowledges the debt that the City owes to those public-spirited citizens who, in the last two decades, devoted their energies and resources to preserving the historic and architectural treasures of New York City. Without their devotion there would have been little left for the Commission to preserve when it came into existence in 1965.

The Community Trust has been in the forefront of those actively concerned with widening public appreciation of New York City's past. It is my feeling that this record of its accomplishment will be an inspiration to generations to come.

Harmon H. Goldstone
Chairman
Landmarks Preservation Commission

Contents

Preface by Whitney North Seymour xiii
Introduction xvii

Manhattan

1. American Academy of Dramatic Arts 4
2. American Fine Arts Society 6
3. American Museum of Natural History 8
4. Assay Office Building Façade 10
5. Association of the Bar of the City of New York 12
6. Astor Library 14
7. Audubon House 16
8. No. 70 Bedford Street 18
9. Bethesda Fountain and Terrace 20
10. Bowery Savings Bank 22
11. Bowling Green Fence 24
12. No. 901 Broadway 26
13. William Cullen Bryant Residence 28
14. Carnegie Hall 30
15. Carnegie House 32
16. Cartier Building 34
17. Cathedral Church of St. John the Divine 36
18. Central Savings Bank 38
19. Central Synagogue 40
20. Chelsea Hotel 42
21. Church Missions House 44
22. Church of St. Bernard 46
23. Church of St. Ignatius Loyola 48
24. Church of the Ascension 50
25. Church of the Heavenly Rest 52
26. Church of the Holy Apostles 54
27. Church of the Holy Communion 56
28. Church of the Holy Trinity 58

29. Church of the Incarnation 60
30. Church of the Sea and Land 62
31. Church of the Transfiguration 64
32. The Cloisters 66
33. Colonnade Row 68
34. Cooper Union 70
35. Cunard Building 72
36. Dakota Apartments 74
37. Dyckman House 76
38. East River Savings Bank 78
39. East 23rd Street Bath House 80
40. Evening Post Building 82
41. Federal Reserve Bank of New York 84
42. First National City Bank Building 86
43. First Presbyterian Church 88
44. Flatiron Building 90
45. General Theological Seminary, West Building 92
46. Grace Church 94
47. Gracie Mansion 96
48. Grand Central Terminal 98
49. Greenwich Savings Bank 100
50. Nos. 4-10 Grove Street 102
51. Guaranty Trust Company Building 104
52. The Harvard Club 106
53. Henry Street Settlement 108
54. President Herbert Hoover Residence 110
55. Institute of Fine Arts 112
56. Institute of Radio Engineers 114
57. Isaacs-Hendricks House 116
58. Jefferson Market Courthouse 118
59. John Street Methodist Church 120
60. Judson Memorial Church 122
61. Knickerbocker Club 124
62. Lotos Club 126
63. Lüchow's Restaurant 128
64. General Douglas MacArthur Residence 130
65. Metropolitan Club 132
66. Metropolitan Life Tower 134
67. Morris-Jumel Mansion 136

68. Municipal Building 138
69. National Arts Club 140
70. New York Academy of Medicine 142
71. New York Chamber of Commerce Building 144
72. New York County Court House 146
73. New York County Lawyers Association 148
74. New York Daily News Building 150
75. New York Life Building 152
76. New York Stock Exchange 154
77. New York Telephone Company Building 156
78. New York Yacht Club 158
79. Nine East 72nd Street 160
80. Old St. Patrick's Cathedral 162
81. Old St. Peter's Church 164
82. Park Avenue Christian Church 166
83. The Players 168
84. Plaza Hotel 170
85. Pulitzer Memorial Fountain 172
86. Regis High School 174
87. President Franklin D. Roosevelt Residence 176
88. Theodore Roosevelt Birthplace 178
89. St. Augustine's Chapel 180
90. St. James' Church 182
91. St. John's Evangelical Lutheran Church 184
92. St. Joseph's Church 186
93. St. Luke's Chapel 188
94. St. Nicholas Historic District 190
95. St. Paul's Chapel 192
96. St. Peter's Episcopal Church 194
97. St. Regis Hotel 196
98. St. Thomas Church 198
99. St. Vincent Ferrer Church 200
100. Salmagundi Club 202
101. Scribner Building 204
102. Serbian Cathedral Church of St. Sava 206
103. Seventh Regiment Armory 208
104. Spring Street Presbyterian Church 210
105. Temple Emanu-El 212
106. Tiffany and Company Stables 214

107. Times Tower 216
108. Treadwell Farm Historic District 218
109. Trinity Church 220
110. United States Custom House 222
111. University Club 224
112. Villard Mansion 226
113. Vincent Office Building 228
114. Wall of New Amsterdam 230
115. No. 22, Washington Square North 232
116. Watson House 234
117. West End Collegiate Church and Collegiate School 236
118. Woolworth Building 238
119. Yivo Institute for Jewish Research 240

Brooklyn

120. Brooklyn Borough Hall 244
121. Brooklyn Botanic Garden, Administration Building 246
122. Brooklyn Children's Museum 248
123. Brooklyn Ethical Culture School 250
124. Brooklyn Municipal Building 252
125. Brooklyn Museum 254
126. Christ Church 256
127. Church of the Saviour 258
128. Dutch Reformed Church of Flatlands 260
129. Erasmus Hall 262
130. Green-Wood Cemetery Gates 264
131. No. 131 Hicks Street 266
132. Hotel Margaret 268
133. Kings County Savings Bank 270
134. Lefferts Homestead 272
135. Litchfield Mansion 274
136. Long Island Historical Society 276
137. Manufacturers Hanover Trust Company 278
138. Montauk Club 280
139. New Utrecht Reformed Church 282
140. Our Lady of Lebanon R.C. Church 284
141. Packer Collegiate Institute 286

142. Plymouth Church of the Pilgrims 288
143. Prospect Park 290
144. St. Ann's Church 292
145. Schenck-Wyckoff House 294
146. United States Post Office 296
147. Johannes Van Nuyse House 298
148. Joost Van Nuyse House 300
149. Robert White House 302
150. Williamsburg Savings Bank 304
151. Nos. 2-8 Willow Place 306
152. Nos. 155-157-159 Willow Street 308
153. The Willows 310

The Bronx

154. Christ Church 314
155. Fonthill Castle 316
156. Fordham University Church 318
157. President John F. Kennedy Residence 320
158. Poe Cottage 322
159. Riverdale Presbyterian Church 324
160. St. Ann's Church of Morrisania 326
161. St. James Church 328
162. St. Peter's Church 330
163. Wave Hill 332

Staten Island

164. Alice Austen House 336
165. Biddle House 338
166. Billopp House 340
167. Cunard Hall 342
168. Original Moravian Church 344
169. Reformed Protestant Dutch Church 346
170. St. John's Church 348
171. St. Mary's Episcopal Church 350
172. St. Paul's Memorial Church 352
173. Voorlezer's House 354

Queens

174.	Bowne House	358
175.	First Presbyterian Church in Jamaica	360
176.	Lent Homestead	362
177.	Old Quaker Meeting House	364
178.	St. George's Church	366

Appendices

A. The Heritage Plaques	369
B. Sites	375
C. Existing Locations Not Illustrated	377
D. Location Maps	379
E. Picture Credits	391

Index 393

Borough Maps

Manhattan	2
Brooklyn	243
The Bronx	313
Staten Island	334
Queens	357

Walking-guide inside back cover

Preface

This book will appeal to old and new lovers of New York. Those who have long loved the great city will be reminded of some of its former and present architectural glories. Those who are seeing it for the first time will be pleased to discover the golden vein of treasure which can still be found in many places by those who seek it out. The structures which endure are worth knowing intimately because they have a quality of timeless beauty and illumine the life and taste of earlier generations—and thus are a revealing part of the history of the city and the human race.

The book stems from the efforts of many determined people to preserve that golden vein for posterity. There were many disappointing failures but also many triumphs, and out of them has come a new awareness of the values involved and the need to preserve them.

The Municipal Art Society—founded in 1892 with Richard Morris Hunt (perhaps best remembered as the Vanderbilts' architect) as its first president—has always crusaded for beauty in New York. It inspired and encouraged many lovely contributions to the city scene, including much of the art in the handsome Appellate Division Courthouse at 25th Street and Madison Avenue.

For many years, a part of its program was to try to preserve the most beautiful architecture of the past, while encouraging the architects of new buildings to combine artistic excellence with utility. The pressure for more offices and apartments, coupled with a commercial disdain for the decorative arts, led to the destruction of many fine buildings and their replacement with metal-and-glass substitutes of little, if any, distinction. A stroll down Park Avenue today tells the story: St. Bartholomew's, the Racquet and Tennis Club, and a few others remain to remind us of the Avenue's notable past; the Seagram Building is an oasis among the newcomers.

Rebelling at the dreary blandness of the new and the disregard of the need to preserve distinguished remnants of the past, the Society tried to mobilize opinion to help save the best of the remaining examples of the architecture of an earlier day. A Society show of photographs assembled over many years, held at the University Club some years ago, was already nostalgic because twenty per cent of the buildings shown were gone before the show opened. Many of the departed are to be seen in Nathan Silver's handsome *Lost New York*.* The Society began an *Index* of buildings of architectural importance

*Boston: Houghton Mifflin, 1967.

which ultimately appeared in several editions. This placed the buildings in categories, beginning with nine "of national importance which should be preserved at all costs."

Ralph Hayes, then the imaginative active, now the emeritus, director of the New York Community Trust, induced the Trust to furnish financial support for the Society's *Index*. More importantly, Ralph Hayes and the Community Trust proceeded to put flesh on the *Index* for the education and benefit of the public. A series of handsome plaques, originally designated "Landmarks of New York" and more recently "Heritage of New York," were placed on the buildings regarded as landmarks by the Society. The crisp and remarkably informative texts were prepared largely by architectural and historical experts. This book, referring to these plaques and the buildings involved, provides a fine guide to the beauties and history of New York.

Two other events deserve to be remembered in this connection. The year 1963 saw the publication of the beautiful *New York Landmarks*† by that fine architectural historian Alan Burnham. That the tide of destruction has not fully subsided is pointed up by the fact that, in the few years since publication, some of the fine buildings pictured have gone down: these include Pennsylvania Station, the Manhattan Club, the Singer Building, the old Times Tower, the Brokaw Mansion, and the old Black, Starr Building.

But Cassandra can no longer dominate the stage, because, inspired again largely by the Municipal Art Society but supported by many others, New York finally put its foot down in 1965 by establishing the Landmarks Preservation Commission. It thus followed New Orleans, Boston, Nantucket, and others in recognizing that the public has a stake in preserving architectural and historic treasures. As the law may properly protect against hazards to health, so it may also protect the community's architectural and historic heritage against unnecessary commercial vandalism. With James Grote Van Derpool as Executive Director and Alan Burnham his successor, and a small, dedicated staff, with a most distinguished Commission, initially under the chairmanship of Geoffrey Platt and now of Harmon H. Goldstone, the Landmarks Preservation Commission has already listed many important buildings and districts for preservation. While, under the law, such listings cannot provide absolute assurance of perpetuity, they do provide adequate opportunity for the sounding of alarms and the summoning of the help of concerned citizens before the wreckers can have their way unimpeded. The Commission is being upheld regularly in the courts. When a lower court

† Published by Wesleyan University Press, Middletown, Connecticut, this is a must for those who want handsome pictures and fuller descriptive text about the architecture of landmarks.

authorized the trustees of Sailor's Snug Harbor — a complex of fine Greek Revival buildings on Staten Island — to proceed with their destruction over the objection of the Commission, a large group of public-spirited lawyers recruited chiefly by Terence H. Benbow, Esq., of the Municipal Art Society (whom Mayor John V. Lindsay had the inspiration to appoint to the Commission) supported the Commission as *amici curiae*; the Appellate Division, First Department, reversed the decision.

The lesson of all this is that eternal vigilance is the price not only of liberty but of the maintenance of the quality of our cities and their treasures. While we know that our ghettos and the people who live in them have a very high priority in their calls upon all citizens, we should look forward to a day when those problems are nearing solution. Meanwhile, the amenities of life in the city should not be neglected, so that there are no lovely springs at which all citizens can refresh themselves. Beauty — not ugliness — must be available to lift the eyes and heart of those who live in and visit New York. If the past is prologue, its most beautiful and clear expressions must help us to understand and give noble dimensions to the present and the future. As Arnold Whitridge, the scholarly and well-loved former chairman of the Art Commission of the City of New York and trustee of the Metropolitan Museum of Art, wrote in the dedication of his fine biography *Rochambeau*: "To my grandchildren, in the hope that the present and the future, however engrossing, will not preclude a glance at the past."‡

Those who use this book to savor some of the flavor of New York history will be grateful to Fordham University Press and the others who laid the groundwork for and helped to make this attractive book available.

Whitney North Seymour

‡ New York: Macmillan, 1965.

Introduction

"'Twas the night before Christmas
And all through the house. . ."

Clement Clarke Moore may be remembered best as the author of *A Visit from St. Nicholas* of 1822, but he was actually one of the most distinguished citizens of old Chelsea when New York City was a collection of villages growing into neighborhoods. His family stemmed from a man who had arrived on the *Half Moon*; his father, despite his loyalty to King George III during the American Revolution, became rector of Trinity Church and, later, president of Columbia College. Clement Moore was an accomplished scholar and a student of the city. Some of the world he knew a century and a half ago in old New York may still be seen in the West Building of General Theological Seminary, erected on land which he donated, and in St. Peter's Episcopal Church, that hallmark of the Gothic Revival in American ecclesiastical architecture, built partially from his designs. He left his mark on old Chelsea.

Of such tales is the real New York made—tales multiplied many times over, as unfortunately too few people, even New Yorkers themselves, realize. In the midst of the dusty turmoil of summer or the windy hustle of winter, the old town still remains, to a degree, a collection of tiny communities. The New Yorker or the visitor need only look carefully to find Moore's Chelsea, Pierpont Morgan's Murray Hill, George Washington's Wall Street, or James Fenimore Cooper's Bowery—not to mention the later Chelsea of Thomas Wolfe, the newspaper offices and restaurants of Christopher Morley, or the homes, clubs, offices, shops, and taverns of millions of lesser lights who, from generation to generation, somehow manage to keep the whole concern going.

Admittedly, the search is frequently not an easy one. Many buildings of importance or just of charm have been destroyed, and many others have been hidden behind the hardware of advertising; the diversions of street level are often strong enough to keep us from looking above the glass and lights of the ground floors. But, whether by design or by chance, many historic structures have been preserved for the education and pleasure of later generations.

Appearances would indicate that demolition and rebuilding have continued over the years in New York with little or no effective opposition from conservation-minded citizens or groups. While it is certainly true that far too much has been destroyed, it should be stated that many individuals felt the loss which the leveling of fine old buildings caused to the aesthetic life of the city. One problem was the difficulty in organizing this desire to conserve the city's treasures and in finding persons of sufficient public influence to turn these feelings into effective action. When sufficiently influential opinion was organized, its effects were soon felt.

Now, at the beginning of the 1970s, this tide of unimpeded destruction has in some cases been stemmed, and in a few cases has been stopped altogether. Success in this work has been hard-won, and only in the very recent past at that. What success has been achieved is the result of the cooperative efforts of many people within and without the city. Yet, the primary encouragement to many of these people was the first appearance of the plaques which are illustrated in this volume. Once someone actually did something concrete and produced tangible evidence of a desire to protect New York's landmarks in a way that all could see, others were encouraged to make their own feelings known.

There was a precedent for this work in London, where a similar undertaking, begun in 1825 under the aegis of the Royal Society, was later made an official activity of the London County Council. It was in 1956 that the New York Community Trust, the community foundation of New York City, began preparatory work on the landmarks project. The program was announced on March 3, 1957, as a memorial to Andrew C. McKenzie, a prominent Brooklyn architect who had died in 1926 (his work included the old Times Tower); his widow, Isabel C. McKenzie, had left a fund to the Community Trust on her death in 1951, and, as she shared her husband's interests in the architectural field, this landmark-designation project was felt to be a fitting tribute to the McKenzies and a singularly apt use of the fund bearing their name.

The first twenty plaques were unveiled at an inaugural luncheon held at the Waldorf-Astoria Hotel on November 21, 1957. The speakers included Bernard Gimbel who expressed his conviction that the plaques would be an asset to all four types of New Yorkers: "to natives, to commuters, to migrants, and to transients." Like most of those which were to follow, the first plaques were selected on the basis of the *Index of Architecturally Historic Structures* —a list of some 300 structures whose preservation is regarded as of great importance—published the previous January by the Municipal Art Society with the aid of a grant from the Community Trust. (It is not without significance that, during the time the *Index* was in preparation, one-fifth of the buildings to be included were razed.) Representatives of the Society of

Architectural Historians and of the Art Commission of the City of New York were consulted prior to the adoption of a standard form of marker: a bronze or aluminum hand-tooled rectangular plaque chemically treated to mark the passage of time without itself becoming a victim of time. Locations were selected primarily from the *Index*, and the inscriptions for the plaques were adopted after being reviewed by a committee of historians affiliated with the Department of History of New York University and with the Museum of the City of New York, as well as by others from the organizations already mentioned.

The plaques originally bore the general title "Landmarks of New York." However, in 1962 Mayor Robert F. Wagner appointed a committee to study landmark legislation. As a result of the work of this committee, the Landmarks Preservation Commission of the City of New York was legally established in 1965. In Mayor John V. Lindsay's reorganization of the city government, the Landmarks Preservation Commission was made a part of the Parks, Recreation and Cultural Affairs Administration.

Since it appeared likely that confusion about the plaques' origin might arise, their title was changed to "Heritage of New York." Cooperation between the official city agency and the non-governmental though public-spirited Community Trust has grown increasingly close.

By 1969 it became apparent that the objectives of the plaque program of the New York Community Trust were fully parallel with those of the Landmarks Preservation Commission. The organizations thereupon agreed to merge their efforts, with the Community Trust providing future plaques for the buildings that the Landmarks Preservation Commission officially designates. The Commission is responsible for drafting the plaque texts. These new plaques all bear the New York City seal and the words "Designated Landmark — New York City." Furthermore, in the case of buildings which are officially designated landmarks and which have already been marked by Community Trust plaques, a similar official medallion and seal will eventually be installed above each of the existing plaques. In this way, the Community Trust will be able to continue its program of public education, and, by cooperating with the Landmarks Preservation Commission, lend valuable support to the work of this agency.

Before the new program becomes fully launched it seems appropriate to review what has already been accomplished. By the end of 1968 (the terminal date of the designations preserved here and the last full year of the Community Trust's independent program), two hundred and twelve locations had received one of the Trust's plaques, as listed in Appendix A.* One hundred and seventy-eight of these locations have been illustrated, and, unless otherwise designated, the photographs have been taken within the last few years. The remaining locations which have not been or could not be illustrated are arranged in Appendices B and C.

The Heritage of New York is intended to be a permanent pictorial and written record of the first twelve years' work of the Community Trust in a project which has itself become a contribution to the cultural history of New York. These plaques make it possible for even the casually interested passerby to acquire a knowledge of historically important buildings. For example, the plaque on the Billopp House in Staten Island commemorates the conference at which Benjamin Franklin and John Adams met with Lord Howe in a vain attempt to halt the American Revolution. On a larger scale, entire neighborhoods which have been designated historic districts may be visited. In these areas of the city, the viewer can get a vibrant picture of the harmonious variety which earlier generations built into their communities—such as the St. Nicholas, Treadwell Farm, and Greenwich Village districts in Manhattan, and Brooklyn Heights in the borough of homes and churches.

Many important structures continue to be torn down, and one need look no further than the present volume for proof of this unhappy fact. Within the very recent past, however, there have been encouraging signs that the aesthetic progress of artistic conservation has been overcoming the commercial progress of demolition. Even so, much has been destroyed that should have been preserved to offer the city beauty, history, and a feeling for tradition which would make it, in Henry Hudson's words to the Dutch East India Company in 1609, "a good land to fall in with and a pleasant place to see." In the vanguard of this conservation movement is, of course, the Landmarks Preservation Commission.

There are also other ambitious undertakings in the city which deserve to be singled out for their enthusiasm and vision—the Richmondtown Restoration project of the Staten Island Historical Society and the New York City Department of Parks, gathering and refurbishing the architecture and artifacts of three centuries of community life, now brought together in a green valley in the center of Staten Island; and the South Street Seaport project on Fulton Street in lower Manhattan. This project is recreating the nineteenth-century waterfront south of the Brooklyn Bridge when Manhattan's East River pierline was a forest of masts and rigging.

---

* Two Manhattan locations marked in 1969 before the Commission undertook the selection of locations, but not included in this volume, are the Appellate Division of the Supreme Court at 27 Madison Avenue, and the Junior League of the City of New York at 130 East 80th Street.

If *The Heritage of New York* serves to increase your enjoyment of the rich legacy of this city, its purpose will have been fulfilled. The practical goal which the instigators of this landmarks project set themselves—the appreciation and enjoyment by New Yorkers of their home—has been well expressed by Ralph Hayes, first Director of the New York Community Trust and the project's most vigorous proponent: "What in modest measure this landmark plan can hope to do is to seize upon our heritage of historical and structural and cultural lore, and, by these plaques, spell out some fragments of our past upon the very walls wherein that past took shape. Along the sidewalks of New York, these vignettes can one day tell the stirring story of our town."

A Note on the Arrangement

The Heritage Plaques with their buildings and monuments are arranged alphabetically within the respective boroughs, the sequence reflecting the number of plaques in each borough. Each group of photographs for one borough is preceded by a map of the entire borough. On the borough maps, the numbered shaded areas indicate the sections depicted in detail on the similarly numbered location maps (see Appendix D), pinpointing the exact street location of each historic structure. A separate walking-guide incorporating all the maps will be found in a pocket inside the back cover.

The Heritage of New York

Manhattan

MANHATTAN (NORTH HALF)

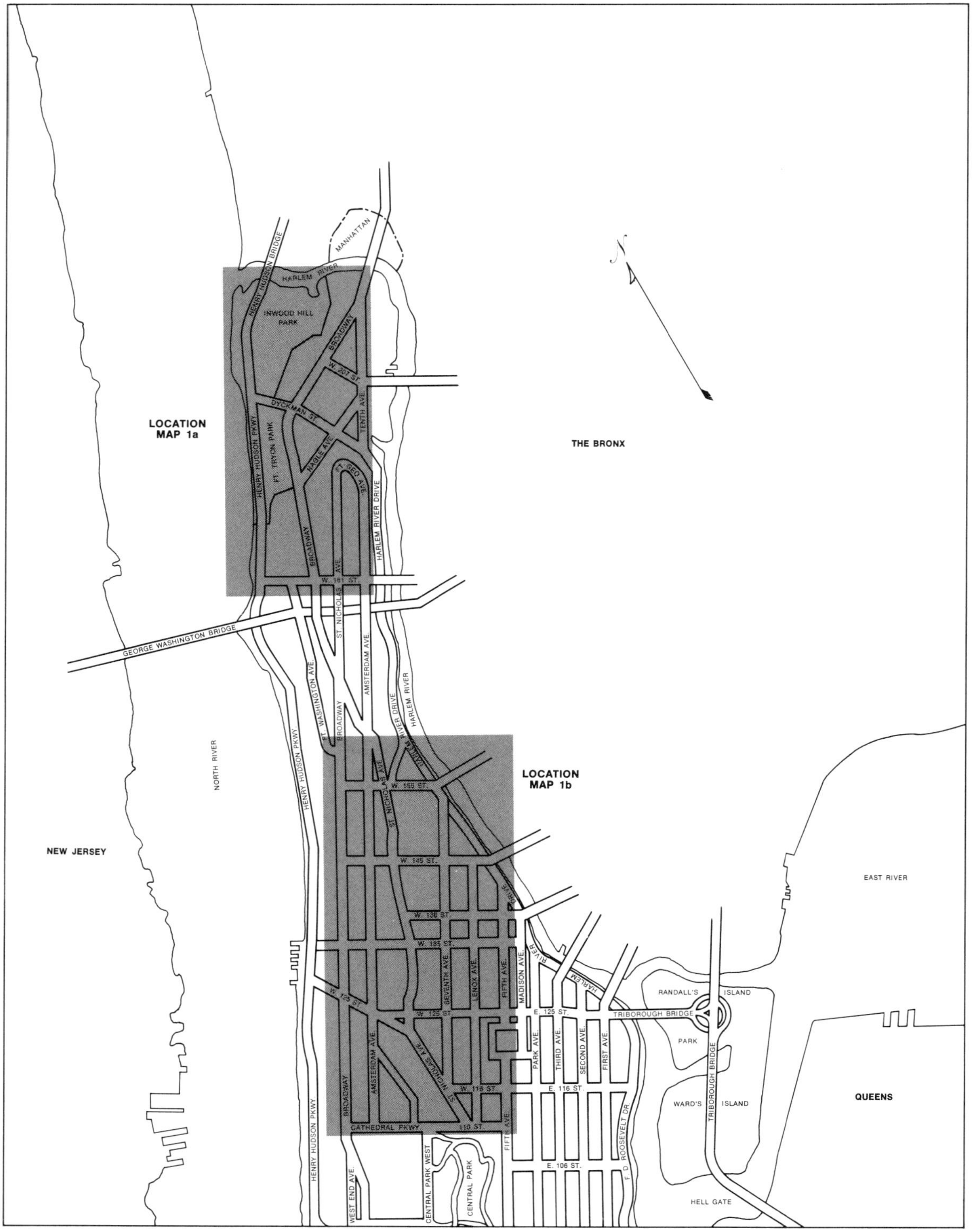

LOCATION
MAP 1a
LOCATION
MAP 1b
THE BRONX
NEW JERSEY
QUEENS
EAST RIVER
NORTH RIVER
HARLEM RIVER
MANHATTAN
INWOOD HILL
PARK
HENRY HUDSON BRIDGE
BROADWAY
W. 207 ST.
DYCKMAN ST.
TENTH AVE.
HENRY HUDSON PKWY.
FT. TRYON PARK
NAGLE AVE.
FT. GEO AVE.
HARLEM RIVER DRIVE
ST. NICHOLAS AVE.
W. 181 ST.
GEORGE WASHINGTON BRIDGE
AMSTERDAM AVE.
FT. WASHINGTON AVE.
W. 155 ST.
W. 145 ST.
W. 138 ST.
W. 135 ST.
W. 125 ST.
SEVENTH AVE.
LENOX AVE.
FIFTH AVE.
MADISON AVE.
E. 125 ST.
PARK AVE.
THIRD AVE.
SECOND AVE.
FIRST AVE.
TRIBOROUGH BRIDGE
RANDALL'S
ISLAND
PARK
WARD'S
ISLAND
W. 116 ST.
E. 116 ST.
CATHEDRAL PKWY
110 ST.
F. D. ROOSEVELT DR.
E. 106 ST.
HELL GATE
WEST END AVE.
CENTRAL PARK WEST
CENTRAL PARK

MANHATTAN (SOUTH HALF)

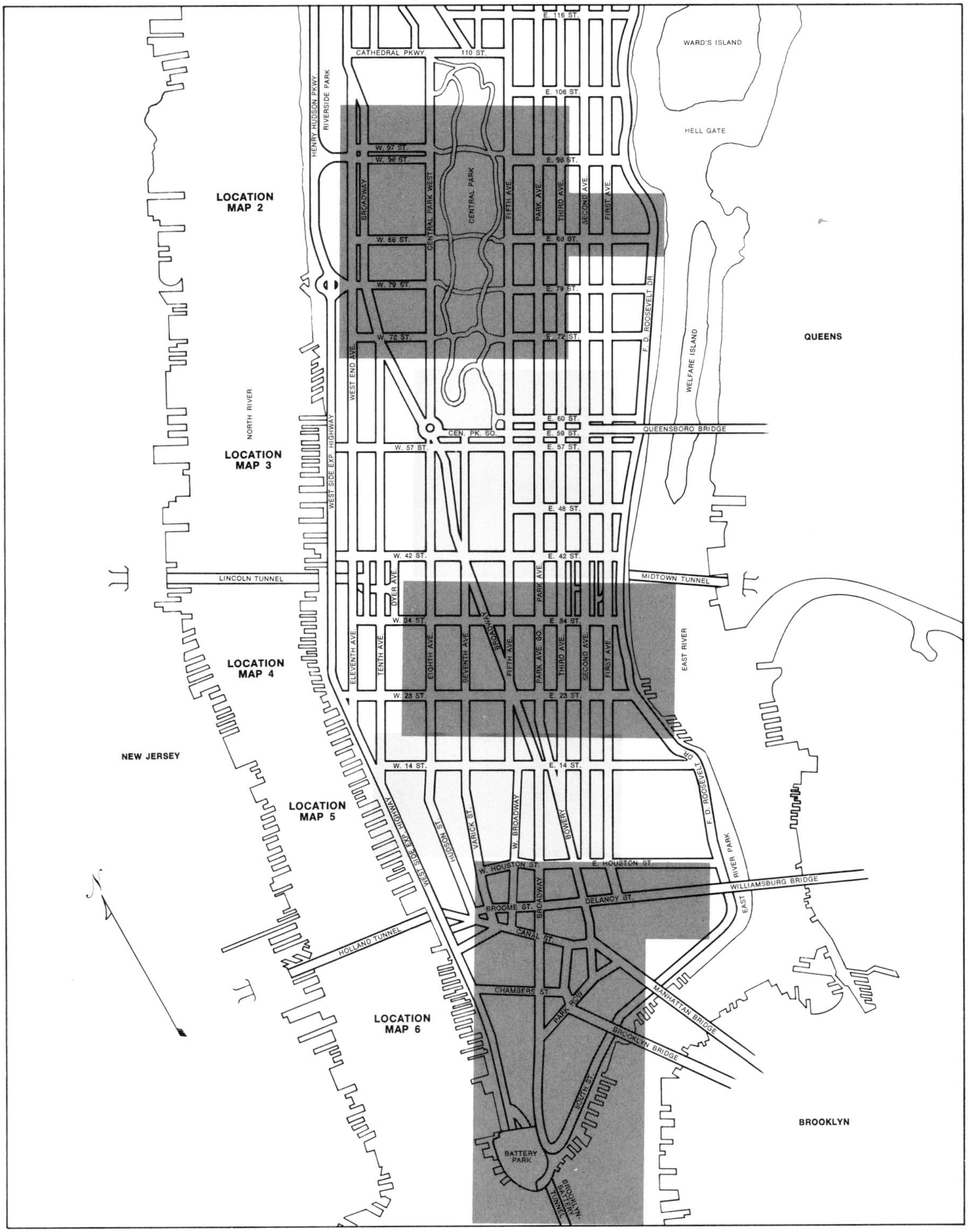
E. 116 ST.
WARD'S ISLAND
CATHEDRAL PKWY.
110 ST.
HENRY HUDSON PKWY.
RIVERSIDE PARK
E. 106 ST.
HELL GATE
W. 97 ST.
W. 96 ST.
E. 96 ST.
LOCATION MAP 2
BROADWAY
CENTRAL PARK WEST
CENTRAL PARK
FIFTH AVE.
PARK AVE.
THIRD AVE.
SECOND AVE.
FIRST AVE.
W. 86 ST.
E. 86 ST.
W. 79 ST.
E. 79 ST.
F. D. ROOSEVELT DR.
W. 72 ST.
E. 72 ST.
QUEENS
WELFARE ISLAND
WEST END AVE.
NORTH RIVER
E. 60 ST.
CEN. PK. SO.
E. 59 ST.
QUEENSBORO BRIDGE
W. 57 ST.
E. 57 ST.
LOCATION MAP 3
WEST SIDE EXP. HIGHWAY
E. 48 ST.
W. 42 ST.
E. 42 ST.
LINCOLN TUNNEL
MIDTOWN TUNNEL
DYER AVE.
W. 34 ST.
E. 34 ST.
LOCATION MAP 4
ELEVENTH AVE.
TENTH AVE.
EIGHTH AVE.
SEVENTH AVE.
BROADWAY
FIFTH AVE.
PARK AVE. SO.
THIRD AVE.
SECOND AVE.
FIRST AVE.
EAST RIVER
W. 23 ST.
E. 23 ST.
NEW JERSEY
W. 14 ST.
E. 14 ST.
LOCATION MAP 5
WEST SIDE EXP. HIGHWAY
HUDSON ST.
VARICK ST.
W. BROADWAY
BOWERY
F. D. ROOSEVELT DR.
EAST RIVER PARK
W. HOUSTON ST.
E. HOUSTON ST.
WILLIAMSBURG BRIDGE
BROOME ST.
BROADWAY
DELANCY ST.
HOLLAND TUNNEL
CANAL ST.
CHAMBERS ST.
PARK ROW
MANHATTAN BRIDGE
LOCATION MAP 6
BROOKLYN BRIDGE
SOUTH ST.
BROOKLYN
BATTERY PARK
BROOKLYN-BATTERY TUNNEL

1
American Academy of Dramatic Arts
120 Madison Avenue (30th Street)
Manhattan

LANDMARKS OF NEW YORK
AMERICAN ACADEMY OF DRAMATIC ARTS
CONSTRUCTED IN 1907, THIS WAS THE ORIGINAL HOME OF THE COLONY CLUB. STANFORD WHITE WAS THE ARCHITECT AND ELSIE DE WOLFE THE INTERIOR DECORATOR. IN 1963, THE BUILDING WAS ACQUIRED BY THE AMERICAN ACADEMY OF DRAMATIC ARTS, FOUNDED IN 1884 BY FRANKLIN HAVEN SARGENT.
PLAQUE ERECTED 1964 BY
THE NEW YORK COMMUNITY TRUST

VIP 120 VIP

2

American Fine Arts Society

215 West 57th Street (7th Avenue)

Manhattan

LANDMARKS OF NEW YORK
AMERICAN FINE ARTS SOCIETY
THIS BUILDING IN THE FRENCH RENAISSANCE STYLE, AN ADAPTATION BY HENRY J. HARDENBERGH OF A FRANCIS I HOUSE, WAS COMPLETED IN 1892 FOR THE SOCIETY WHICH INCLUDED THE ARCHITECTURAL LEAGUE OF NEW YORK, THE SOCIETY OF AMERICAN ARTISTS, AND THE ART STUDENTS' LEAGUE OF NEW YORK.
PLAQUE ERECTED 1958 BY
THE NEW YORK COMMUNITY TRUST

EXCELSIOR SAVINGS BANK

3

American Museum of Natural History

West 77th Street Façade
Central Park West and 77th Street
Manhattan

LANDMARKS OF NEW YORK
AMERICAN MUSEUM OF NATURAL HISTORY
FOUNDED IN 1869, THIS INSTITUTION HOUSES NOTABLE COLLECTIONS OF EXHIBITS IN ALMOST EVERY BRANCH OF NATURAL SCIENCE. THE CORNERSTONE OF THE FIRST BUILDING, DESIGNED BY J. C. CADY & COMPANY AND FACING 77TH STREET, WAS LAID BY PRESIDENT ULYSSES S. GRANT IN 1874 AND PRESIDENT RUTHERFORD B. HAYES OFFICIATED AT ITS FORMAL OPENING IN 1877.
THE NEW YORK COMMUNITY TRUST

4

Assay Office Building Façade

Metropolitan Museum of Art, American Wing
Fifth Avenue and 82nd Street
Manhattan

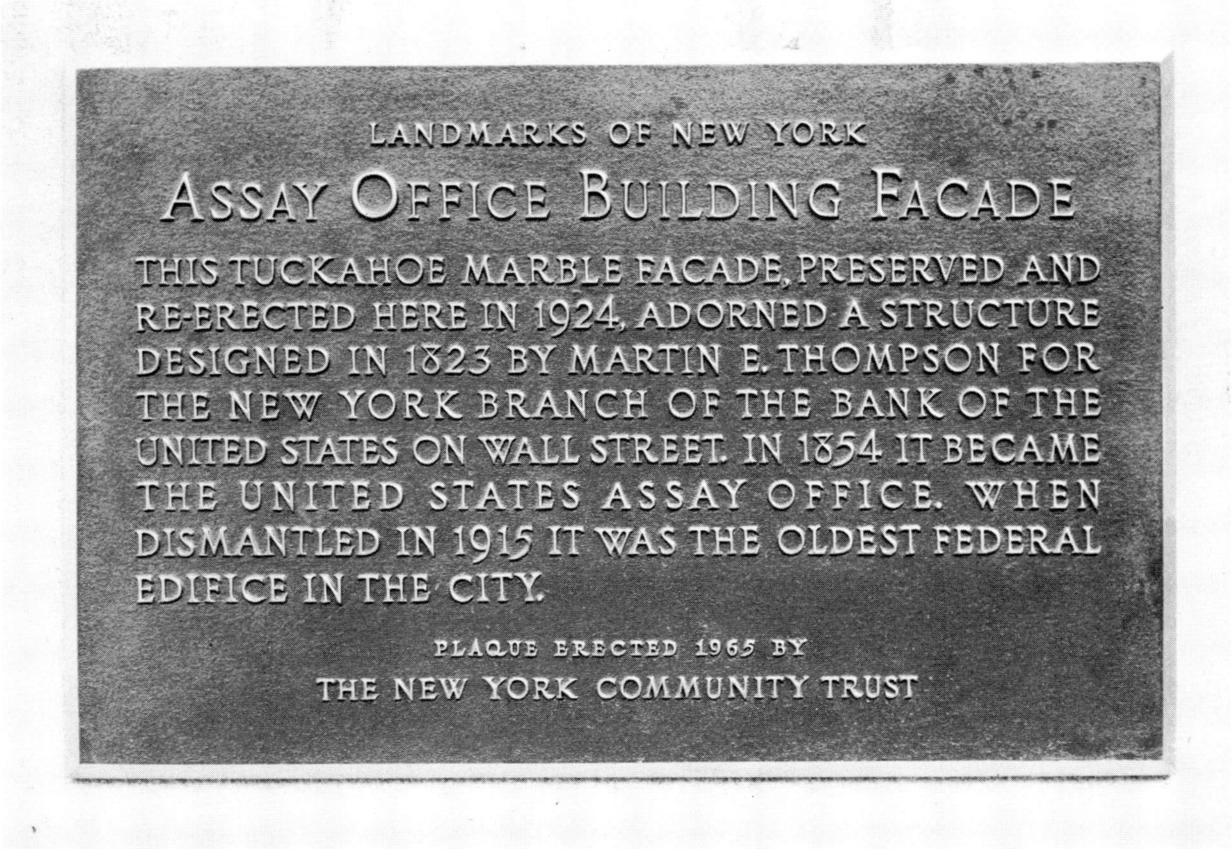
LANDMARKS OF NEW YORK
ASSAY OFFICE BUILDING FACADE
THIS TUCKAHOE MARBLE FACADE, PRESERVED AND RE-ERECTED HERE IN 1924, ADORNED A STRUCTURE DESIGNED IN 1823 BY MARTIN E. THOMPSON FOR THE NEW YORK BRANCH OF THE BANK OF THE UNITED STATES ON WALL STREET. IN 1854 IT BECAME THE UNITED STATES ASSAY OFFICE. WHEN DISMANTLED IN 1915 IT WAS THE OLDEST FEDERAL EDIFICE IN THE CITY.
PLAQUE ERECTED 1965 BY
THE NEW YORK COMMUNITY TRUST

5

Association of the Bar of the City of New York

42 West 44th Street (5th Avenue)

Manhattan

LANDMARKS OF NEW YORK
THE ASSOCIATION OF THE BAR
OF THE CITY OF NEW YORK
DESIGNED BY CYRUS L.W. EIDLITZ IN CLASSICAL
STYLE. THIS BUILDING OF INDIANA LIMESTONE
AND MARBLE WAS COMPLETED IN 1896. THE
ASSOCIATION, ORGANIZED IN 1870, HERE DIRECTS
ITS PROFESSIONAL AND PUBLIC ACTIVITIES AND
MAINTAINS ONE OF THE LARGEST LAW LIBRARIES
IN THE COUNTRY.
PLAQUE ERECTED 1960 BY
THE NEW YORK COMMUNITY TRUST

BAR·BUILDING·
BAR
FIGHT CANCER
DESKS
HOTEL ROYALTON
TAXI

6

Astor Library

425 Lafayette Street (Astor Place)

Manhattan

"HERITAGE OF NEW YORK"
ASTOR LIBRARY
THIS ITALIANATE STRUCTURE, BEGUN IN 1849 AND COMPLETED IN 1881, WAS BUILT BY JOHN JACOB ASTOR, WHOSE SONS LATER ADDED THE NORTH AND CENTER SECTIONS. THREE ARCHITECTS CONTRIBUTED TO ITS DESIGN: ALEXANDER SAELTZER (SOUTH WING, 1849-1853); GRIFFITH THOMAS (CENTER SECTION, 1856-1859); AND THOMAS STENT (NORTH WING, 1879-1881). ORIGINALLY THE CITY'S FIRST MAJOR LIBRARY BROADLY ACCESSIBLE TO THE PUBLIC, THE ASTOR COLLECTION WAS COMBINED WITH THE TILDEN TRUST AND THE LENOX LIBRARY IN 1912 TO FORM THE NUCLEUS OF THE NEW YORK PUBLIC LIBRARY.
PLAQUE ERECTED 1967 BY
THE NEW YORK COMMUNITY TRUST

DRIVEWAY
NO PARKING

7

Audubon House (former Willard Straight Residence)

1130 Fifth Avenue (94th Street)
Manhattan

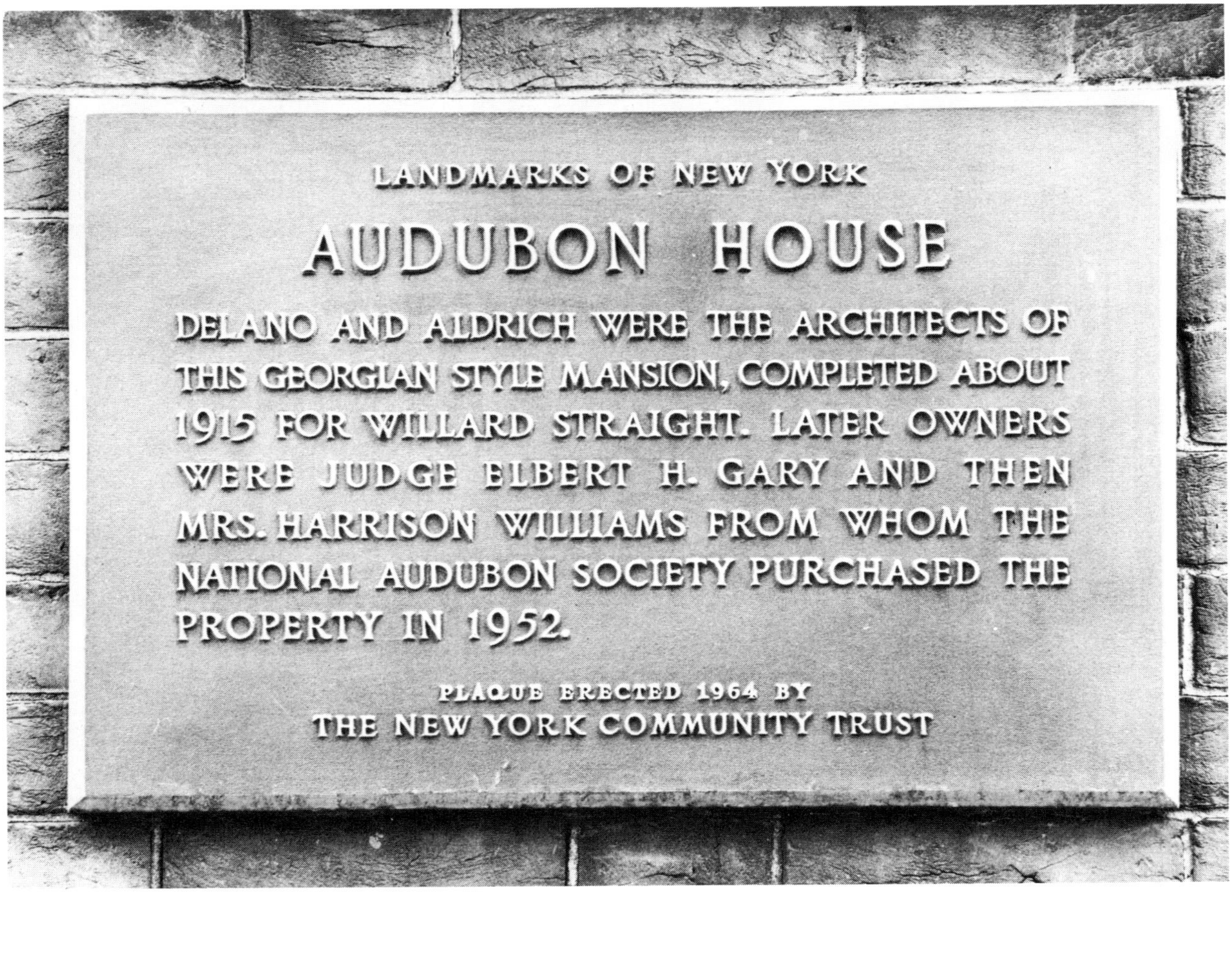
LANDMARKS OF NEW YORK
AUDUBON HOUSE
DELANO AND ALDRICH WERE THE ARCHITECTS OF THIS GEORGIAN STYLE MANSION, COMPLETED ABOUT 1915 FOR WILLARD STRAIGHT. LATER OWNERS WERE JUDGE ELBERT H. GARY AND THEN MRS. HARRISON WILLIAMS FROM WHOM THE NATIONAL AUDUBON SOCIETY PURCHASED THE PROPERTY IN 1952.
PLAQUE ERECTED 1964 BY
THE NEW YORK COMMUNITY TRUST

E 94 ST
SCHOOL
CROSSING
STOP
HERE ON
RED
SIGNAL

8

No. 70 Bedford Street

near Commerce Street, Greenwich Village
Manhattan

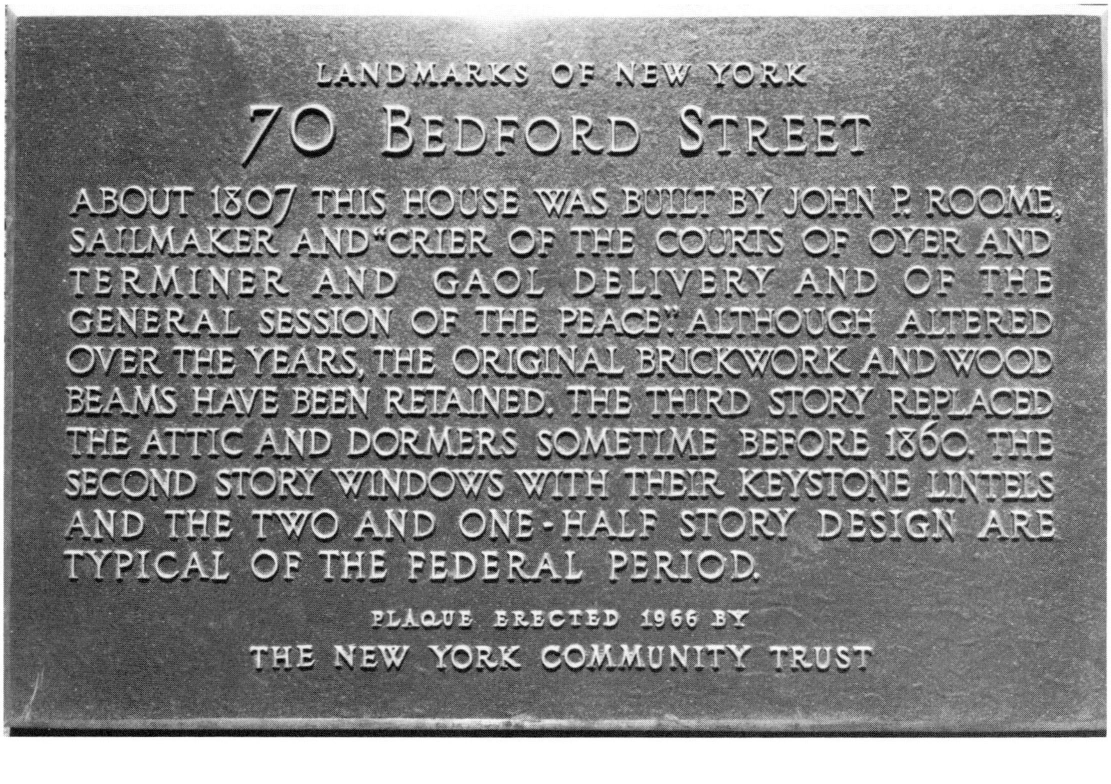
LANDMARKS OF NEW YORK
70 BEDFORD STREET
ABOUT 1807 THIS HOUSE WAS BUILT BY JOHN P. ROOME, SAILMAKER AND "CRIER OF THE COURTS OF OYER AND TERMINER AND GAOL DELIVERY AND OF THE GENERAL SESSION OF THE PEACE." ALTHOUGH ALTERED OVER THE YEARS, THE ORIGINAL BRICKWORK AND WOOD BEAMS HAVE BEEN RETAINED. THE THIRD STORY REPLACED THE ATTIC AND DORMERS SOMETIME BEFORE 1860. THE SECOND STORY WINDOWS WITH THEIR KEYSTONE LINTELS AND THE TWO AND ONE-HALF STORY DESIGN ARE TYPICAL OF THE FEDERAL PERIOD.
PLAQUE ERECTED 1966 BY
THE NEW YORK COMMUNITY TRUST

9

Bethesda Fountain and Terrace

Central Park (5th Avenue and 72nd Street)
Manhattan

LANDMARKS OF NEW YORK
BETHESDA FOUNTAIN AND TERRACE
DESIGNED BY CALVERT VAUX AND JACOB WREY MOULD, THESE STAIRWAYS, TERRACE AND FOUNTAIN WERE FOCAL FEATURES OF THE ORIGINAL PLAN FOR CENTRAL PARK BY VAUX AND FREDERICK LAW OLMSTED. THE FOUNTAIN SCULPTURE BY EMMA STEBBINS, INSPIRED BY THE BIBLICAL ACCOUNT OF THE MIRACULOUS POOL OF BETHESDA, WAS INSTALLED IN 1873.
PLAQUE ERECTED 1965 BY
THE NEW YORK COMMUNITY TRUST

1894

10
Bowery Savings Bank Building
110 East 42nd Street (Park Avenue)
Manhattan

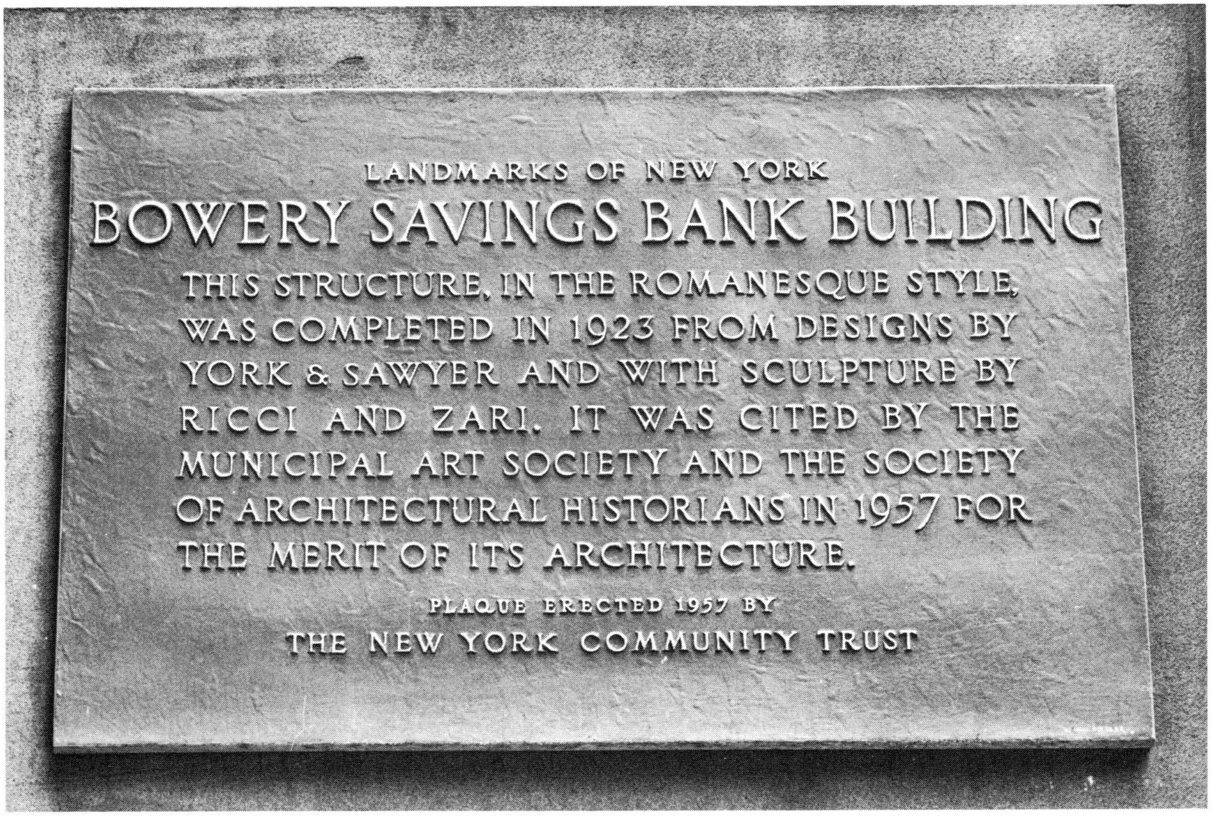
LANDMARKS OF NEW YORK
BOWERY SAVINGS BANK BUILDING
THIS STRUCTURE, IN THE ROMANESQUE STYLE, WAS COMPLETED IN 1923 FROM DESIGNS BY YORK & SAWYER AND WITH SCULPTURE BY RICCI AND ZARI. IT WAS CITED BY THE MUNICIPAL ART SOCIETY AND THE SOCIETY OF ARCHITECTURAL HISTORIANS IN 1957 FOR THE MERIT OF ITS ARCHITECTURE.
PLAQUE ERECTED 1957 BY
THE NEW YORK COMMUNITY TRUST

Sterling National Bank
& Trust Company
aliant

11

Bowling Green Fence

Broadway, Battery Place, State and Whitehall Streets

Manhattan

LANDMARKS OF NEW YORK
BOWLING GREEN FENCE
ERECTED BY THE COMMON COUNCIL IN 1771, THIS FENCE SURROUNDS NEW YORK'S EARLIEST PARK. THE PARK WAS LEASED IN 1733 FOR USE AS A BOWLING GREEN AT A RENTAL OF ONE PEPPERCORN A YEAR. PATRIOTS, WHO IN 1776 DESTROYED AN EQUESTRIAN STATUE OF GEORGE III WHICH STOOD HERE, ARE SAID TO HAVE REMOVED THE CROWNS WHICH CAPPED THE FENCE POSTS BUT THE FENCE ITSELF REMAINS
PLAQUE ERECTED 1964 BY
THE NEW YORK COMMUNITY TRUST

1797

1830

12

No. 901 Broadway (former Lord and Taylor Store)

Broadway and 20th Street

Manhattan

LANDMARKS OF NEW YORK
901 BROADWAY
FORMER LORD & TAYLOR STORE
DESIGNED BY JAMES H. GILES FOR LORD & TAYLOR, AND CONSTRUCTED IN 1869, THIS BUILDING HOUSED THEIR RETAIL STORE FROM 1872 TO 1914. WITH ITS CAST IRON FACADE IN THE SECOND EMPIRE STYLE, THE STRUCTURE IS AMONG THE SURVIVING EXAMPLES OF THE "COMMERCIAL PALACES" BUILT IN THE DECADE FOLLOWING THE CIVIL WAR.
PLAQUE ERECTED 1963 BY
THE NEW YORK COMMUNITY TRUST

13
William Cullen Bryant Residence
24 West 16th Street (6th Avenue), Chelsea
Manhattan

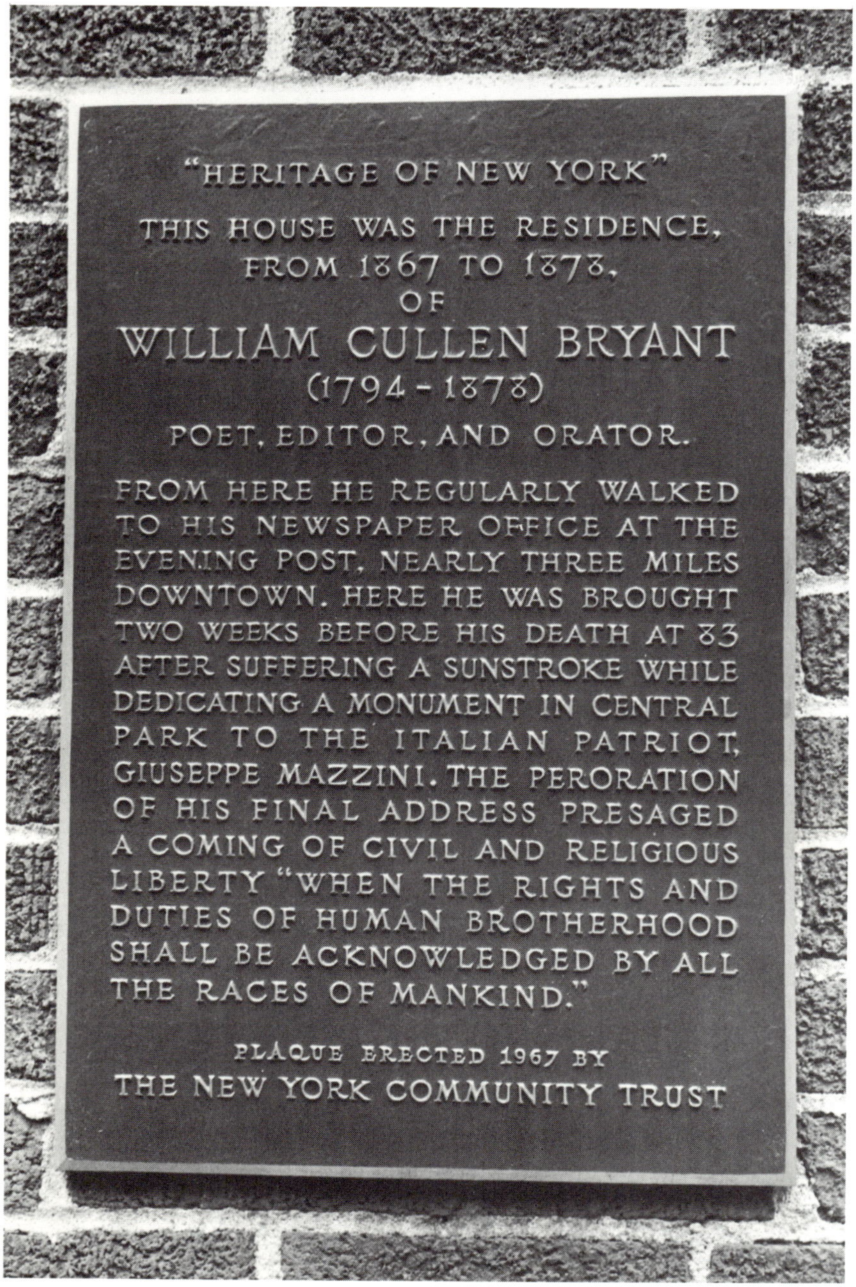
"HERITAGE OF NEW YORK"
THIS HOUSE WAS THE RESIDENCE, FROM 1867 TO 1878, OF
WILLIAM CULLEN BRYANT
(1794-1878)
POET, EDITOR, AND ORATOR.
FROM HERE HE REGULARLY WALKED TO HIS NEWSPAPER OFFICE AT THE EVENING POST, NEARLY THREE MILES DOWNTOWN. HERE HE WAS BROUGHT TWO WEEKS BEFORE HIS DEATH AT 83 AFTER SUFFERING A SUNSTROKE WHILE DEDICATING A MONUMENT IN CENTRAL PARK TO THE ITALIAN PATRIOT, GIUSEPPE MAZZINI. THE PERORATION OF HIS FINAL ADDRESS PRESAGED A COMING OF CIVIL AND RELIGIOUS LIBERTY "WHEN THE RIGHTS AND DUTIES OF HUMAN BROTHERHOOD SHALL BE ACKNOWLEDGED BY ALL THE RACES OF MANKIND."
PLAQUE ERECTED 1967 BY
THE NEW YORK COMMUNITY TRUST

14
Carnegie Hall
154 West 57th Street (7th Avenue)
Manhattan

"HERITAGE OF NEW YORK"
CARNEGIE HALL
DESIGNED IN THE ITALIAN RENAISSANCE STYLE BY WILLIAM BURNET TUTHILL AS SUPERVISING ARCHITECT AND DANKMAR ADLER AS ACOUSTICAL CONSULTANT, THIS BUILDING OPENED AS THE "MUSIC HALL" ON MAY 5, 1891 WITH A GALA WEEK OF PROGRAMS INCLUDING SEVERAL OF TCHAIKOVSKY'S WORKS CONDUCTED BY THE COMPOSER. IN THE SAME SEASON PADEREWSKI GAVE HIS FIRST AMERICAN PERFORMANCE HERE. EXTENSIVELY ALTERED IN 1896 AND 1925, THE HALL WAS ACQUIRED BY THE CITY OF NEW YORK IN 1960. IT WAS GIVEN ITS PRESENT NAME IN 1892 IN TRIBUTE TO ITS BENEFACTOR, ANDREW CARNEGIE.
PLAQUE ERECTED 1966 BY
THE NEW YORK COMMUNITY TRUST

NO
LEFT
TURN
COFFEE SHOP
COFFEE SHOP

15
Carnegie House
Fifth Avenue at 91st Street
Manhattan

LANDMARKS OF NEW YORK
THE CARNEGIE HOUSE
THIS STRUCTURE, DESIGNED BY BABB, COOK
& WILLARD AS A RESIDENCE FOR MR. AND MRS.
ANDREW CARNEGIE, WAS BUILT IN 1900-01.
IN 1957 IT WAS CITED BY THE MUNICIPAL
ART SOCIETY AND THE SOCIETY OF
ARCHITECTURAL HISTORIANS FOR THE MERIT
OF ITS GEORGIAN ARCHITECTURE.
PLAQUE ERECTED 1957 BY
THE NEW YORK COMMUNITY TRUST

16

Cartier Building

653 Fifth Avenue (52nd Street)

Manhattan

LANDMARKS OF NEW YORK
CARTIER BUILDING
DESIGNED BY ROBERT W. GIBSON AS THE RESIDENCE OF MORTON F. PLANT, THIS BUILDING WAS CONSTRUCTED IN 1904. MESSRS. CARTIER ACQUIRED IT IN 1917 AND, AFTER MODIFICATION BY WILLIAM WELLES BOSWORTH, IT WAS OCCUPIED BY THE FIRM OF CARTIER, FOUNDED IN PARIS IN 1847.
PLAQUE ERECTED 1962 BY
THE NEW YORK COMMUNITY TRUST

Cartier
E 52

17

Cathedral Church of St. John the Divine (Episcopal)

Amsterdam Avenue and Morningside Drive (West 113th Street), Cathedral Heights
Manhattan

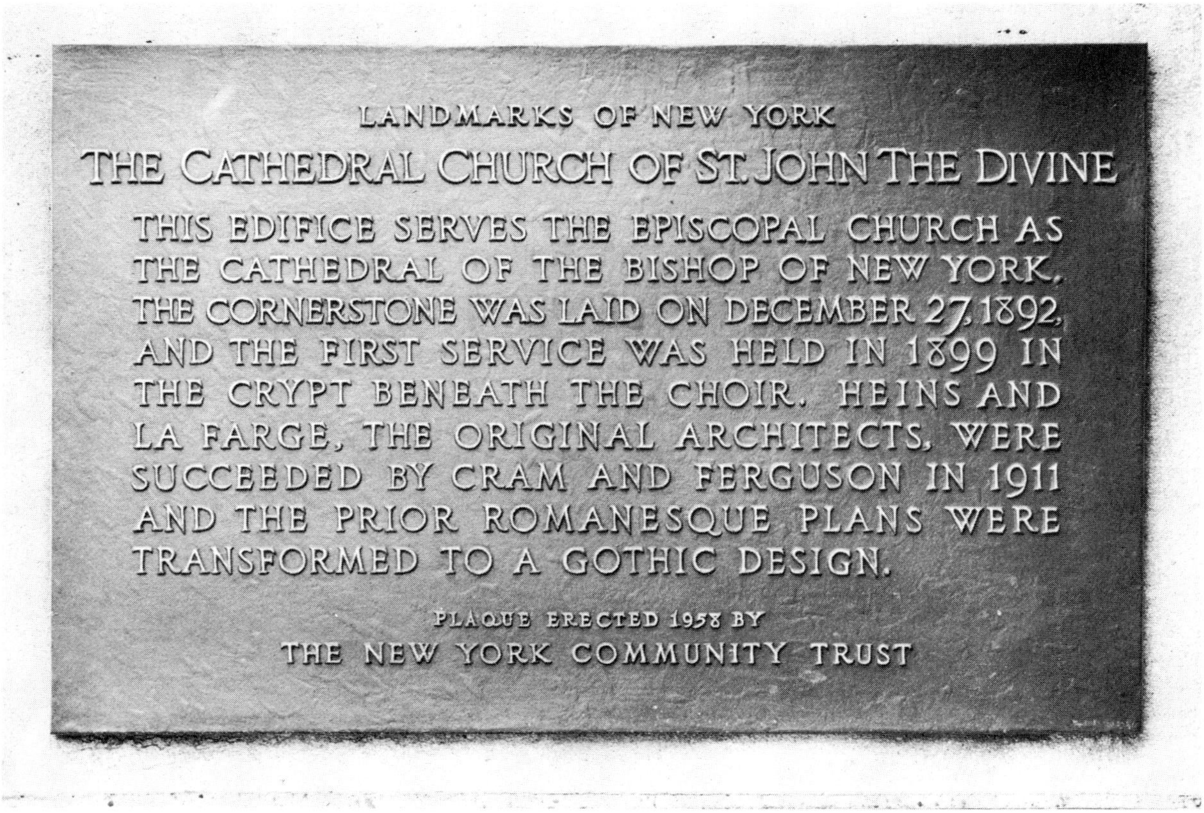
LANDMARKS OF NEW YORK
THE CATHEDRAL CHURCH OF ST. JOHN THE DIVINE
THIS EDIFICE SERVES THE EPISCOPAL CHURCH AS THE CATHEDRAL OF THE BISHOP OF NEW YORK. THE CORNERSTONE WAS LAID ON DECEMBER 27, 1892, AND THE FIRST SERVICE WAS HELD IN 1899 IN THE CRYPT BENEATH THE CHOIR. HEINS AND LA FARGE, THE ORIGINAL ARCHITECTS, WERE SUCCEEDED BY CRAM AND FERGUSON IN 1911 AND THE PRIOR ROMANESQUE PLANS WERE TRANSFORMED TO A GOTHIC DESIGN.
PLAQUE ERECTED 1958 BY
THE NEW YORK COMMUNITY TRUST

18
Central Savings Bank
Broadway at 73rd Street
Manhattan

LANDMARKS OF NEW YORK
CENTRAL SAVINGS BANK
THIS BUILDING, DESIGNED IN THE STYLE OF THE ITALIAN RENAISSANCE BY YORK AND SAWYER, WAS COMPLETED IN 1928. IT IS THE THIRD HOME OF THE BANK, ORGANIZED IN 1859, WHICH MOVED ITS PRINCIPAL OFFICES TO THIS SITE IN 1928 FROM FOURTEENTH STREET AND FOURTH AVENUE WHERE IT HAD FIRST OCCUPIED SPACE IN THE OLD NAPIER HOTEL THAT WAS RAZED IN 1871.
PLAQUE ERECTED 1961 BY
THE NEW YORK COMMUNITY TRUST

CENTRAL SAVINGS BANK
HARDWARE

19
Central Synagogue
Lexington Avenue at 55th Street
Manhattan

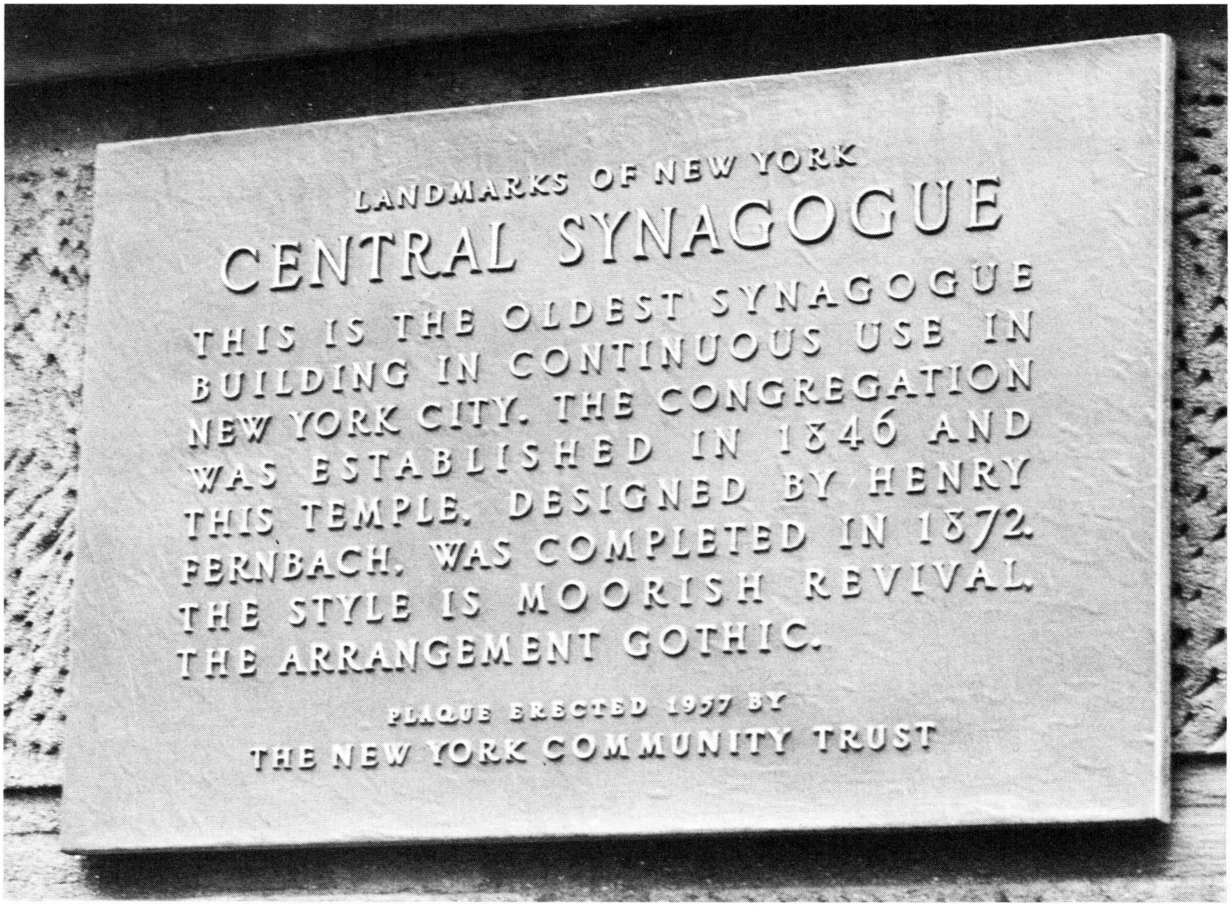
LANDMARKS OF NEW YORK
CENTRAL SYNAGOGUE
THIS IS THE OLDEST SYNAGOGUE BUILDING IN CONTINUOUS USE IN NEW YORK CITY. THE CONGREGATION WAS ESTABLISHED IN 1846 AND THIS TEMPLE, DESIGNED BY HENRY FERNBACH, WAS COMPLETED IN 1872. THE STYLE IS MOORISH REVIVAL. THE ARRANGEMENT GOTHIC.
PLAQUE ERECTED 1957 BY
THE NEW YORK COMMUNITY TRUST

20
Chelsea Hotel
222 West 23rd Street (7th Avenue)
Manhattan

LANDMARKS OF NEW YORK
CHELSEA HOTEL
DESIGNED BY HUBERT & PIRSSON, THE CHELSEA WAS OPENED IN 1884 AS ONE OF THE CITY'S EARLIEST COOPERATIVE APARTMENT HOUSES. IT BECAME A HOTEL ABOUT 1905. THE FLORID CAST IRON BALCONIES WERE MADE BY THE FIRM OF J. B. & J. M. CORNELL. ARTISTS AND WRITERS WHO HAVE LIVED HERE INCLUDE ARTHUR B. DAVIES, JAMES T. FARRELL, ROBERT FLAHERTY, O. HENRY, JOHN SLOAN, DYLAN THOMAS AND THOMAS WOLFE.
PLAQUE ERECTED 1962 BY
THE NEW YORK COMMUNITY TRUST

HOTEL
CHELSEA
LAUNDERERS
CLEANERS
FISHING TACKLE
TEL CHELSEA
TELEPHONE

21
Church Missions House (P.E.)
281 Park Avenue South (22nd Street)
Manhattan

LANDMARKS OF NEW YORK
CHURCH MISSIONS HOUSE
DESIGNED BY ROBERT W. GIBSON IN ROMANESQUE STYLE, THIS BUILDING WAS COMPLETED IN 1893 AS HEADQUARTERS FOR THE DOMESTIC AND FOREIGN MISSIONARY SOCIETY OF THE PROTESTANT EPISCOPAL CHURCH. THE SOCIETY WAS FOUNDED IN 1821 AND INCORPORATED IN 1846.
PLAQUE ERECTED 1960 BY
THE NEW YORK COMMUNITY TRUST

22

Church of St. Bernard (R.C.)

328 West 14th Street (Hudson Street), Greenwich Village
Manhattan

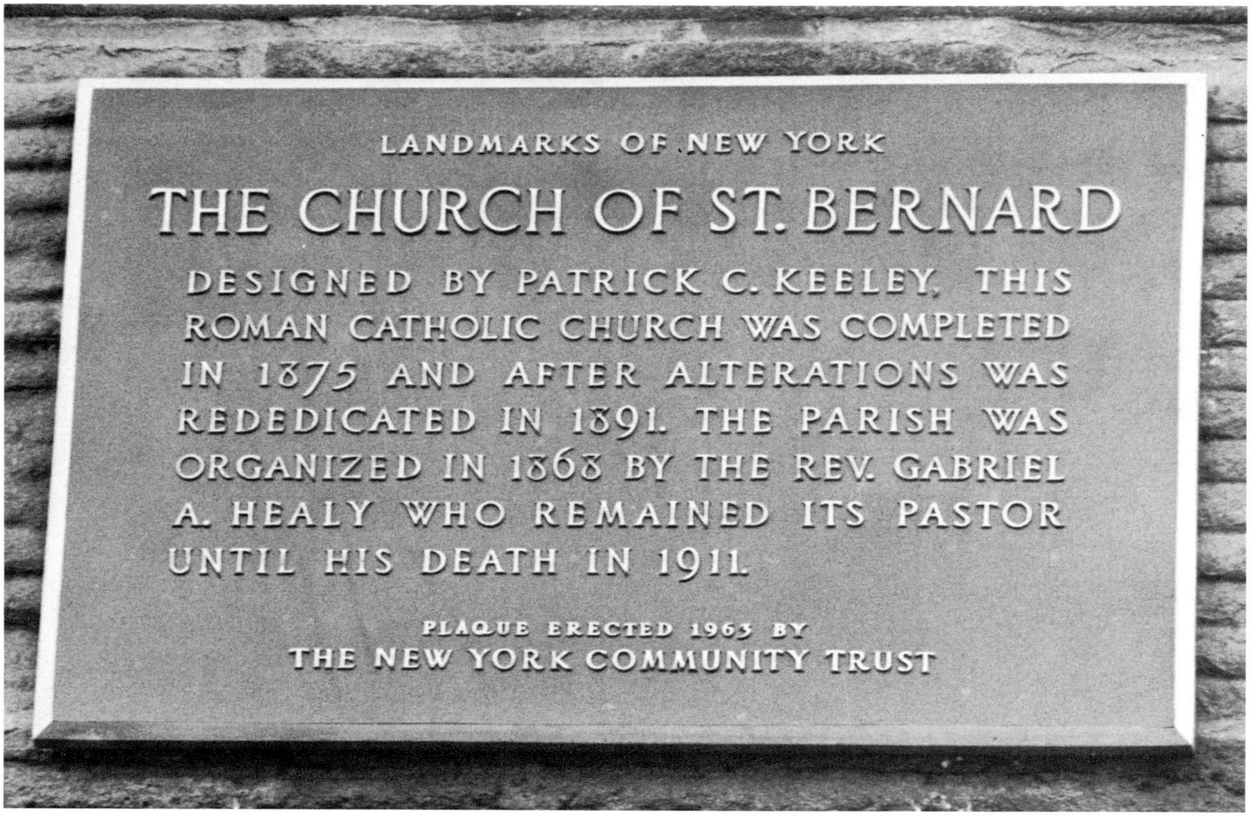
LANDMARKS OF NEW YORK
THE CHURCH OF ST. BERNARD
DESIGNED BY PATRICK C. KEELEY, THIS ROMAN CATHOLIC CHURCH WAS COMPLETED IN 1875 AND AFTER ALTERATIONS WAS REDEDICATED IN 1891. THE PARISH WAS ORGANIZED IN 1868 BY THE REV. GABRIEL A. HEALY WHO REMAINED ITS PASTOR UNTIL HIS DEATH IN 1911.
PLAQUE ERECTED 1963 BY
THE NEW YORK COMMUNITY TRUST

23
Church of St. Ignatius Loyola (R.C.)
980 Park Avenue (84th Street)
Manhattan

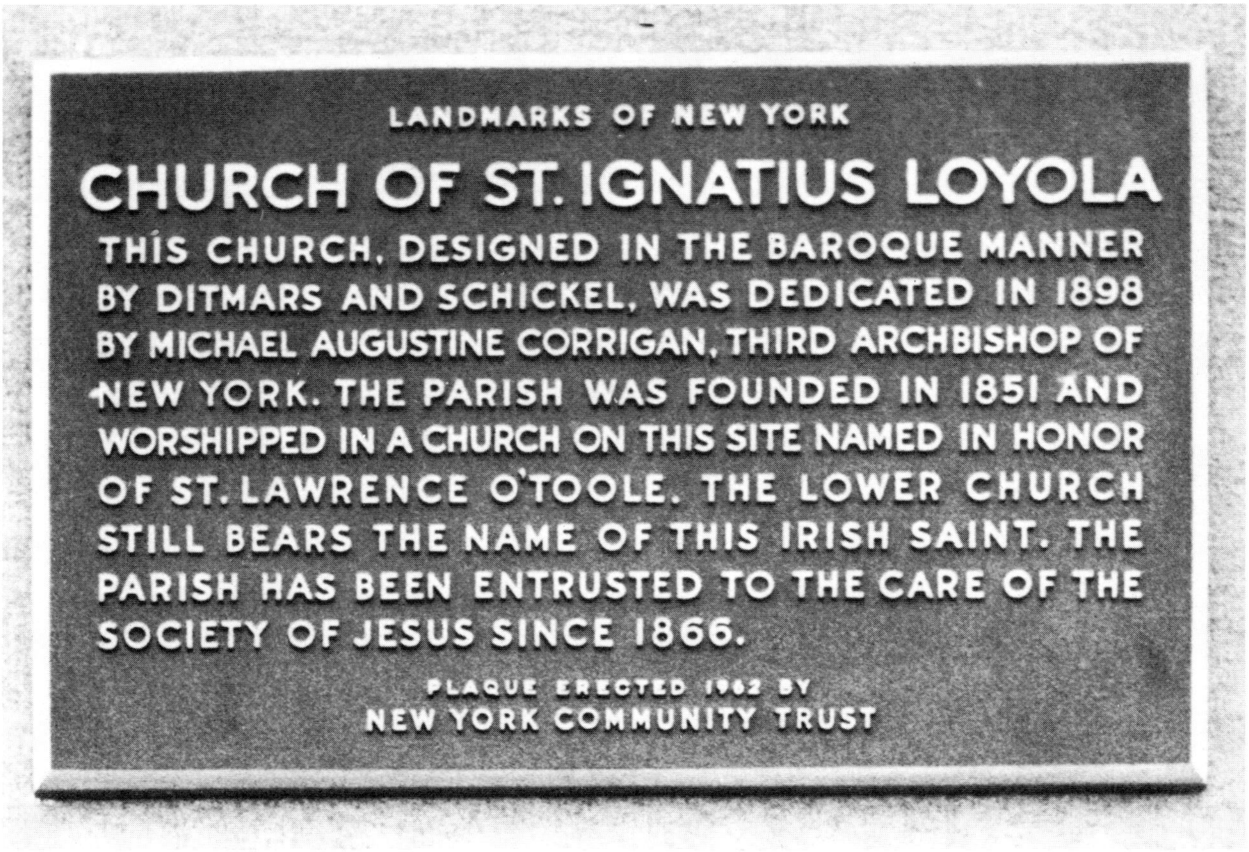
LANDMARKS OF NEW YORK
CHURCH OF ST. IGNATIUS LOYOLA
THIS CHURCH, DESIGNED IN THE BAROQUE MANNER BY DITMARS AND SCHICKEL, WAS DEDICATED IN 1898 BY MICHAEL AUGUSTINE CORRIGAN, THIRD ARCHBISHOP OF NEW YORK. THE PARISH WAS FOUNDED IN 1851 AND WORSHIPPED IN A CHURCH ON THIS SITE NAMED IN HONOR OF ST. LAWRENCE O'TOOLE. THE LOWER CHURCH STILL BEARS THE NAME OF THIS IRISH SAINT. THE PARISH HAS BEEN ENTRUSTED TO THE CARE OF THE SOCIETY OF JESUS SINCE 1866.
PLAQUE ERECTED 1962 BY
NEW YORK COMMUNITY TRUST

AD MAJOREM DEI GLORIAM

24
Church of the Ascension (Episcopal)
Fifth Avenue and 10th Street, Greenwich Village
Manhattan

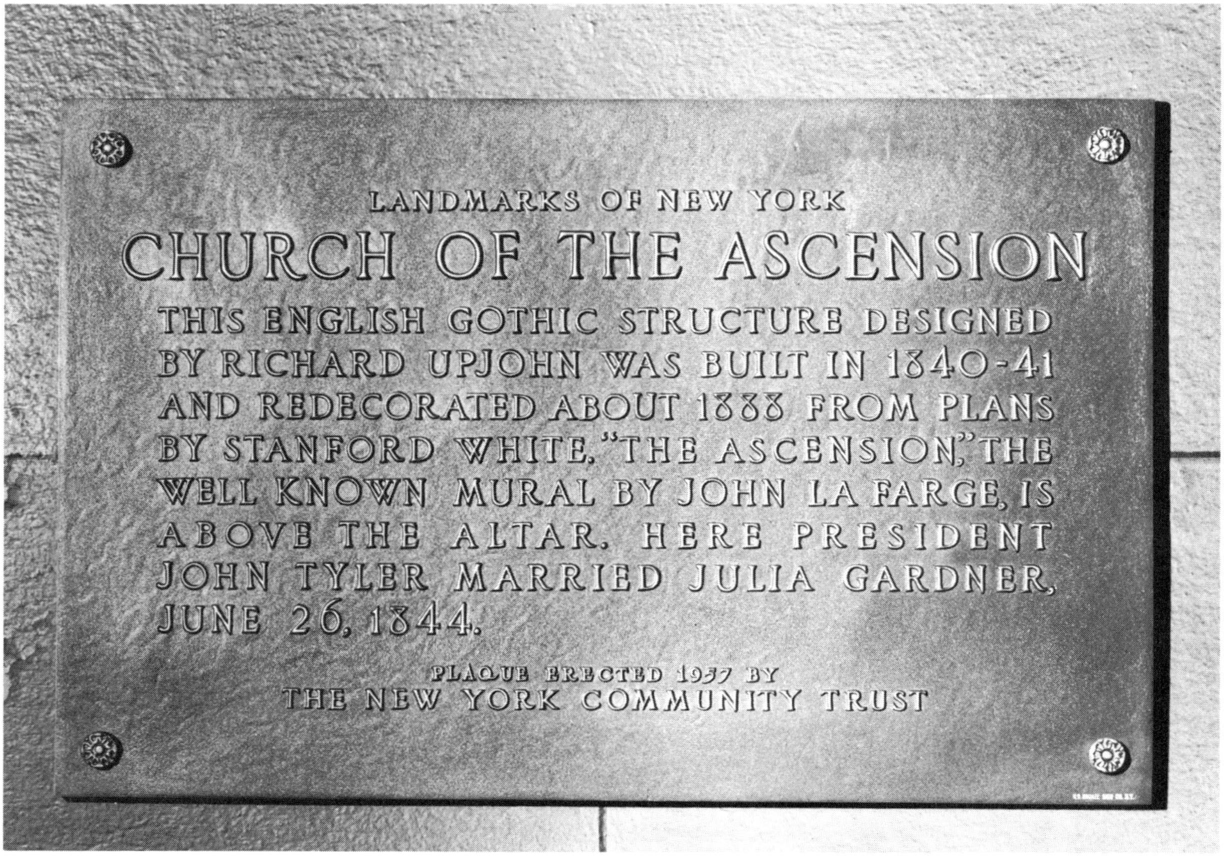
LANDMARKS OF NEW YORK
CHURCH OF THE ASCENSION
THIS ENGLISH GOTHIC STRUCTURE DESIGNED BY RICHARD UPJOHN WAS BUILT IN 1840-41 AND REDECORATED ABOUT 1888 FROM PLANS BY STANFORD WHITE. "THE ASCENSION," THE WELL KNOWN MURAL BY JOHN LA FARGE, IS ABOVE THE ALTAR. HERE PRESIDENT JOHN TYLER MARRIED JULIA GARDNER, JUNE 26, 1844.
PLAQUE ERECTED 1957 BY
THE NEW YORK COMMUNITY TRUST

5TH AV
E 10 ST

25
Church of the Heavenly Rest (P.E.)
Fifth Avenue and 90th Street
Manhattan

LANDMARKS OF NEW YORK
CHURCH OF THE HEAVENLY REST
CHAPEL OF THE BELOVED DISCIPLE
DESIGNED IN A GOTHIC STYLE BY HARDIE PHILLIP, THIS PROTESTANT EPISCOPAL CHURCH WAS OPENED FOR WORSHIP EASTER SUNDAY, 1929. THE ROSE WINDOW WAS EXECUTED BY J. GORDON GUTHRIE. THE CLERESTORY WINDOWS, DESIGNED BY J. H. HOGAN, WERE PRODUCED IN ENGLAND. THE PARISH, ORGANIZED IN 1868, UNITED WITH THE CHURCH OF THE BELOVED DISCIPLE IN 1925.
PLAQUE ERECTED 1964 BY
THE NEW YORK COMMUNITY TRUST

5TH AV
E 90 ST

26

Church of the Holy Apostles (P.E.)

360 West 28th Street (9th Avenue), Chelsea
Manhattan

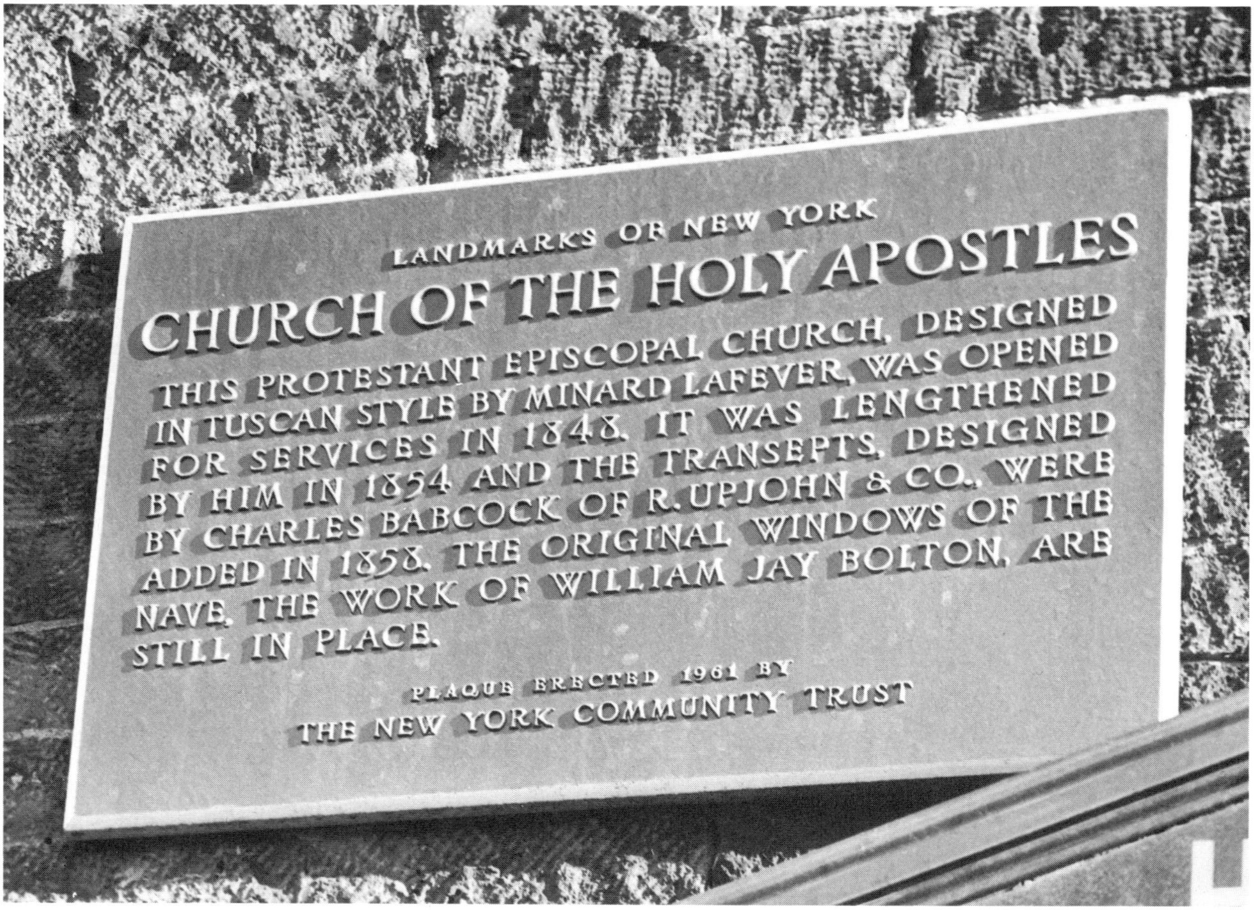
LANDMARKS OF NEW YORK
CHURCH OF THE HOLY APOSTLES
THIS PROTESTANT EPISCOPAL CHURCH, DESIGNED IN TUSCAN STYLE BY MINARD LAFEVER, WAS OPENED FOR SERVICES IN 1848. IT WAS LENGTHENED BY HIM IN 1854 AND THE TRANSEPTS, DESIGNED BY CHARLES BABCOCK OF R. UPJOHN & CO., WERE ADDED IN 1858. THE ORIGINAL WINDOWS OF THE NAVE, THE WORK OF WILLIAM JAY BOLTON, ARE STILL IN PLACE.
PLAQUE ERECTED 1961 BY
THE NEW YORK COMMUNITY TRUST

27
Church of the Holy Communion (Episcopal)
49 West 20th Street (6th Avenue)
Manhattan

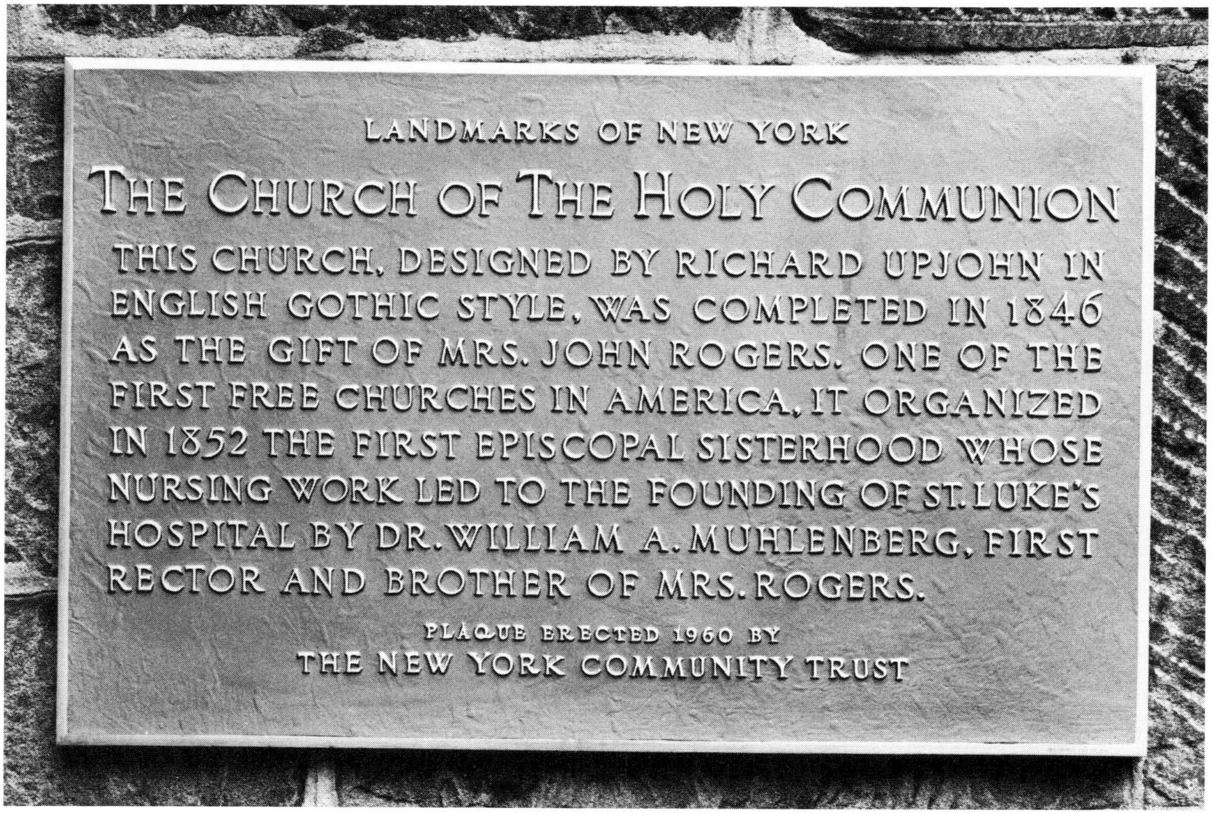
LANDMARKS OF NEW YORK
THE CHURCH OF THE HOLY COMMUNION
THIS CHURCH, DESIGNED BY RICHARD UPJOHN IN ENGLISH GOTHIC STYLE, WAS COMPLETED IN 1846 AS THE GIFT OF MRS. JOHN ROGERS. ONE OF THE FIRST FREE CHURCHES IN AMERICA, IT ORGANIZED IN 1852 THE FIRST EPISCOPAL SISTERHOOD WHOSE NURSING WORK LED TO THE FOUNDING OF ST. LUKE'S HOSPITAL BY DR. WILLIAM A. MUHLENBERG, FIRST RECTOR AND BROTHER OF MRS. ROGERS.
PLAQUE ERECTED 1960 BY
THE NEW YORK COMMUNITY TRUST

28

Church of the Holy Trinity (Rhinelander Memorial)

316 East 88th Street (1st Avenue)

Manhattan

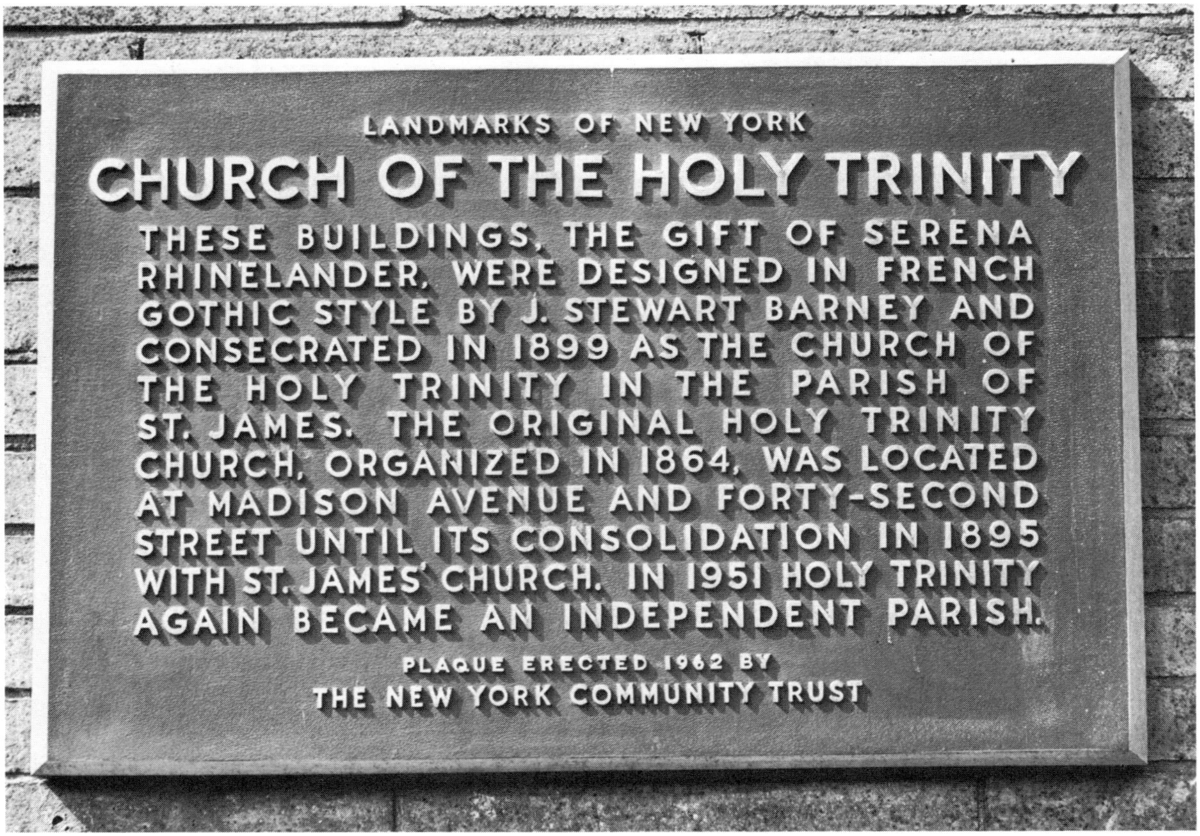
LANDMARKS OF NEW YORK
CHURCH OF THE HOLY TRINITY
THESE BUILDINGS, THE GIFT OF SERENA RHINELANDER, WERE DESIGNED IN FRENCH GOTHIC STYLE BY J. STEWART BARNEY AND CONSECRATED IN 1899 AS THE CHURCH OF THE HOLY TRINITY IN THE PARISH OF ST. JAMES. THE ORIGINAL HOLY TRINITY CHURCH, ORGANIZED IN 1864, WAS LOCATED AT MADISON AVENUE AND FORTY-SECOND STREET UNTIL ITS CONSOLIDATION IN 1895 WITH ST. JAMES' CHURCH. IN 1951 HOLY TRINITY AGAIN BECAME AN INDEPENDENT PARISH.
PLAQUE ERECTED 1962 BY
THE NEW YORK COMMUNITY TRUST

29
Church of the Incarnation (P.E.)
Madison Avenue and 35th Street
Manhattan

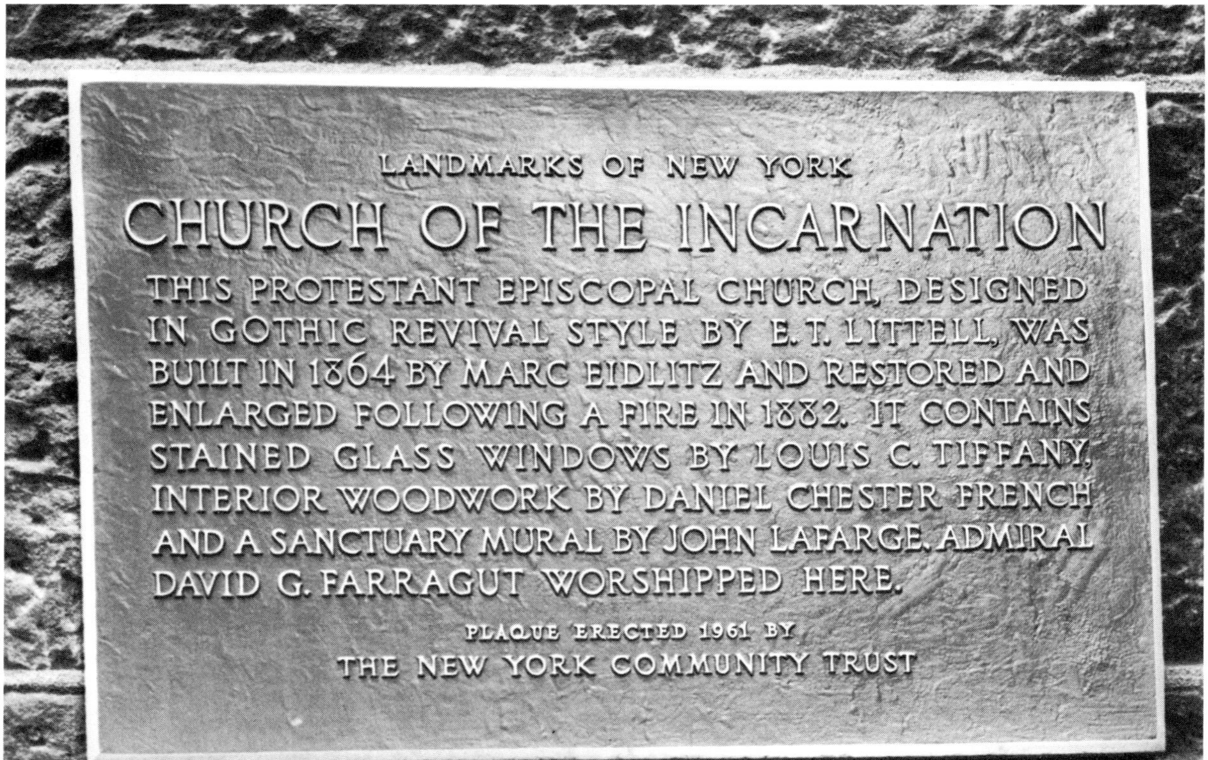
LANDMARKS OF NEW YORK
CHURCH OF THE INCARNATION
THIS PROTESTANT EPISCOPAL CHURCH, DESIGNED IN GOTHIC REVIVAL STYLE BY E. T. LITTELL, WAS BUILT IN 1864 BY MARC EIDLITZ AND RESTORED AND ENLARGED FOLLOWING A FIRE IN 1882. IT CONTAINS STAINED GLASS WINDOWS BY LOUIS C. TIFFANY, INTERIOR WOODWORK BY DANIEL CHESTER FRENCH AND A SANCTUARY MURAL BY JOHN LAFARGE. ADMIRAL DAVID G. FARRAGUT WORSHIPPED HERE.
PLAQUE ERECTED 1961 BY
THE NEW YORK COMMUNITY TRUST

30
Church of the Sea and Land (Presbyterian)
Henry and Market Streets
Manhattan

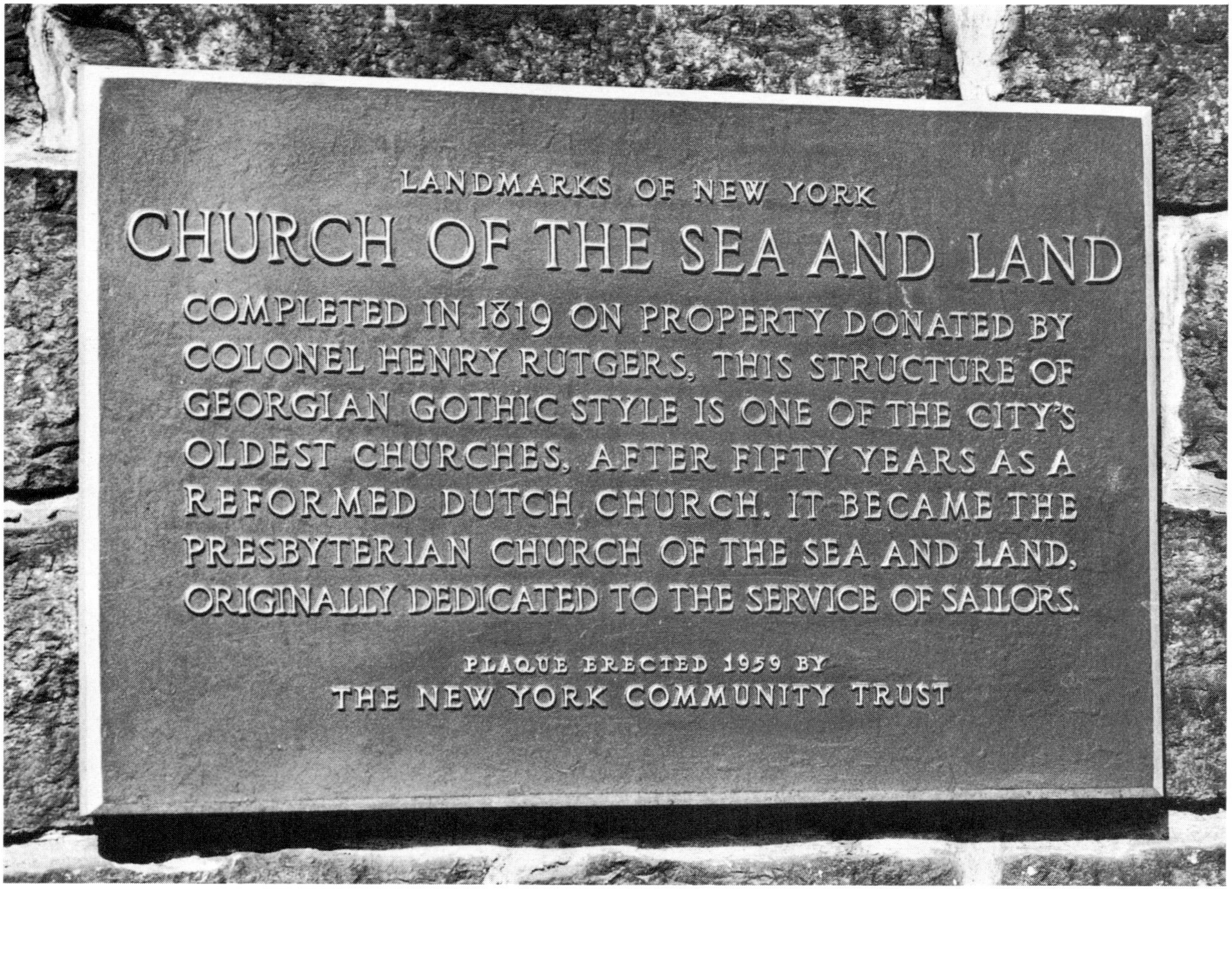
LANDMARKS OF NEW YORK
CHURCH OF THE SEA AND LAND
COMPLETED IN 1819 ON PROPERTY DONATED BY COLONEL HENRY RUTGERS, THIS STRUCTURE OF GEORGIAN GOTHIC STYLE IS ONE OF THE CITY'S OLDEST CHURCHES. AFTER FIFTY YEARS AS A REFORMED DUTCH CHURCH, IT BECAME THE PRESBYTERIAN CHURCH OF THE SEA AND LAND, ORIGINALLY DEDICATED TO THE SERVICE OF SAILORS.
PLAQUE ERECTED 1959 BY
THE NEW YORK COMMUNITY TRUST

for
ASTORI

31

Church of the Transfiguration—"Little Church Around the Corner" (P.E.)

29th Street near Fifth Avenue

Manhattan

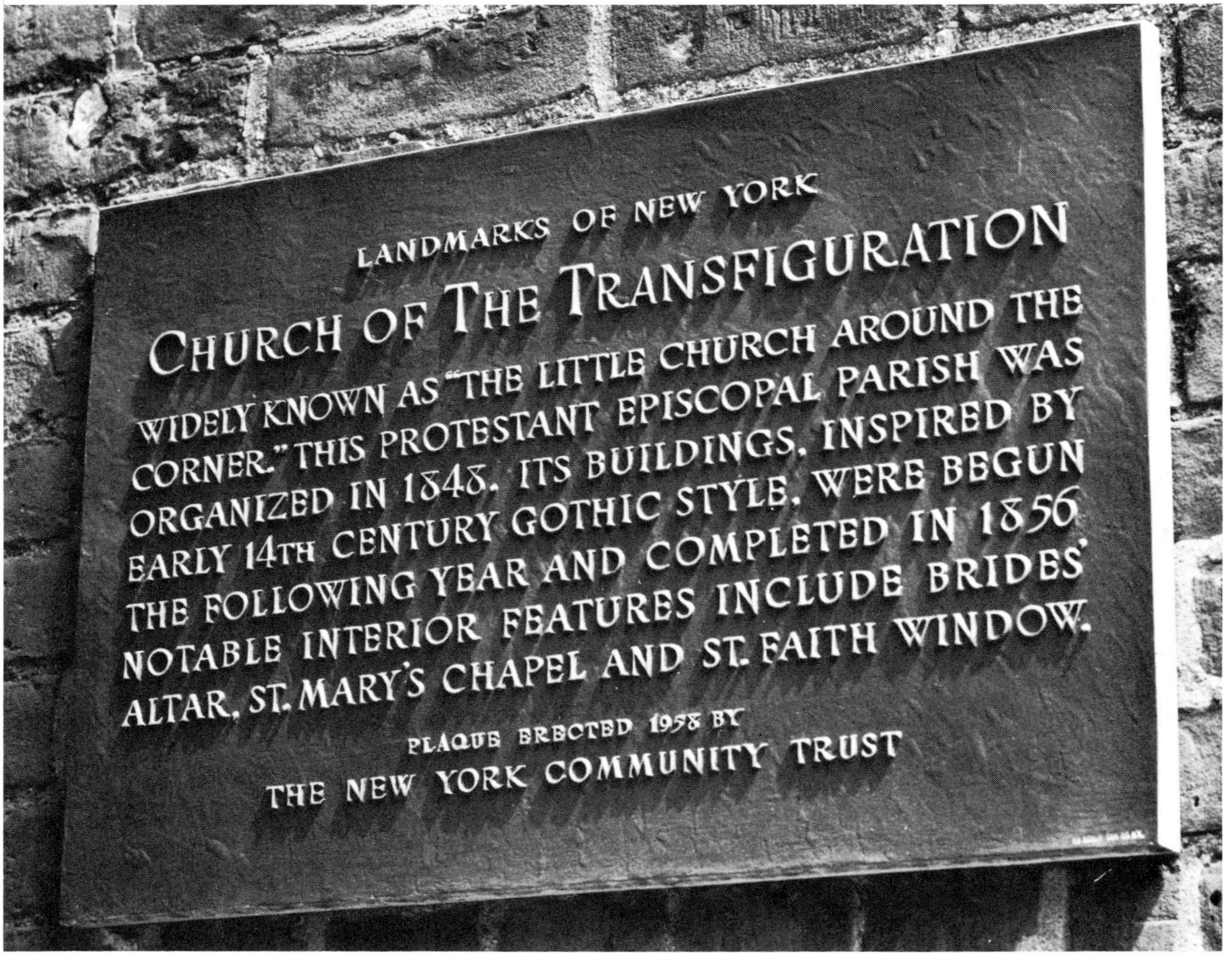

LANDMARKS OF NEW YORK
CHURCH OF THE TRANSFIGURATION
WIDELY KNOWN AS "THE LITTLE CHURCH AROUND THE CORNER." THIS PROTESTANT EPISCOPAL PARISH WAS ORGANIZED IN 1848. ITS BUILDINGS, INSPIRED BY EARLY 14TH CENTURY GOTHIC STYLE, WERE BEGUN THE FOLLOWING YEAR AND COMPLETED IN 1856. NOTABLE INTERIOR FEATURES INCLUDE BRIDES' ALTAR, ST. MARY'S CHAPEL AND ST. FAITH WINDOW.
PLAQUE ERECTED 1958 BY
THE NEW YORK COMMUNITY TRUST

CRAVATS
Mastercraft
FOUNDATIONS
HEADWEAR
MICHAEL ADDISON
SILK UNDERWEAR
NO PARKING
C-6393

32
The Cloisters
Fort Tryon Park (200th Street), Inwood
Manhattan

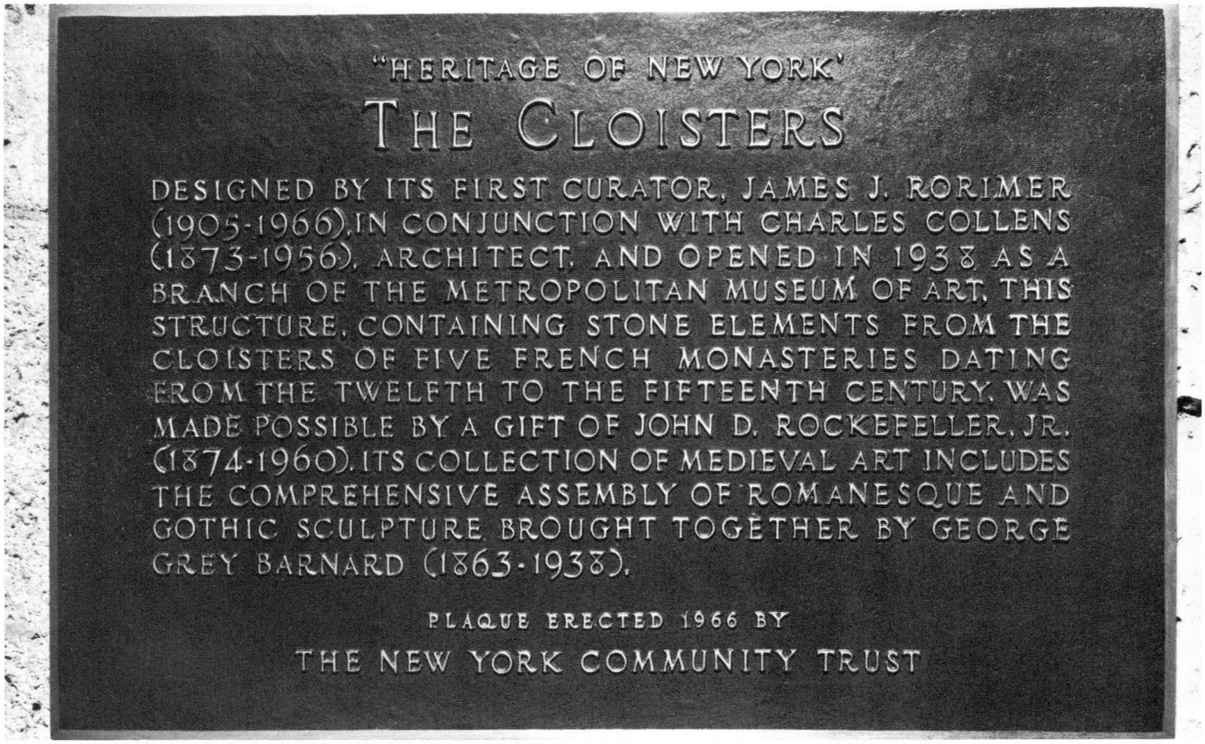
"HERITAGE OF NEW YORK"
THE CLOISTERS
DESIGNED BY ITS FIRST CURATOR, JAMES J. RORIMER (1905-1966), IN CONJUNCTION WITH CHARLES COLLENS (1873-1956), ARCHITECT, AND OPENED IN 1938 AS A BRANCH OF THE METROPOLITAN MUSEUM OF ART, THIS STRUCTURE, CONTAINING STONE ELEMENTS FROM THE CLOISTERS OF FIVE FRENCH MONASTERIES DATING FROM THE TWELFTH TO THE FIFTEENTH CENTURY, WAS MADE POSSIBLE BY A GIFT OF JOHN D. ROCKEFELLER, JR. (1874-1960). ITS COLLECTION OF MEDIEVAL ART INCLUDES THE COMPREHENSIVE ASSEMBLY OF ROMANESQUE AND GOTHIC SCULPTURE BROUGHT TOGETHER BY GEORGE GREY BARNARD (1863-1938).
PLAQUE ERECTED 1966 BY
THE NEW YORK COMMUNITY TRUST

33
Colonnade Row
432 Lafayette Street (Astor Place)
Manhattan

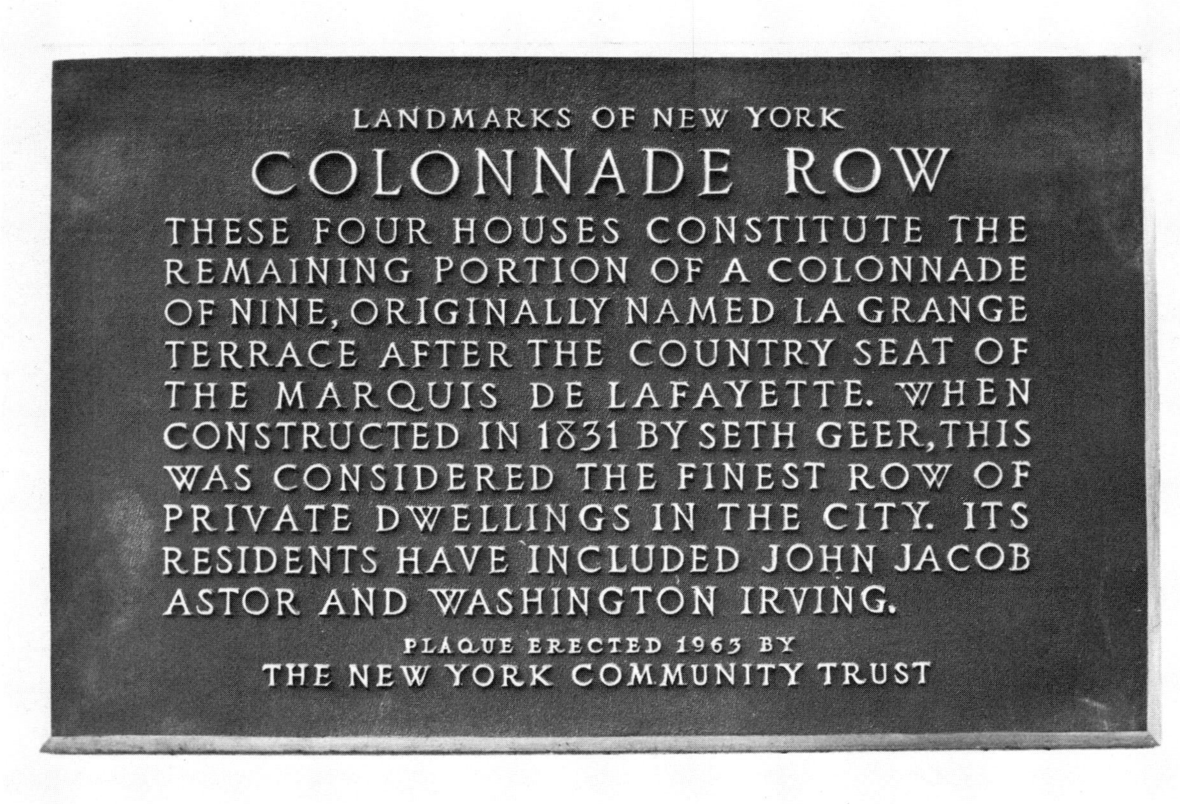
LANDMARKS OF NEW YORK
COLONNADE ROW
THESE FOUR HOUSES CONSTITUTE THE REMAINING PORTION OF A COLONNADE OF NINE, ORIGINALLY NAMED LA GRANGE TERRACE AFTER THE COUNTRY SEAT OF THE MARQUIS DE LAFAYETTE. WHEN CONSTRUCTED IN 1831 BY SETH GEER, THIS WAS CONSIDERED THE FINEST ROW OF PRIVATE DWELLINGS IN THE CITY. ITS RESIDENTS HAVE INCLUDED JOHN JACOB ASTOR AND WASHINGTON IRVING.
PLAQUE ERECTED 1963 BY
THE NEW YORK COMMUNITY TRUST

CONTE
CONTE RESTAURANT
CONTE RESTAURANT
CONTE 432
ASTOR PL

34
Cooper Union
Cooper Square and Astor Place, Greenwich Village
Manhattan

LANDMARKS OF NEW YORK
COOPER UNION
FOR THE ADVANCEMENT OF SCIENCE AND ART
PETER COOPER, INVENTOR, CIVIC LEADER, PHILANTHROPIST, FOUNDED THIS INSTITUTION OFFERING FREE EDUCATION TO ALL. IN ITS GREAT HALL, BIRTHPLACE OF MANY IMPORTANT SOCIAL AND POLITICAL MOVEMENTS, AMERICA'S LEADING CITIZENS HAVE SPOKEN, AMONG THEM ABRAHAM LINCOLN, WHOSE 1860 ADDRESS HERE CONTRIBUTED TO HIS PRESIDENTIAL NOMINATION. DESIGNED BY FREDERICK A. PETERSON, THIS BUILDING WAS OPENED IN 1859.
PLAQUE ERECTED 1959 BY
THE NEW YORK COMMUNITY TRUST

COOPER UNION

35
Cunard Building
25 Broadway (Bowling Green)
Manhattan

LANDMARKS OF NEW YORK
CUNARD BUILDING
THE CUNARD LINE, WHICH FIRST OPENED A NEW YORK OFFICE IN 1848, OCCUPIED THIS BUILDING ON ITS COMPLETION IN 1921. BENJAMIN W. MORRIS WAS THE ARCHITECT, AND THOMAS HASTINGS SERVED AS CONSULTANT IN THE DESIGN OF THE GREAT HALL, INSPIRED BY ROMAN AND ITALIAN RENAISSANCE EXAMPLES. THE SITE WAS FORMERLY OCCUPIED BY DELMONICO'S HOTEL, OPENED IN 1846, LATER RE-NAMED THE STEVENS HOUSE AND DEMOLISHED IN 1919.
PLAQUE ERECTED 1962 BY
THE NEW YORK COMMUNITY TRUST

BEAVER ST
WAY
ONE WAY
ALL TRAFFIC
STOP

36

Dakota Apartments

1 West 72nd Street (Central Park West)
Manhattan

LANDMARKS OF NEW YORK
DAKOTA APARTMENTS
COMPLETED IN 1884 FROM DESIGNS BY HENRY J. HARDENBERGH, THIS WAS ONE OF THE CITY'S EARLIEST LUXURY APARTMENTS AND AMONG THE FIRST TO INCLUDE AN ELEVATOR. BUILT FOR EDWARD CLARK, PRESIDENT OF THE SINGER SEWING MACHINE COMPANY, IT WAS NAMED FOR THE DAKOTA TERRITORY WITH IRONIC REFERENCE TO ITS REMOTENESS FROM THE THEN FASHIONABLE AREA.
PLAQUE ERECTED 1962 BY
THE NEW YORK COMMUNITY TRUST

37
Dyckman House
Broadway at 204th Street, Inwood
Manhattan

LANDMARKS OF NEW YORK
DYCKMAN HOUSE
THIS IS THE ONLY REMAINING MANHATTAN FARMHOUSE OF THE EIGHTEENTH CENTURY. BUILT BY WILLIAM DYCKMAN IN 1783, IT REPLACED HIS EARLIER HOME ON THIS SITE WHICH WAS DESTROYED DURING THE REVOLUTIONARY WAR. IN 1915, FOLLOWING RESTORATION OF THE HOUSE AND GROUNDS, IT WAS GIVEN TO THE CITY BY DESCENDANTS OF THE BUILDER.
PLAQUE ERECTED 1959 BY
THE NEW YORK COMMUNITY TRUST

38

East River Savings Bank

743 Amsterdam Avenue (West 96th Street)
Manhattan

LANDMARKS OF NEW YORK
EAST RIVER SAVINGS BANK
CITED FOR ARCHITECTURAL DISTINCTION BY THE MUNICIPAL ART SOCIETY IN ITS "NEW YORK LANDMARKS," THIS FIRST BRANCH OF THE EAST RIVER SAVINGS BANK, ORGANIZED IN 1848, WAS OPENED IN 1927. THE ARCHITECTS, WALKER & GILLETTE, FOLLOWED A MODIFIED GREEK STYLE IN ITS DESIGN.
PLAQUE ERECTED 1961 BY
THE NEW YORK COMMUNITY TRUST

· 1848 · EAST RIVER SAVINGS BANK · 1926 ·
EAST RIVER SAVINGS BANK
EAST RIVER SAVINGS BANK

39

East 23rd Street Bath House

Asser Levy Place near Franklin D. Roosevelt (East River) Drive
Manhattan

LANDMARKS OF NEW YORK
EAST 23RD STREET BATH HOUSE
THIS BUILDING WAS ERECTED BY THE CITY IN 1906 AS ONE OF ITS FREE PUBLIC BATH FACILITIES. INFLUENCED BY CLASSIC ROMAN ARCHITECTURE, IT WAS THE WORK OF MARTIN AIKEN AND ARNOLD W. BRUNNER. IN 1939 THE DEPARTMENT OF PARKS RECONSTRUCTED THE INTERIOR.
PLAQUE ERECTED 1965 BY
THE NEW YORK COMMUNITY TRUST

FREE PUBLIC BATHS

40
Evening Post Building
20 Vesey Street (Church Street)
Manhattan

"HERITAGE OF NEW YORK"
EVENING POST BUILDING
DESIGNED BY ROBERT D. KOHN AND OCCUPIED BY THE NEW YORK EVENING POST FROM 1907 TO 1926, THIS BUILDING IS ONE OF NEW YORK'S RARE EXAMPLES OF "ART NOUVEAU." THE BRONZE-FINISHED, CAST-IRON WINDOW SPANDRELS ARE ORNAMENTED WITH THE MARKS OF FAMOUS PRINTERS OF THE 16TH AND 17TH CENTURIES. THE STATUES ON THE 9TH FLOOR, EXECUTED BY GUTZON BORGLUM AND ESTELLE RUMBOLD KOHN, REPRESENT "FOUR PERIODS OF PUBLICITY."
PLAQUE ERECTED 1966 BY
THE NEW YORK COMMUNITY TRUST

UNDERWOOD BUILD
UNIFORMS HARRY SADOW CLOTHIER
FOUNTAIN PEN HOSPITAL
STATIONERS
KEYS

41
Federal Reserve Bank of New York
33 Liberty Street (Nassau Street)
Manhattan

LANDMARKS OF NEW YORK
FEDERAL RESERVE BANK OF NEW YORK
INSPIRED BY FLORENTINE RENAISSANCE PALACES AND COMPLETED IN 1924, THIS STRUCTURE OF INDIANA LIMESTONE AND OHIO SANDSTONE WITH IRONWORK BY SAMUEL YELLIN WAS DESIGNED BY YORK AND SAWYER AND BUILT BY MARC EIDLITZ & SON, INC. FIVE STORIES ARE BELOW STREET LEVEL WITH SUBTERRANEAN VAULTS RESTING ON BEDROCK.
PLAQUE ERECTED 1960 BY
THE NEW YORK COMMUNITY TRUST

55
55 LIBERTY STREET
STOP
STOP
THE CHASE M

42

First National City Bank Building

55 Wall Street (William Street)

Manhattan

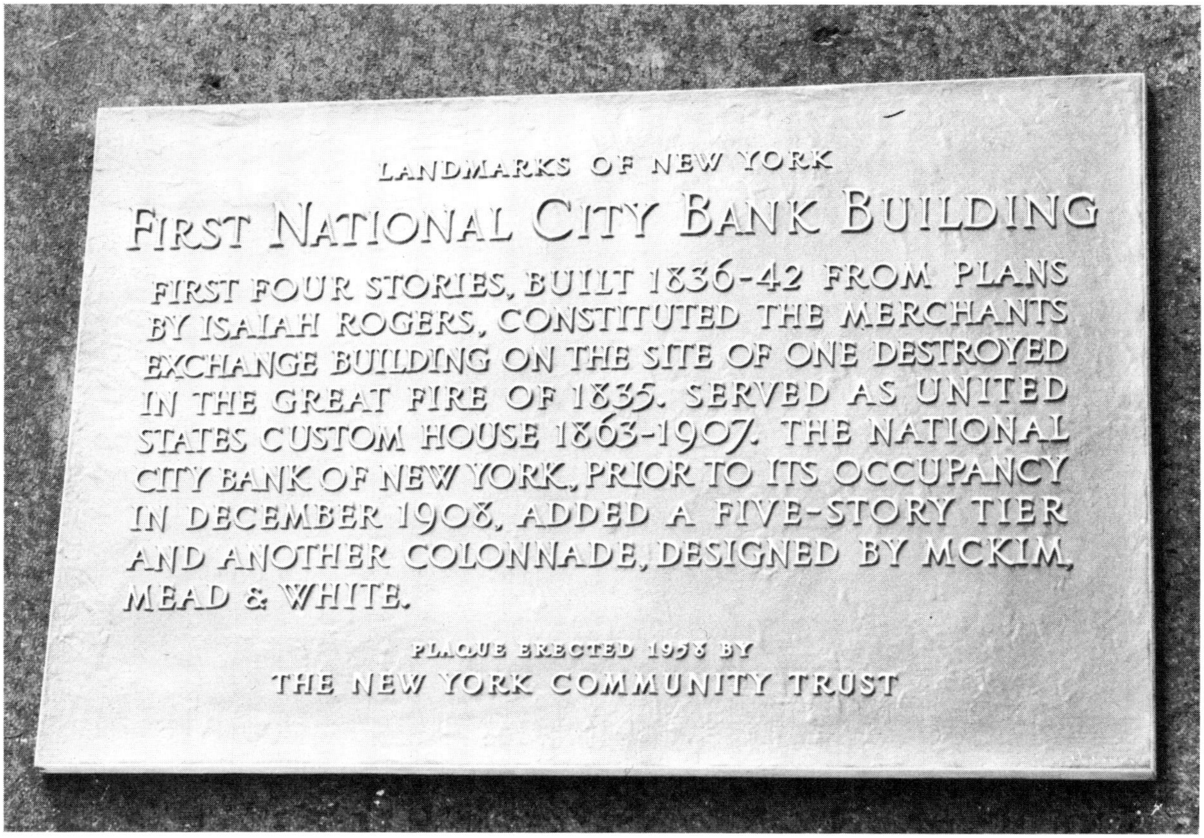

LANDMARKS OF NEW YORK
FIRST NATIONAL CITY BANK BUILDING
FIRST FOUR STORIES, BUILT 1836-42 FROM PLANS BY ISAIAH ROGERS, CONSTITUTED THE MERCHANTS EXCHANGE BUILDING ON THE SITE OF ONE DESTROYED IN THE GREAT FIRE OF 1835. SERVED AS UNITED STATES CUSTOM HOUSE 1863-1907. THE NATIONAL CITY BANK OF NEW YORK, PRIOR TO ITS OCCUPANCY IN DECEMBER 1908, ADDED A FIVE-STORY TIER AND ANOTHER COLONNADE, DESIGNED BY MCKIM, MEAD & WHITE.
PLAQUE ERECTED 1958 BY
THE NEW YORK COMMUNITY TRUST

43
First Presbyterian Church
12 West 12th Street (5th Avenue), Greenwich Village
Manhattan

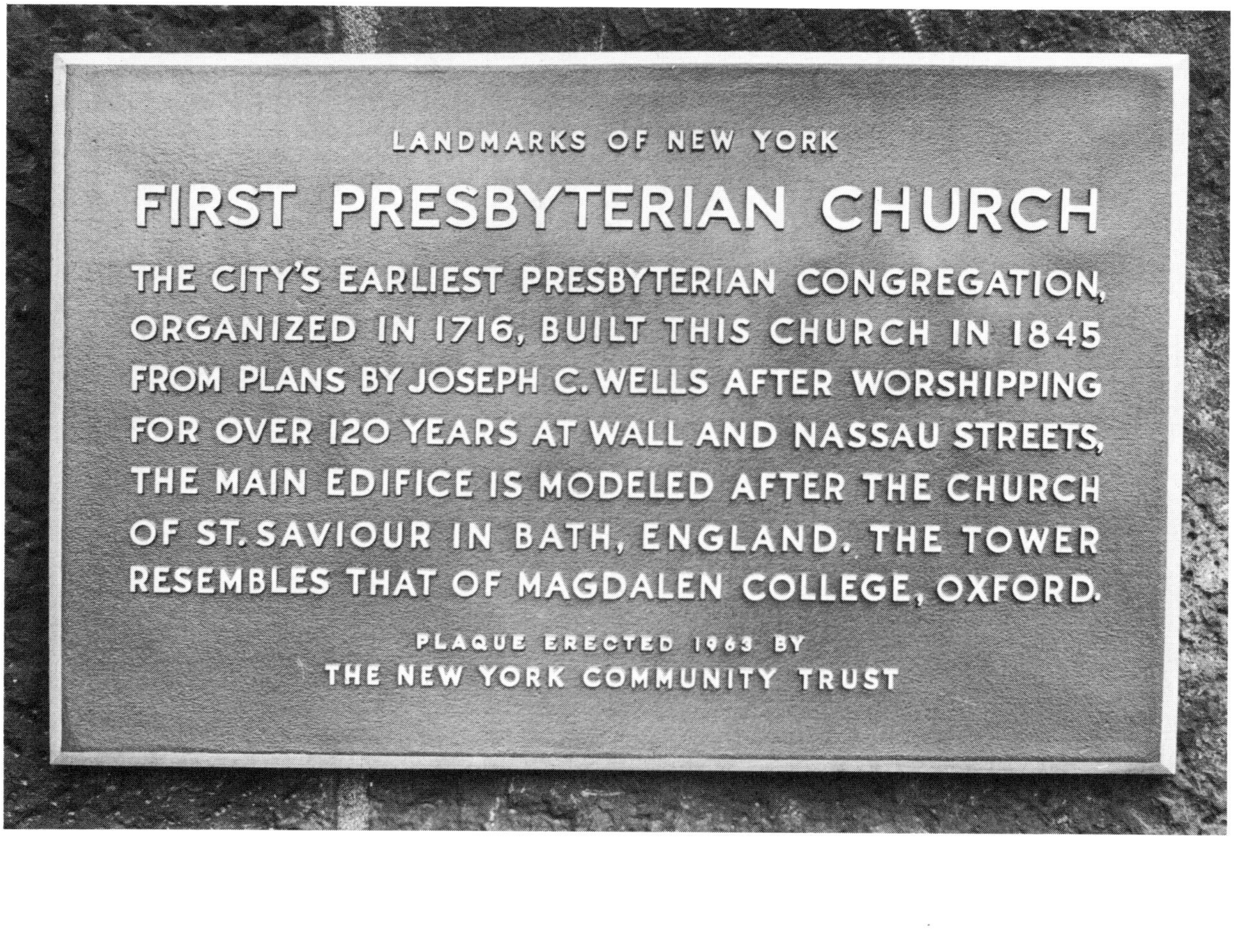
LANDMARKS OF NEW YORK
FIRST PRESBYTERIAN CHURCH
THE CITY'S EARLIEST PRESBYTERIAN CONGREGATION, ORGANIZED IN 1716, BUILT THIS CHURCH IN 1845 FROM PLANS BY JOSEPH C. WELLS AFTER WORSHIPPING FOR OVER 120 YEARS AT WALL AND NASSAU STREETS. THE MAIN EDIFICE IS MODELED AFTER THE CHURCH OF ST. SAVIOUR IN BATH, ENGLAND. THE TOWER RESEMBLES THAT OF MAGDALEN COLLEGE, OXFORD.
PLAQUE ERECTED 1963 BY
THE NEW YORK COMMUNITY TRUST

44
The Flatiron Building

Broadway, Fifth Avenue, and 23rd Street (Madison Square)
Manhattan

LANDMARKS OF NEW YORK
THE FLATIRON BUILDING
THIS EARLY SKYSCRAPER, ORIGINALLY NAMED THE FULLER BUILDING, WAS COMPLETED IN 1902 FROM PLANS OF D. H. BURNHAM & COMPANY. ITS TRIANGULAR SHAPE CAUSED IT TO BECOME GENERALLY KNOWN AS THE FLATIRON BUILDING. THIS WAS ONE OF THE EARLY BUILDINGS TO EMPLOY A STEEL FRAME ON WHICH THE EXTERIOR WALLS WERE HUNG, A PRINCIPLE WIDELY USED IN THE LATER ERECTION OF LOFTY STRUCTURES.
PLAQUE ERECTED 1958 BY
THE NEW YORK COMMUNITY TRUST

THE
NEW YORK
BANK
FOR
SAVINGS
PARK AV. SO.
at 22nd ST.

45
General Theological Seminary, West Building
175 Ninth Avenue (20th Street), Chelsea
Manhattan

LANDMARKS OF NEW YORK
WEST BUILDING
GENERAL THEOLOGICAL SEMINARY
THIS OLDEST EXISTING STRUCTURE OF THE GENERAL
THEOLOGICAL SEMINARY HAS BEEN IN CONTINUOUS
USE SINCE ITS COMPLETION IN 1836. AT THAT
TIME IT CONTAINED LECTURE ROOMS AND A CHAPEL
AS WELL AS LIVING QUARTERS FOR STUDENTS AND
A PROFESSOR. DESIGNED IN GOTHIC REVIVAL STYLE,
IT WAS MODELED AFTER THE EAST BUILDING, COMPLETED
IN 1827 AND DEMOLISHED IN 1892.
PLAQUE ERECTED 1961 BY
THE NEW YORK COMMUNITY TRUST

46
Grace Church (P.E.)
Broadway and 10th Street, Greenwich Village
Manhattan

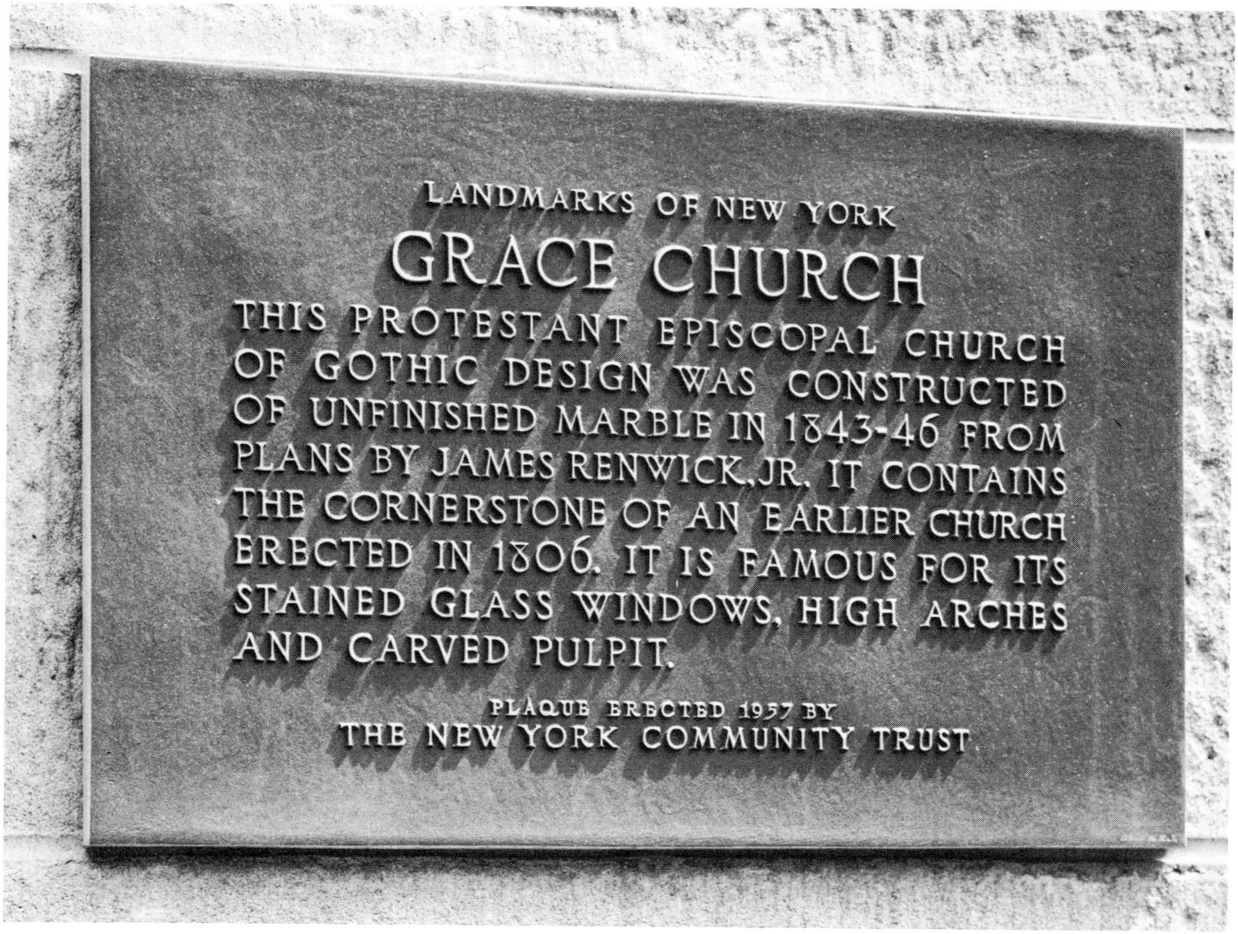
LANDMARKS OF NEW YORK
GRACE CHURCH
THIS PROTESTANT EPISCOPAL CHURCH OF GOTHIC DESIGN WAS CONSTRUCTED OF UNFINISHED MARBLE IN 1843-46 FROM PLANS BY JAMES RENWICK, JR. IT CONTAINS THE CORNERSTONE OF AN EARLIER CHURCH ERECTED IN 1806. IT IS FAMOUS FOR ITS STAINED GLASS WINDOWS, HIGH ARCHES AND CARVED PULPIT.
PLAQUE ERECTED 1957 BY
THE NEW YORK COMMUNITY TRUST

47

Gracie Mansion

East End Avenue and 88th Street (Carl Schurz Park)
Manhattan

LANDMARKS OF NEW YORK
GRACIE MANSION
BUILT ABOUT 1799 ON THE SITE OF A REVOLUTIONARY FORT AS THE COUNTRY HOUSE OF ARCHIBALD GRACIE, SCOTTISH MERCHANT, THIS COLONIAL STRUCTURE WAS RESTORED IN 1927 UNDER THE SUPERVISION OF THE PARK DEPARTMENT. FROM 1923 TO 1932 IT HOUSED THE MUSEUM OF THE CITY OF NEW YORK. IT IS NOW THE OFFICIAL RESIDENCE OF THE MAYOR OF NEW YORK.
PLAQUE ERECTED 1960 BY
THE NEW YORK COMMUNITY TRUST

48
Grand Central Terminal
42nd Street and Park Avenue
Manhattan

LANDMARKS OF NEW YORK
GRAND CENTRAL TERMINAL
COMPLETED IN 1913 FROM PLANS OF
WARREN & WETMORE AND REED & STEM
ON SITE OF EARLIER DEPOT BUILT BY
COMMODORE CORNELIUS VANDERBILT
IN 1871. STATUARY GROUP OVER MAIN
ENTRANCE EXECUTED BY JULES COUTAN
PLAQUE ERECTED 1957 BY
THE NEW YORK COMMUNITY TRUST

49

Greenwich Savings Bank

Broadway, Sixth Avenue, and 33rd Street
Manhattan

LANDMARKS OF NEW YORK
THE GREENWICH SAVINGS BANK
DESIGNED IN CORINTHIAN CLASSICAL STYLE
BY YORK & SAWYER AND BUILT BY MARC EIDLITZ
& SON. THIS IS THE SEVENTH SITE OF ONE OF
NEW YORK'S OLDEST SAVINGS BANKS, ORGANIZED
IN 1833. THE CORNERSTONE WAS LAID IN 1922
AND THE STRUCTURE COMPLETED IN 1924.
PLAQUE ERECTED 1960 BY
THE NEW YORK COMMUNITY TRUST

THE GREENWICH SAVINGS BANK
THE GREENWICH

50

Nos. 4-10 Grove Street

near Bedford Street, Greenwich Village

Manhattan

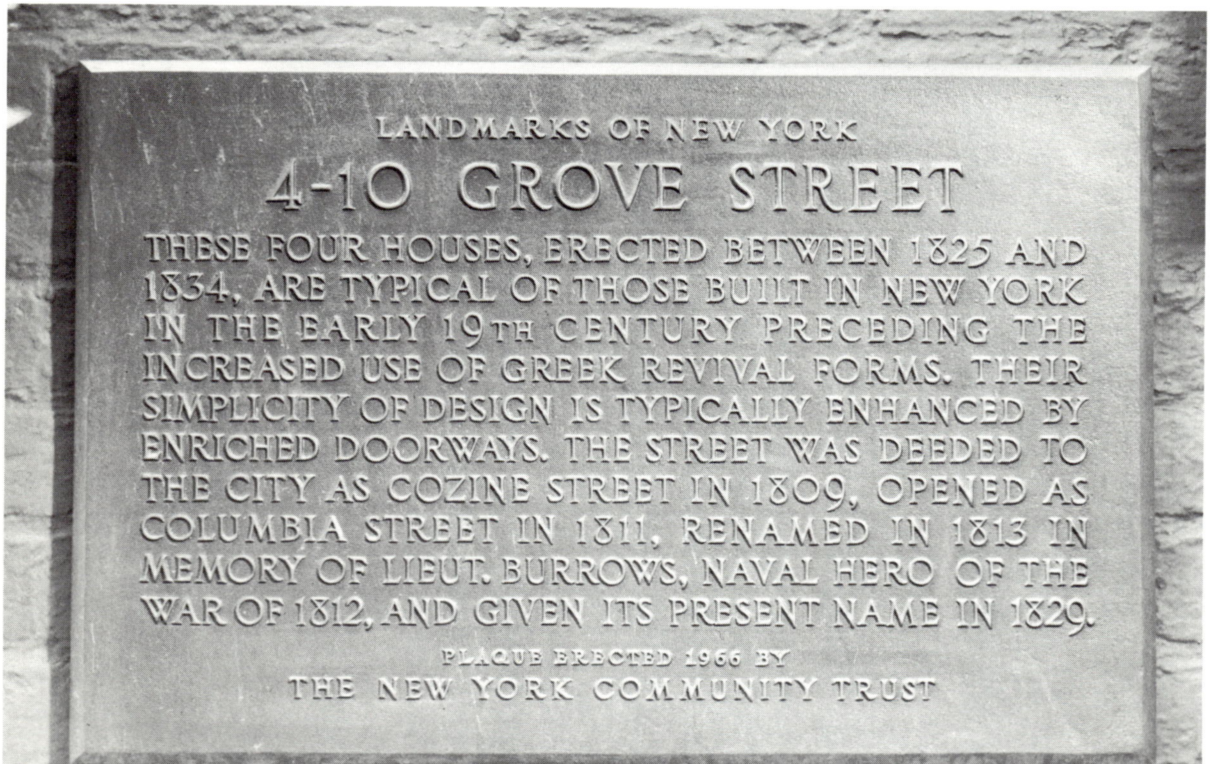
LANDMARKS OF NEW YORK
4-10 GROVE STREET
THESE FOUR HOUSES, ERECTED BETWEEN 1825 AND 1834, ARE TYPICAL OF THOSE BUILT IN NEW YORK IN THE EARLY 19TH CENTURY PRECEDING THE INCREASED USE OF GREEK REVIVAL FORMS. THEIR SIMPLICITY OF DESIGN IS TYPICALLY ENHANCED BY ENRICHED DOORWAYS. THE STREET WAS DEEDED TO THE CITY AS COZINE STREET IN 1809, OPENED AS COLUMBIA STREET IN 1811, RENAMED IN 1813 IN MEMORY OF LIEUT. BURROWS, NAVAL HERO OF THE WAR OF 1812, AND GIVEN ITS PRESENT NAME IN 1829.
PLAQUE ERECTED 1966 BY
THE NEW YORK COMMUNITY TRUST

51
Guaranty Trust Company Building
140 Broadway (Liberty Street) [demolished]
Manhattan

LANDMARKS OF NEW YORK
GUARANTY TRUST COMPANY BUILDING
THIS STRUCTURE OF ROMAN STYLE, DESIGNED
BY YORK & SAWYER AND BUILT BY MARC
EIDLITZ & SON IN 1912-13, RECEIVED
AMERICAN INSTITUTE OF ARCHITECTS' MEDAL
FOR DISTINGUISHED ARCHITECTURE IN 1914.
NEW ENGLAND GRANITE FORMS THE EXTERIOR
AND HAUTEVILLE MARBLE LINES THE MAIN
BANKING ROOM.
PLAQUE ERECTED 1957 BY
THE NEW YORK COMMUNITY TRUST

GVARANTY TRVST COMPANY

52

The Harvard Club

32 West 45th Street (5th Avenue)

Manhattan

LANDMARKS OF NEW YORK
THE HARVARD CLUB
THIS BUILDING WAS DESIGNED BY McKIM, MEAD & WHITE IN AN ARCHITECTURAL STYLE EMPLOYED IN THE LATE NINETEENTH CENTURY AT HARVARD. ITS EXTERIOR IS HARVARD BRICK LAID IN FLEMISH BOND WITH TRIM OF INDIANA LIMESTONE. THE CLUB HOUSE, OPENED IN 1894, WAS EXTENDED TO 45TH STREET IN 1905 AND FURTHER ENLARGED IN 1915.
PLAQUE ERECTED 1959 BY
THE NEW YORK COMMUNITY TRUST

27

53
Henry Street Settlement
265 Henry Street (Montgomery Street)
Manhattan

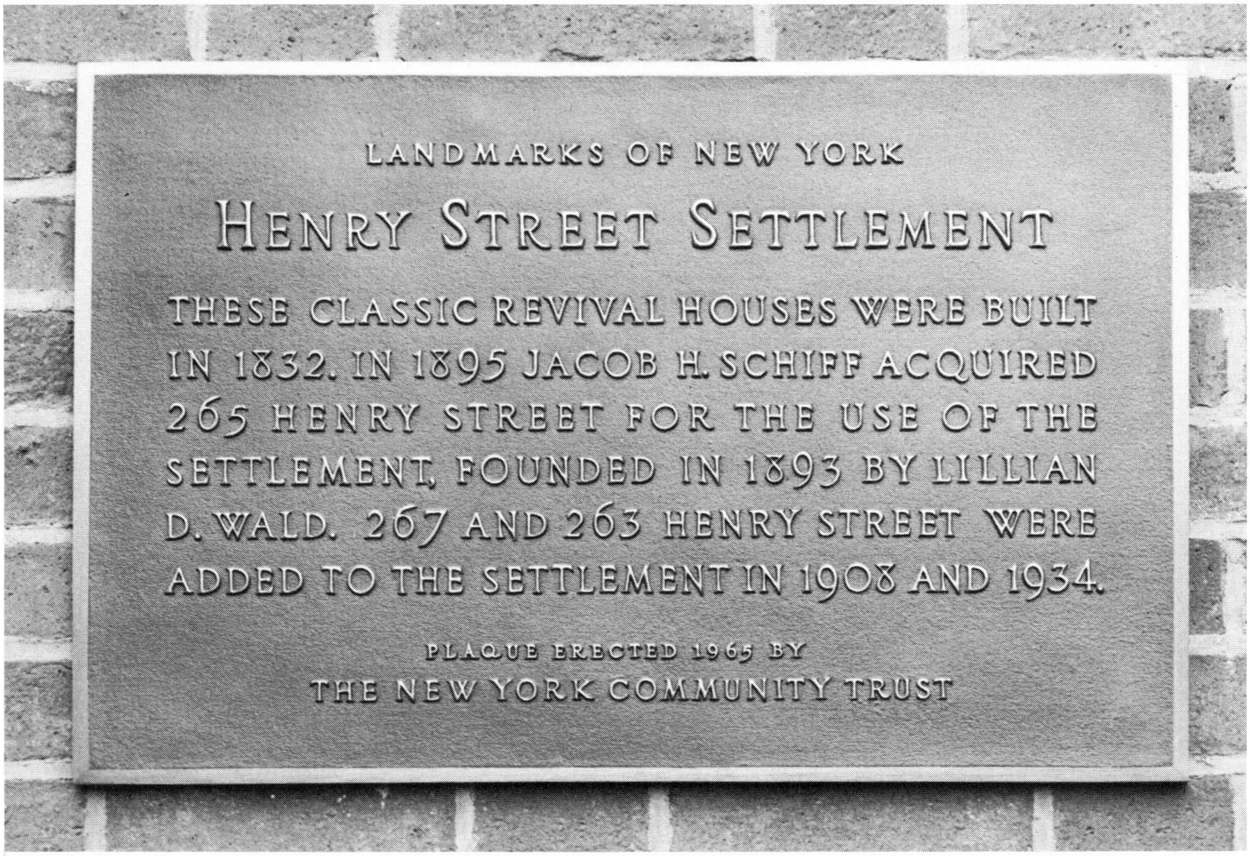
LANDMARKS OF NEW YORK
HENRY STREET SETTLEMENT
THESE CLASSIC REVIVAL HOUSES WERE BUILT IN 1832. IN 1895 JACOB H. SCHIFF ACQUIRED 265 HENRY STREET FOR THE USE OF THE SETTLEMENT, FOUNDED IN 1893 BY LILLIAN D. WALD. 267 AND 263 HENRY STREET WERE ADDED TO THE SETTLEMENT IN 1908 AND 1934.
PLAQUE ERECTED 1965 BY
THE NEW YORK COMMUNITY TRUST

54

President Herbert Hoover Residence

Waldorf Towers, Park Avenue and 50th Street
Manhattan

"NEW YORK OF THE PRESIDENTS"
HERBERT HOOVER
AUGUST 10, 1874 - OCTOBER 20, 1964
THIRTY-FIRST PRESIDENT
OF THE UNITED STATES, 1929-1933
CHAIRMAN, COMMISSION FOR RELIEF IN BELGIUM, 1915-1919
U.S. FOOD ADMINISTRATOR, 1917-1919
SECRETARY OF COMMERCE, 1921-1928
THE WALDORF TOWERS WAS THE RESIDENCE OF
MR. HOOVER FOR THIRTY YEARS PRECEDING HIS DEATH
PLAQUE ERECTED 1965
BY THE NEW YORK COMMUNITY TRUST

55

Institute of Fine Arts (former Duke Mansion)

1 East 78th Street (5th Avenue)

Manhattan

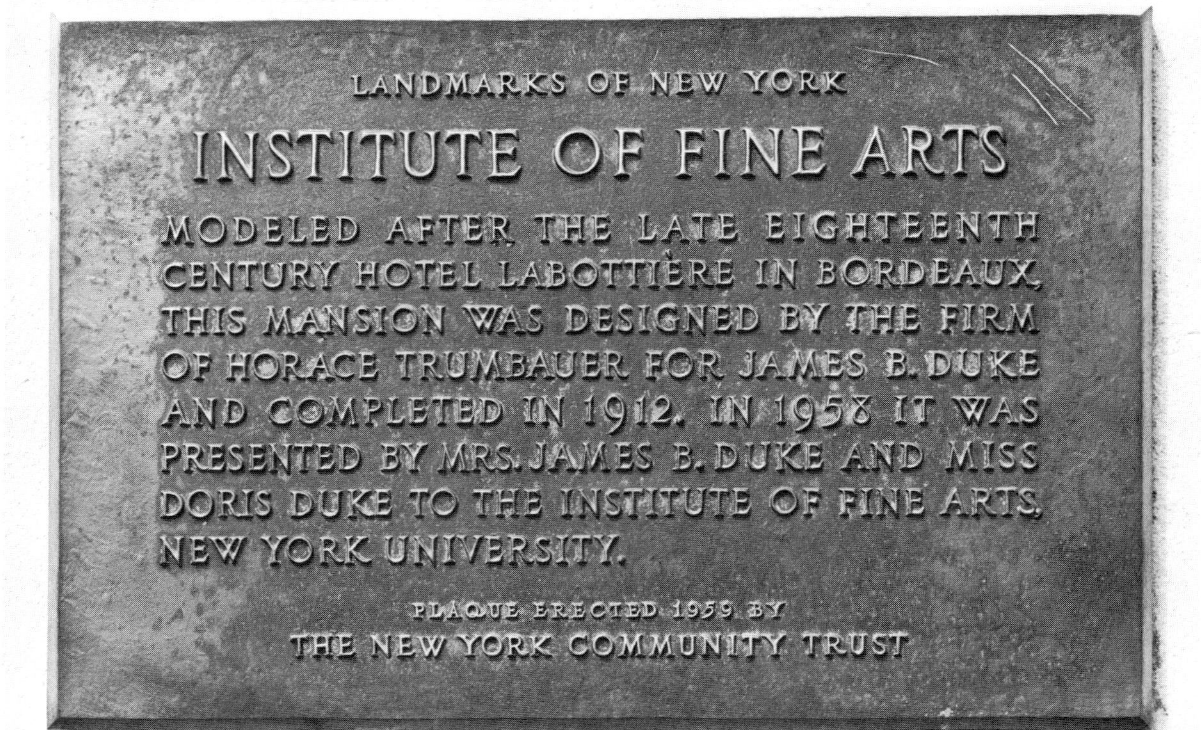
LANDMARKS OF NEW YORK
INSTITUTE OF FINE ARTS
MODELED AFTER THE LATE EIGHTEENTH CENTURY HOTEL LABOTTIÈRE IN BORDEAUX, THIS MANSION WAS DESIGNED BY THE FIRM OF HORACE TRUMBAUER FOR JAMES B. DUKE AND COMPLETED IN 1912. IN 1958 IT WAS PRESENTED BY MRS. JAMES B. DUKE AND MISS DORIS DUKE TO THE INSTITUTE OF FINE ARTS, NEW YORK UNIVERSITY.
PLAQUE ERECTED 1959 BY
THE NEW YORK COMMUNITY TRUST

56

Institute of Radio Engineers (former Isaac Vail Brokaw Residence)

79th Street and Fifth Avenue [demolished]
Manhattan

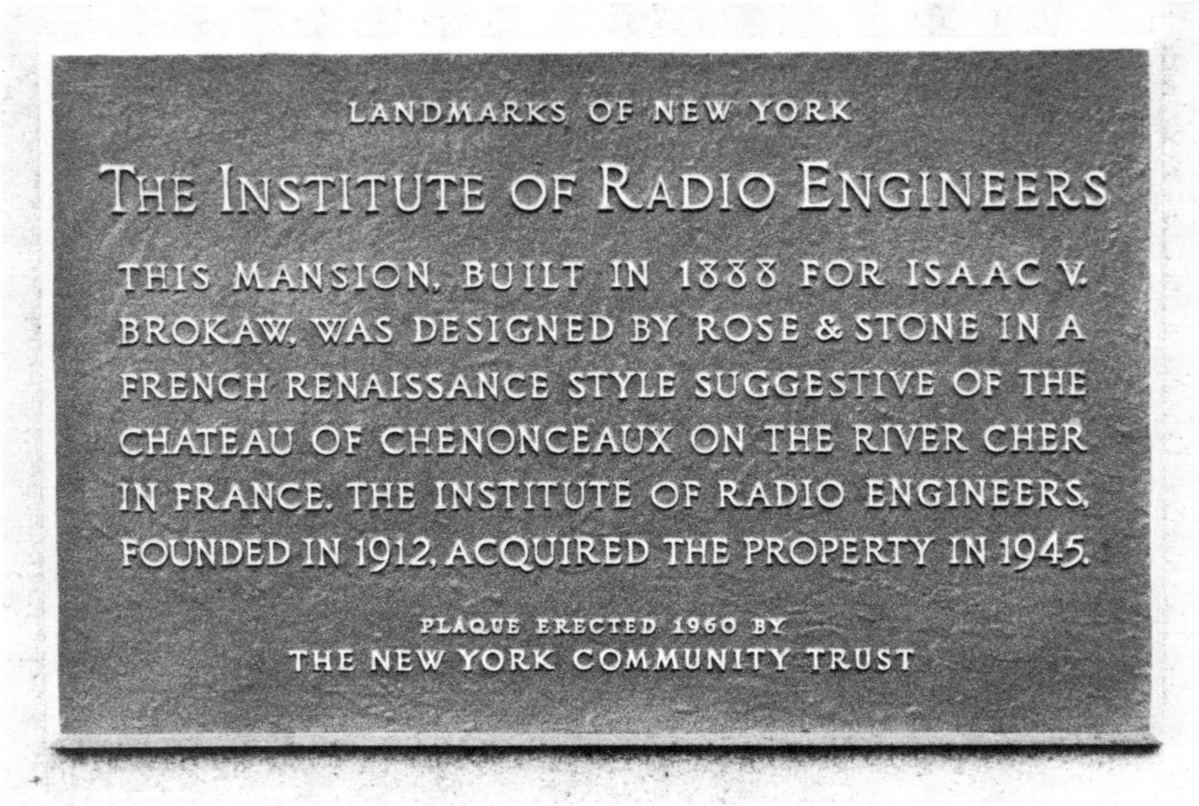
LANDMARKS OF NEW YORK
THE INSTITUTE OF RADIO ENGINEERS
THIS MANSION, BUILT IN 1888 FOR ISAAC V. BROKAW, WAS DESIGNED BY ROSE & STONE IN A FRENCH RENAISSANCE STYLE SUGGESTIVE OF THE CHATEAU OF CHENONCEAUX ON THE RIVER CHER IN FRANCE. THE INSTITUTE OF RADIO ENGINEERS, FOUNDED IN 1912, ACQUIRED THE PROPERTY IN 1945.
PLAQUE ERECTED 1960 BY
THE NEW YORK COMMUNITY TRUST

E 79 ST
WEST
SIDE

57

Isaacs-Hendricks House

77 Bedford Street (Commerce Street), Greenwich Village
Manhattan

"HERITAGE OF NEW YORK"
ISAACS-HENDRICKS HOUSE
THIS FRAME HOUSE WAS CONSTRUCTED IN 1799 FOR JOSHUA ISAACS, OF LANCASTER, PA., ON PROPERTY PURCHASED FROM ELBERT ROOSEVELT. IN 1801 ISAACS' SON-IN-LAW, HARMON HENDRICKS, A COPPER MERCHANT, BOUGHT THE HOUSE, WHICH WITH NEIGHBORING PROPERTY WAS HELD BY THE HENDRICKS FAMILY UNTIL 1928. THE GREEK REVIVAL FACADE WAS ADDED TO THE ORIGINAL TWO AND ONE HALF STORY FEDERAL HOUSE IN 1836 AND A THIRD STORY REPLACED PREVIOUS DORMERS IN 1928.
PLAQUE ERECTED 1966 BY
THE NEW YORK COMMUNITY TRUST

58

Jefferson Market Courthouse

Sixth Avenue and 10th Street, Greenwich Village
Manhattan

LANDMARKS OF NEW YORK
JEFFERSON MARKET COURTHOUSE
THIS BUILDING, DESIGNED ALONG VICTORIAN GOTHIC LINES BY VAUX & WITHERS, WAS CONSTRUCTED IN 1876 AND SERVED AS THE WOMEN'S COURT UNTIL 1932. OF PARTICULAR INTEREST ARE ITS TURRETS, TRACERIED WINDOWS, IRONWORK AND SCULPTURE.
PLAQUE ERECTED 1958 BY
THE NEW YORK COMMUNITY TRUST

59
John Street Methodist Church
44 John Street (Nassau Street)
Manhattan

LANDMARKS OF NEW YORK
JOHN STREET METHODIST CHURCH
THE OLDEST METHODIST SOCIETY IN AMERICA, ORGANIZED IN 1766 BY PHILIP EMBURY AND BARBARA HECK, CONSTRUCTED HERE IN 1768 WESLEY CHAPEL, THE FIRST METHODIST MEETING HOUSE IN AMERICA. THE PRESENT CHURCH, THE THIRD ON THIS SITE, WAS COMPLETED IN 1841.
PLAQUE ERECTED 1964 BY
THE NEW YORK COMMUNITY TRUST

JOHN STREET
METHODIST
CHURCH
ORGANIZED 1766
JOHN STREET
METHODIST CHURCH
SUNDAY
11 A.M. MORNING WORSHIP
WEDNESDAY
FRIDAY
PASTOR
REV. RICHARD L. FRANCIS
NO
PARKING
ANY
TIME
FOR
RENT

60
Judson Memorial Church (Baptist)
55 Washington Square South (Thompson Street), Greenwich Village
Manhattan

LANDMARKS OF NEW YORK
JUDSON MEMORIAL CHURCH
CONSTRUCTED IN 1892, THIS BAPTIST CHURCH, NAMED IN MEMORY OF ADONIRAM JUDSON, WAS DESIGNED IN A GRECO-ROMANESQUE STYLE BY MCKIM, MEAD AND WHITE, WITH STAINED GLASS WINDOWS BY JOHN LA FARGE AND A BAPTISTRY EXECUTED BY HERBERT ADAMS FROM PLANS OF ST. GAUDENS. DR. JUDSON WAS ONE OF THE FIRST AMERICAN MISSIONARIES SENT TO FOREIGN LANDS WHEN APPOINTED TO BURMA IN 1811. HIS SON, EDWARD JUDSON, PLACED IN THE CORNERSTONE A COPY OF HIS FATHER'S BURMESE TRANSLATION OF THE BIBLE.
PLAQUE ERECTED 1963 BY
THE NEW YORK COMMUNITY TRUST

61

Knickerbocker Club

807 Fifth Avenue (62nd Street)
Manhattan

LANDMARKS OF NEW YORK
KNICKERBOCKER CLUB
THIS THIRD HOME OF THE KNICKERBOCKER CLUB, ORGANIZED IN 1871, WAS DESIGNED BY DELANO AND ALDRICH AND WAS COMPLETED IN 1915.
PLAQUE ERECTED 1962 BY
THE NEW YORK COMMUNITY TRUST

62
Lotos Club
5 East 66th Street (5th Avenue)
Manhattan

LANDMARKS OF NEW YORK
THE LOTOS CLUB
DESIGNED IN FRENCH RENAISSANCE STYLE BY
RICHARD HOWLAND HUNT IN 1900 AS THE
RESIDENCE OF WILLIAM JAY SCHIEFFELIN.
THIS MANSION BECAME IN 1947 THE HOME
OF THE LOTOS CLUB, FOUNDED IN 1870 AND
DEVOTED TO LITERATURE AND THE ARTS.
PLAQUE ERECTED 1960 BY
THE NEW YORK COMMUNITY TRUST

5
5

63
Lüchow's Restaurant
110 East 14th Street (4th Avenue), Union Square
Manhattan

LANDMARKS OF NEW YORK
LÜCHOW'S RESTAURANT
IN 1882 AUGUST LÜCHOW FOUNDED THIS RESTAURANT WITH AN INTERIOR IN LATE GERMAN RENAISSANCE STYLE. UNTIL THE TURN OF THE CENTURY THIS AREA WAS A CENTER OF THE CITY'S MUSICAL, THEATRICAL, POLITICAL AND MERCHANDISING ACTIVITIES. HERE IN 1914 VICTOR HERBERT AND EIGHT ASSOCIATES FORMED THE ORGANIZATION THAT BECAME THE AMERICAN SOCIETY OF COMPOSERS, AUTHORS AND PUBLISHERS.
PLAQUE ERECTED 1965 BY
THE NEW YORK COMMUNITY TRUST

Lüchow's
LÜCHOW'S

64
General Douglas MacArthur Residence
Waldorf Towers, Park Avenue and 50th Street
Manhattan

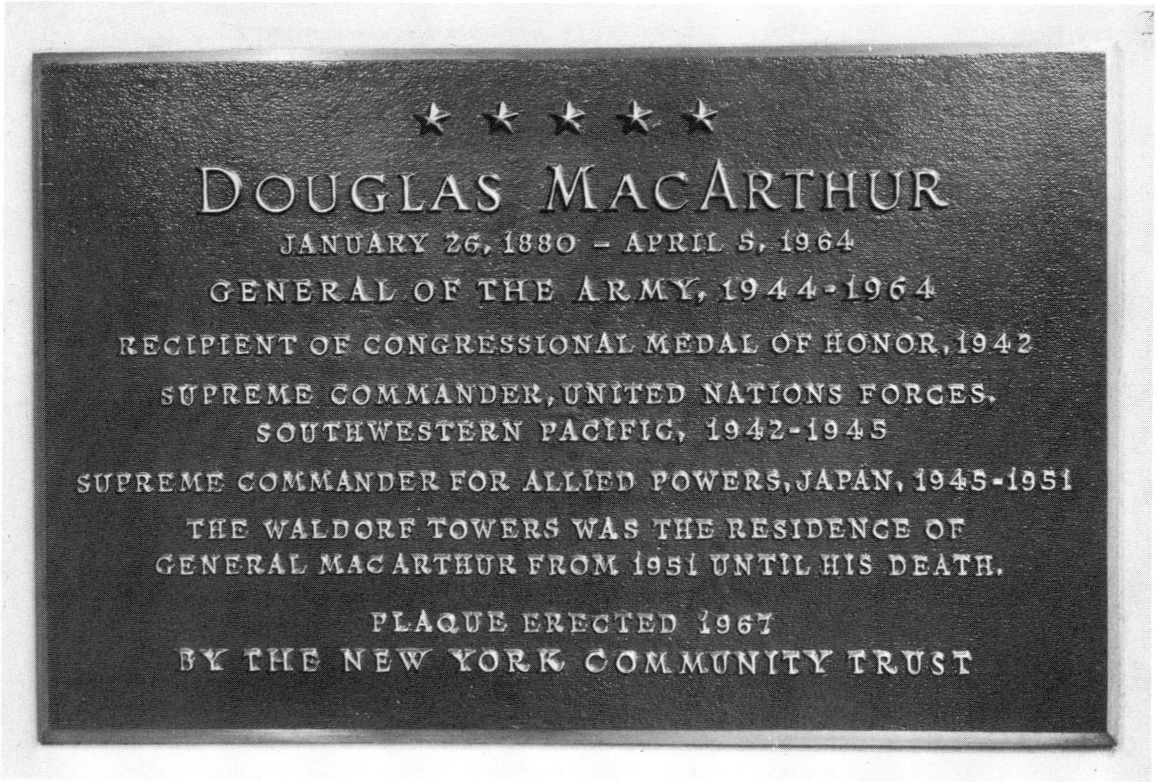
★ ★ ★ ★ ★
DOUGLAS MACARTHUR
JANUARY 26, 1880 – APRIL 5, 1964
GENERAL OF THE ARMY, 1944-1964
RECIPIENT OF CONGRESSIONAL MEDAL OF HONOR, 1942
SUPREME COMMANDER, UNITED NATIONS FORCES,
SOUTHWESTERN PACIFIC, 1942-1945
SUPREME COMMANDER FOR ALLIED POWERS, JAPAN, 1945-1951
THE WALDORF TOWERS WAS THE RESIDENCE OF
GENERAL MACARTHUR FROM 1951 UNTIL HIS DEATH.
PLAQUE ERECTED 1967
BY THE NEW YORK COMMUNITY TRUST

The Waldorf Towers
The Waldorf Towers
114
PRIVATE ENTRANCE
THE TOWERS
OF THE
WALDORF ASTORIA
PRIVATE ENTRANCE
THE TOWERS
OF THE
WALDORF ASTORIA

65
Metropolitan Club
1 East 60th Street (5th Avenue)
Manhattan

LANDMARKS OF NEW YORK
THE METROPOLITAN CLUB
DESIGNED IN ITALIAN RENAISSANCE STYLE BY MCKIM, MEAD & WHITE, THIS BUILDING, ON A SITE FORMERLY OWNED BY THE DUCHESS OF MARLBOROUGH, WAS COMPLETED AS A HOME FOR THE METROPOLITAN CLUB IN 1894. THE CLUB, WHOSE FIRST PRESIDENT WAS J. PIERPONT MORGAN, WAS ORGANIZED IN 1891.
PLAQUE ERECTED 1966 BY
THE NEW YORK COMMUNITY TRUST

66
Metropolitan Life Tower
1 Madison Avenue (24th Street), Madison Square
Manhattan

LANDMARKS OF NEW YORK
METROPOLITAN LIFE TOWER
THIS TOWER, OF MASSIVE SIMPLICITY
IN ITALIAN RENAISSANCE STYLE, WAS
COMPLETED IN 1909 FROM PLANS BY
LE BRUN & SONS. ITS FOUR CLOCK FACES
ARE EACH 26½ FEET IN DIAMETER, WITH
MINUTE HANDS WEIGHING ½ TON. FOUR
CHIMES (THE LARGEST 7000 POUNDS) SOUND
A MEASURE BY HANDEL ON QUARTER HOURS.
PLAQUE ERECTED 1957 BY
THE NEW YORK COMMUNITY TRUST

67

Morris-Jumel Mansion

West 160th Street and Jumel Terrace (Edgecombe Avenue)
Manhattan

LANDMARKS OF NEW YORK
MORRIS-JUMEL MANSION
THIS GEORGIAN COLONIAL STRUCTURE BUILT BY ROGER MORRIS IN 1765 WAS ACQUIRED BY STEPHEN JUMEL IN 1810 AFTER HAVING SERVED AS HEADQUARTERS FOR BOTH GENERAL WASHINGTON AND THE BRITISH-HESSIAN FORCES.
PLAQUE ERECTED 1959 BY
THE NEW YORK COMMUNITY TRUST

68
Municipal Building
Centre and Chambers Streets, City Hall
Manhattan

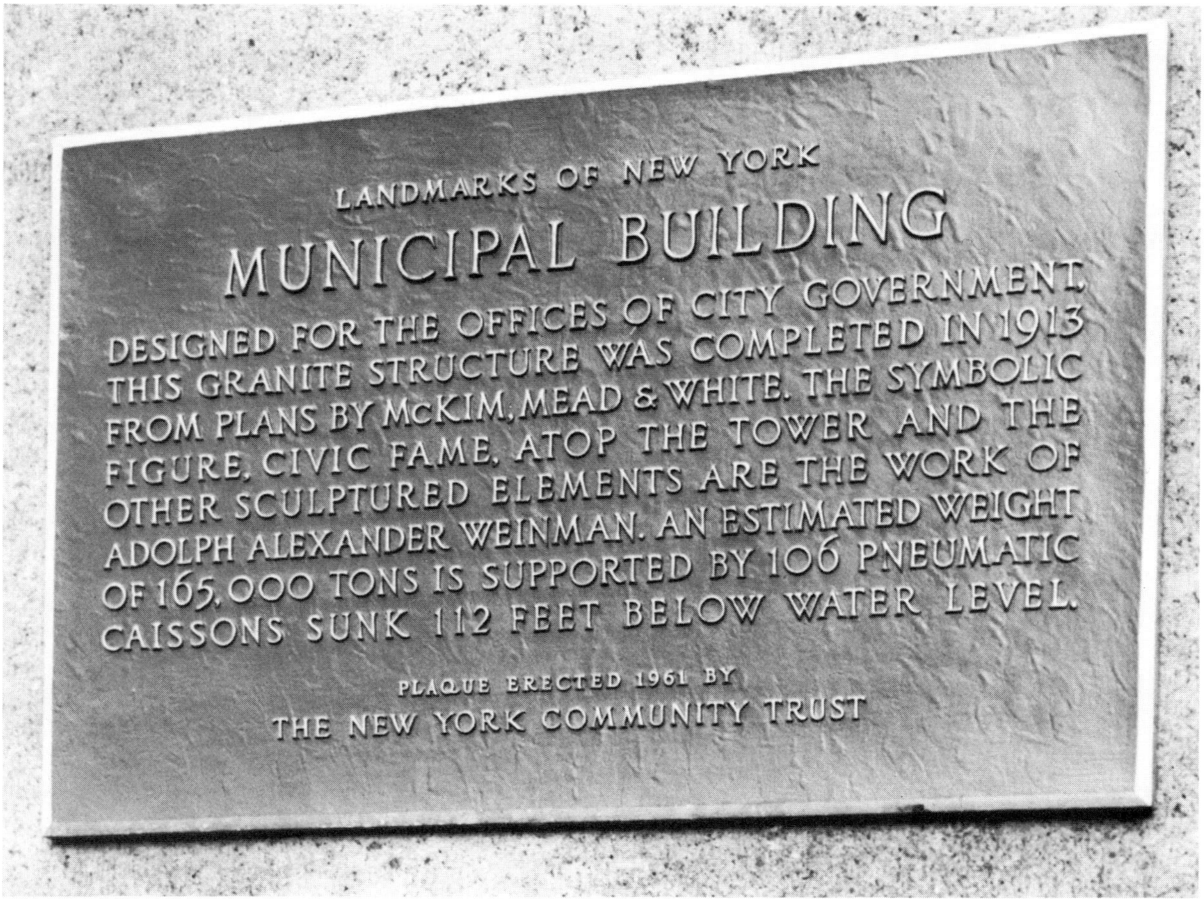
LANDMARKS OF NEW YORK
MUNICIPAL BUILDING
DESIGNED FOR THE OFFICES OF CITY GOVERNMENT,
THIS GRANITE STRUCTURE WAS COMPLETED IN 1913
FROM PLANS BY McKIM, MEAD & WHITE. THE SYMBOLIC
FIGURE, CIVIC FAME, ATOP THE TOWER AND THE
OTHER SCULPTURED ELEMENTS ARE THE WORK OF
ADOLPH ALEXANDER WEINMAN. AN ESTIMATED WEIGHT
OF 165,000 TONS IS SUPPORTED BY 106 PNEUMATIC
CAISSONS SUNK 112 FEET BELOW WATER LEVEL.
PLAQUE ERECTED 1961 BY
THE NEW YORK COMMUNITY TRUST

NEW YORK

69

National Arts Club

15 Gramercy Park (20th Street)

Manhattan

LANDMARKS OF NEW YORK
THE NATIONAL ARTS CLUB
THIS BUILDING, ORIGINALLY TWO PRIVATE HOUSES, WAS REMODELED FOR SAMUEL J. TILDEN IN THE EARLY 1870'S BY CALVERT VAUX, ONE OF THE DESIGNERS OF CENTRAL PARK. TILDEN, GOVERNOR OF NEW YORK, 1874-76, AND CANDIDATE FOR THE PRESIDENCY IN 1876, RESIDED HERE UNTIL HIS DEATH. THE NATIONAL ARTS CLUB, FOUNDED IN 1898, PURCHASED THE PROPERTY IN 1906.
PLAQUE ERECTED 1962 BY
THE NEW YORK COMMUNITY TRUST

ELECTRIC BURGLAR ALARM
CO.
146 LUDLOW ST NEW YORK 2 NY

70
New York Academy of Medicine
2 East 103rd Street (5th Avenue)
Manhattan

LANDMARKS OF NEW YORK
THE NEW YORK ACADEMY OF MEDICINE
THIS STRUCTURE, A GIFT FROM THE CARNEGIE FOUNDATION TO THE NEW YORK ACADEMY OF MEDICINE (FOUNDED IN 1847), WAS DESIGNED IN ROMANESQUE STYLE BY YORK & SAWYER AND BUILT BY MARC EIDLITZ & SON IN 1925-26. IT WAS CITED BY THE MUNICIPAL ART SOCIETY AND SOCIETY OF ARCHITECTURAL HISTORIANS IN 1957 FOR THE MERIT OF ITS ARCHITECTURE.
PLAQUE ERECTED 1957 BY
THE NEW YORK COMMUNITY TRUST

71
New York Chamber of Commerce Building
65 Liberty Street (Broadway)
Manhattan

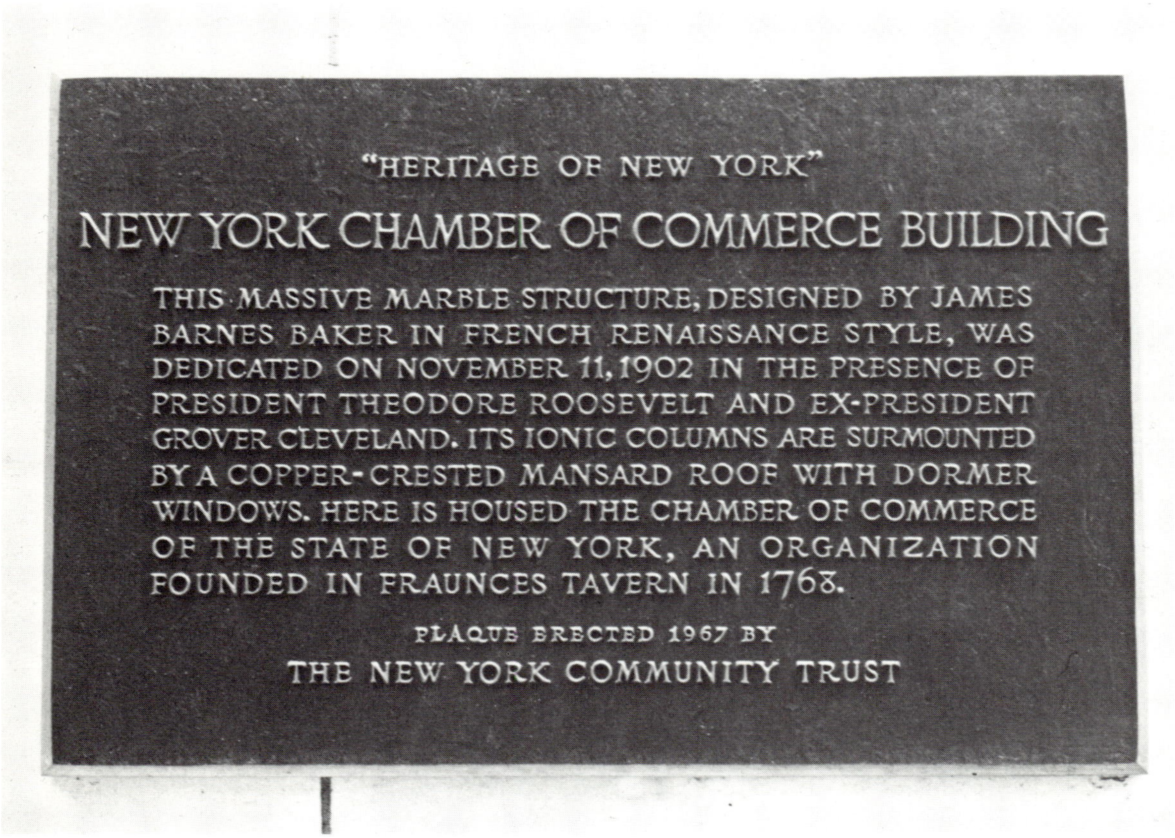
"HERITAGE OF NEW YORK"
NEW YORK CHAMBER OF COMMERCE BUILDING
THIS MASSIVE MARBLE STRUCTURE, DESIGNED BY JAMES BARNES BAKER IN FRENCH RENAISSANCE STYLE, WAS DEDICATED ON NOVEMBER 11, 1902 IN THE PRESENCE OF PRESIDENT THEODORE ROOSEVELT AND EX-PRESIDENT GROVER CLEVELAND. ITS IONIC COLUMNS ARE SURMOUNTED BY A COPPER-CRESTED MANSARD ROOF WITH DORMER WINDOWS. HERE IS HOUSED THE CHAMBER OF COMMERCE OF THE STATE OF NEW YORK, AN ORGANIZATION FOUNDED IN FRAUNCES TAVERN IN 1768.
PLAQUE ERECTED 1967 BY
THE NEW YORK COMMUNITY TRUST

72
New York County Court House
Foley Square
Manhattan

LANDMARKS OF NEW YORK
NEW YORK COUNTY COURT HOUSE
THIS BUILDING, DESIGNED IN NEOCLASSIC STYLE BY GUY LOWELL, WAS COMPLETED IN 1927. THE ORIGINAL PLANS, WHICH WON A COMPETITION HELD IN 1912-1913, WERE FOR A CIRCULAR STRUCTURE, BUT WERE ALTERED TO CREATE THE PRESENT HEXAGONAL FORM.
PLAQUE ERECTED 1962 BY
THE NEW YORK COMMUNITY TRUST

THE·TRUE·ADMINISTRATION·OF·JUSTICE·IS·THE·FIRMEST·PILLAR·OF·GOOD·GOVERNMENT

73

New York County Lawyers Association

14 Vesey Street (Broadway)

Manhattan

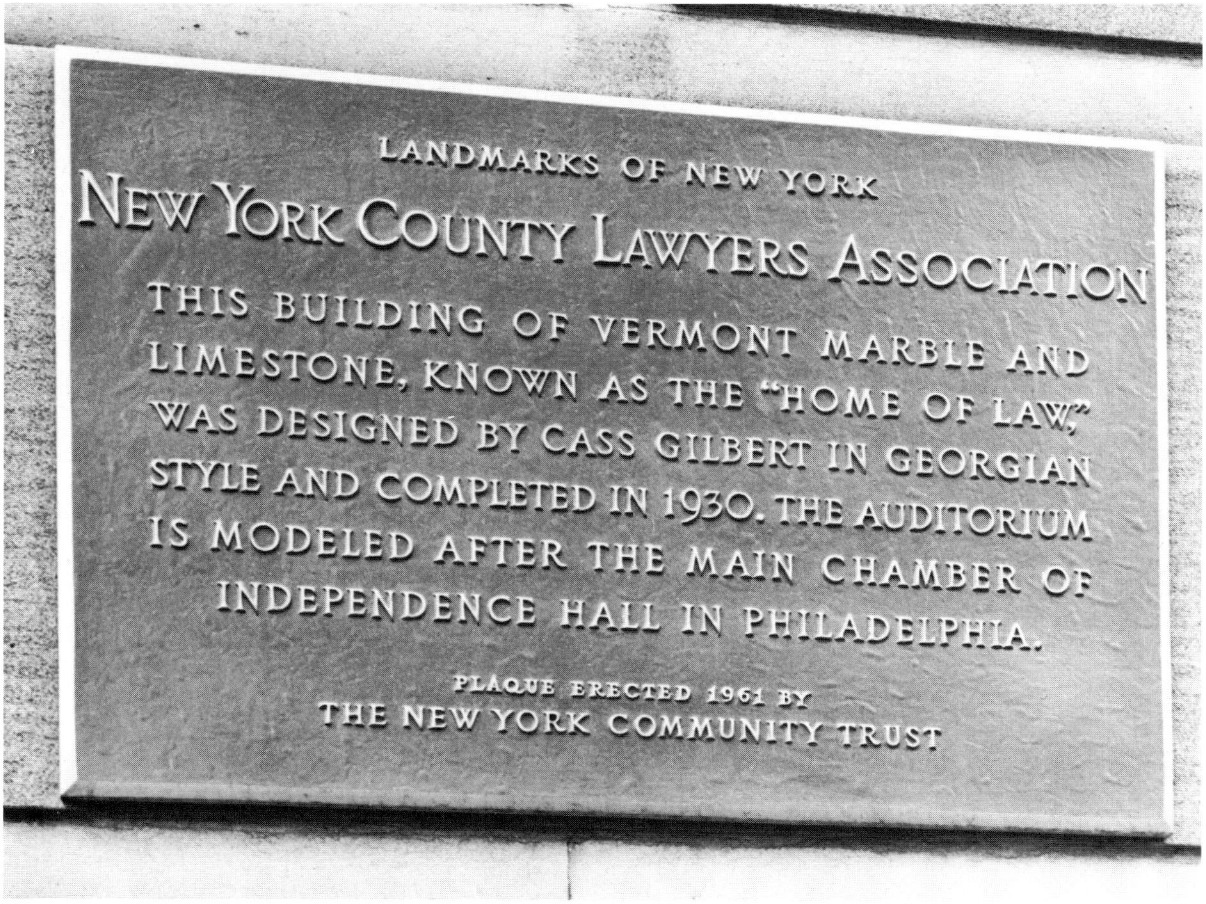
LANDMARKS OF NEW YORK
NEW YORK COUNTY LAWYERS ASSOCIATION
THIS BUILDING OF VERMONT MARBLE AND LIMESTONE, KNOWN AS THE "HOME OF LAW," WAS DESIGNED BY CASS GILBERT IN GEORGIAN STYLE AND COMPLETED IN 1930. THE AUDITORIUM IS MODELED AFTER THE MAIN CHAMBER OF INDEPENDENCE HALL IN PHILADELPHIA.
PLAQUE ERECTED 1961 BY
THE NEW YORK COMMUNITY TRUST

74
New York Daily News Building
220 East 42nd Street (2nd Avenue)
Manhattan

LANDMARKS OF NEW YORK
NEW YORK DAILY NEWS BUILDING
COMPLETED IN 1930 FROM DESIGNS OF JOHN MEAD HOWELLS AND RAYMOND HOOD. THIS STRUCTURE WAS CITED IN 1957 BY THE MUNICIPAL ART SOCIETY AND THE SOCIETY OF ARCHITECTURAL HISTORIANS "FOR ORIGINALITY IN DESIGN AND INFLUENCE ON LATER WORK."
PLAQUE ERECTED 1957 BY
THE NEW YORK COMMUNITY TRUST

DONT
WALK

75
New York Life Building
51 Madison Avenue (26th Street), Madison Square
Manhattan

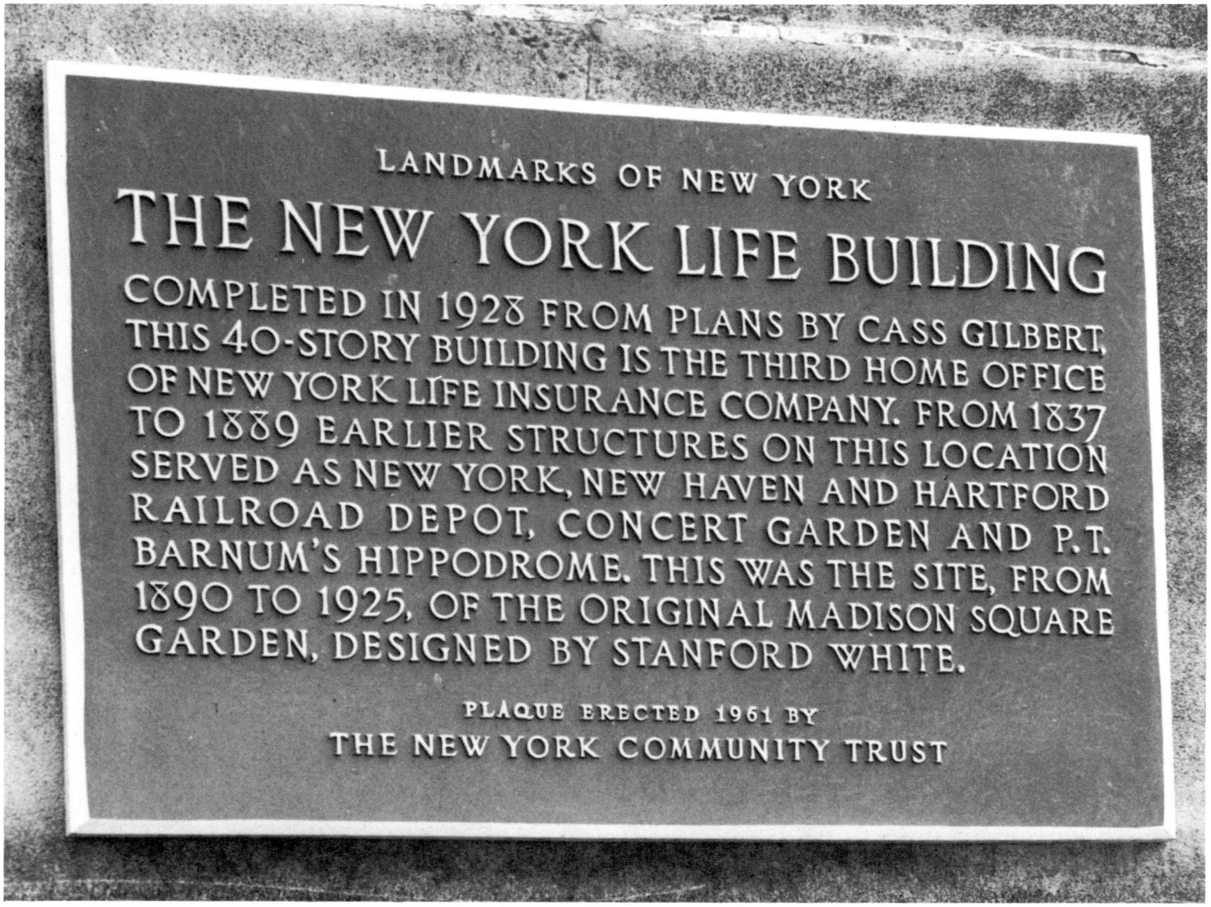
LANDMARKS OF NEW YORK
THE NEW YORK LIFE BUILDING
COMPLETED IN 1928 FROM PLANS BY CASS GILBERT, THIS 40-STORY BUILDING IS THE THIRD HOME OFFICE OF NEW YORK LIFE INSURANCE COMPANY. FROM 1837 TO 1889 EARLIER STRUCTURES ON THIS LOCATION SERVED AS NEW YORK, NEW HAVEN AND HARTFORD RAILROAD DEPOT, CONCERT GARDEN AND P.T. BARNUM'S HIPPODROME. THIS WAS THE SITE, FROM 1890 TO 1925, OF THE ORIGINAL MADISON SQUARE GARDEN, DESIGNED BY STANFORD WHITE.
PLAQUE ERECTED 1961 BY
THE NEW YORK COMMUNITY TRUST

76

New York Stock Exchange

Broad Street at Wall Street
Manhattan

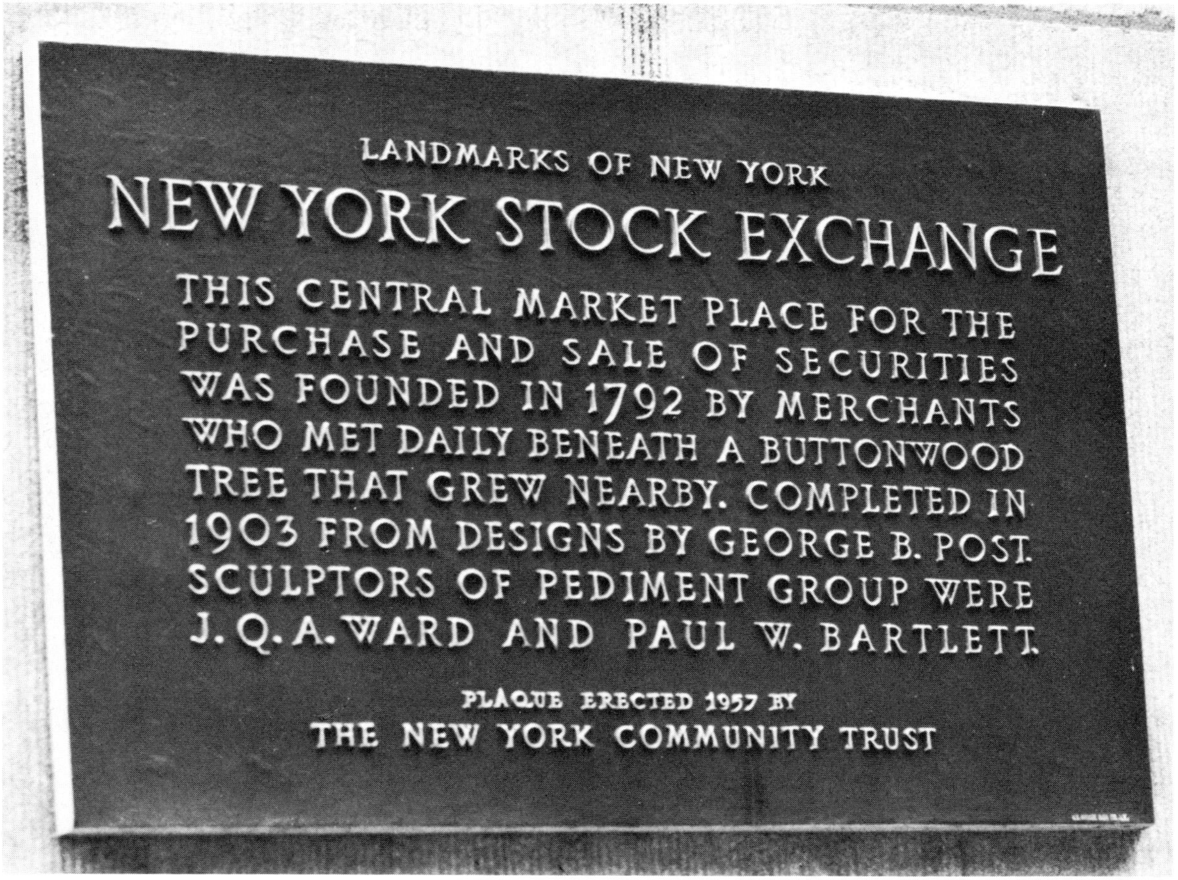
LANDMARKS OF NEW YORK
NEW YORK STOCK EXCHANGE
THIS CENTRAL MARKET PLACE FOR THE
PURCHASE AND SALE OF SECURITIES
WAS FOUNDED IN 1792 BY MERCHANTS
WHO MET DAILY BENEATH A BUTTONWOOD
TREE THAT GREW NEARBY. COMPLETED IN
1903 FROM DESIGNS BY GEORGE B. POST.
SCULPTORS OF PEDIMENT GROUP WERE
J. Q. A. WARD AND PAUL W. BARTLETT.
PLAQUE ERECTED 1957 BY
THE NEW YORK COMMUNITY TRUST

77
New York Telephone Company Building
140 West Street (Barclay Street)
Manhattan

LANDMARKS OF NEW YORK
NEW YORK TELEPHONE COMPANY BUILDING
THIS UNIQUELY ORNAMENTED SKYSCRAPER, PRESENTLY THE LARGEST TELEPHONE BUILDING IN THE WORLD, WAS DESIGNED BY RALPH WALKER OF THE FIRM OF MC KENZIE, VOORHEES AND GMELIN. CONSTRUCTION BEGAN IN 1923 AND WAS COMPLETED THREE YEARS LATER. THE SITE, ONCE A SUBMERGED WATER LOT OWNED BY TRINITY CHURCH, WAS FILLED IN PRIOR TO 1811.
PLAQUE ERECTED 1963 BY
THE NEW YORK COMMUNITY TRUST

FOR SPACE DOWNTOWN

78

New York Yacht Club

37 West 44th Street (5th Avenue)

Manhattan

"HERITAGE OF NEW YORK"
NEW YORK YACHT CLUB
DESIGNED BY WARREN AND WETMORE IN
CLASSIC ECLECTIC STYLE ON LAND
DONATED BY J. PIERPONT MORGAN IN 1898.
THIS BUILDING WAS COMPLETED IN 1901
AS THE SIXTH HOME OF THE NEW YORK
YACHT CLUB. THE CELEBRATED "AMERICA'S CUP",
FIRST WON BY A SCHOONER OF THAT
NAME IN A REGATTA AT COWES, ENGLAND,
IN 1851, WAS DEEDED TO THE CLUB IN 1857.
PLAQUE ERECTED 1966 BY
THE NEW YORK COMMUNITY TRUST

79
Nine East 72nd Street (former Stillman Residence)
near Fifth Avenue
Manhattan

LANDMARKS OF NEW YORK
CARRÈRE & HASTINGS DESIGNED THIS STRUCTURE OF LATE FRENCH RENAISSANCE STYLE. IT WAS BUILT IN 1894 AND CITED BY THE SOCIETY OF ARCHITECTURAL HISTORIANS AND THE MUNICIPAL ART SOCIETY IN 1957 FOR ITS ARCHITECTURAL SIGNIFICANCE.
PLAQUE ERECTED 1957 BY
THE NEW YORK COMMUNITY TRUST

Reed's
CALL

80

Old St. Patrick's Cathedral (R.C.)

Mott and Prince Streets

Manhattan

LANDMARKS OF NEW YORK
OLD ST. PATRICK'S CATHEDRAL
CONSTRUCTION OF THIS FIRST CATHEDRAL OF THE ROMAN CATHOLIC DIOCESE OF NEW YORK WAS BEGUN IN 1809, THE YEAR FOLLOWING THE CREATION OF THE DIOCESE. THE ORIGINAL BUILDING, DESIGNED BY JOSEPH F. MANGIN, WAS DEDICATED IN 1815, ENLARGED IN 1838-42, AND ALMOST TOTALLY DESTROYED BY FIRE IN 1866. THE REBUILT STRUCTURE WAS REDEDICATED TWO YEARS LATER. IN 1879, WHEN THE NEW CATHEDRAL ON FIFTH AVENUE WAS OPENED, OLD ST. PATRICK'S BECAME A PARISH CHURCH. HERE JOHN McCLOSKEY IN 1875 WAS INVESTED AS THE FIRST AMERICAN CARDINAL.
PLAQUE ERECTED 1963 BY
THE NEW YORK COMMUNITY TRUST

ONE WAY

81
Old St. Peter's Church (R.C.)
Barclay and Church Streets
Manhattan

LANDMARKS OF NEW YORK
OLD ST. PETER'S CHURCH
HERE WORSHIPS NEW YORK STATE'S OLDEST ROMAN CATHOLIC PARISH, ORGANIZED IN 1785. THE FIRST CHURCH ON THIS SITE, BUILT A YEAR LATER, REMAINED UNTIL 1836. THE PRESENT BUILDING, WHOSE GREEK REVIVAL DESIGN IS ATTRIBUTED TO ISAIAH ROGERS, WAS BLESSED BY BISHOP JOHN HUGHES IN 1838.
PLAQUE ERECTED 1962 BY
THE NEW YORK COMMUNITY TRUST

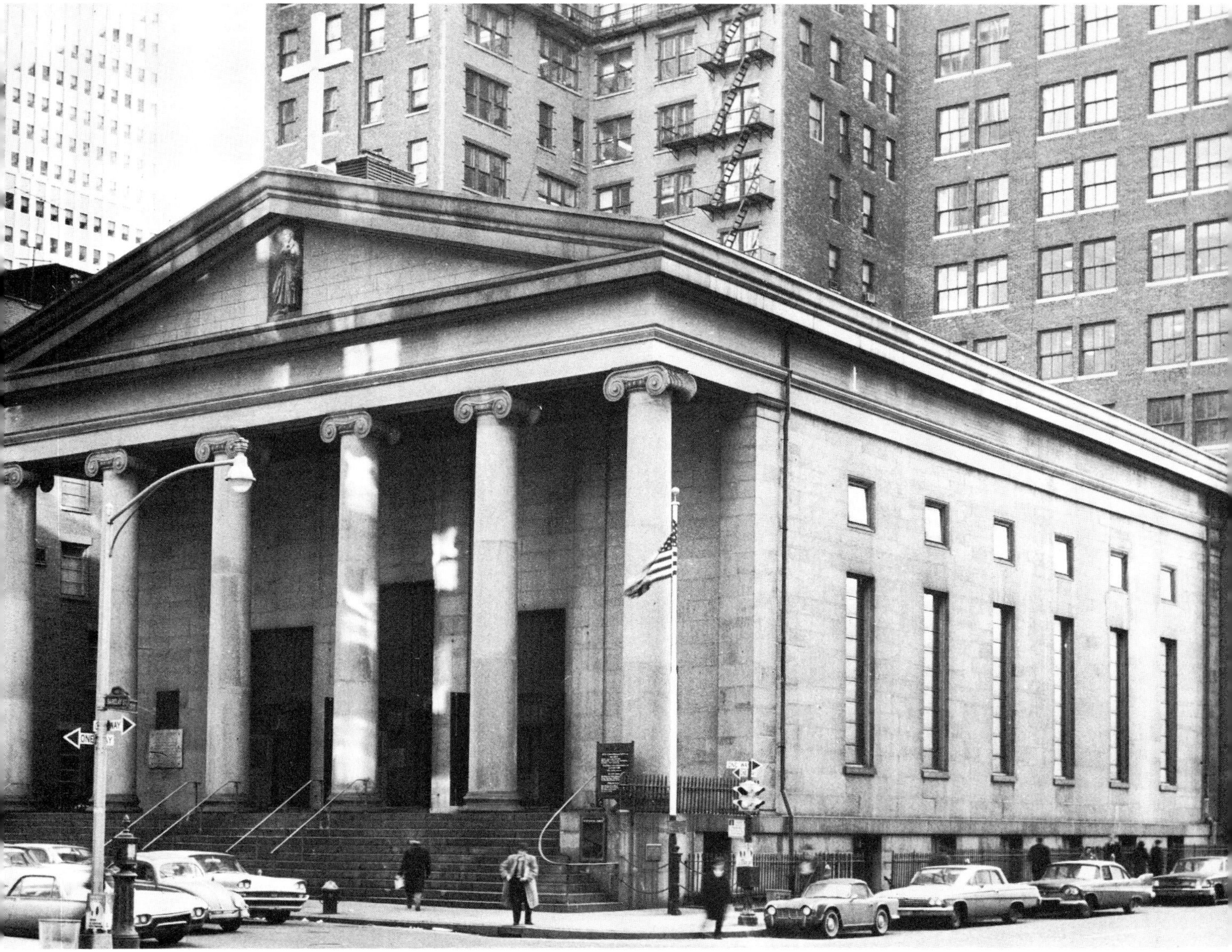

82
Park Avenue Christian Church (Disciples of Christ)
1010 Park Avenue (85th Street)
Manhattan

LANDMARKS OF NEW YORK
PARK AVENUE CHRISTIAN CHURCH
THIS CHURCH, DESIGNED BY CRAM, GOODHUE & FERGUSON IN A GOTHIC STYLE INSPIRED BY THE SAINTE CHAPELLE IN PARIS, WAS OPENED IN 1911 AS THE SOUTH REFORMED CHURCH. PURCHASED BY THE PRESBYTERY OF NEW YORK IN 1914, IT REMAINED A PRESBYTERIAN HOUSE OF WORSHIP UNTIL 1945 WHEN IT WAS ACQUIRED BY THE CHRISTIAN CHURCH (DISCIPLES OF CHRIST) WHOSE CONGREGATION WAS ORGANIZED IN 1810.
PLAQUE ERECTED 1960 BY
THE NEW YORK COMMUNITY TRUST

ONE WAY
SCHOOL
CROSSING

83

The Players

16 Gramercy Park (20th Street)

Manhattan

LANDMARKS OF NEW YORK
THE PLAYERS
THIS HOUSE, BUILT PRIOR TO 1846, WAS PURCHASED BY THE ACTOR EDWIN BOOTH IN 1887 AS A HOME FOR THE PLAYERS. AFTER EXTENSIVE REMODELLING OF THE EXTERIOR AND INTERIOR BY STANFORD WHITE, IT WAS DEEDED TO THE CLUB ON DECEMBER 31, 1888. BOOTH'S ROOM WHERE HE LIVED UNTIL HIS DEATH FIVE YEARS LATER HAS BEEN KEPT UNCHANGED. THE LIBRARY CONTAINS ONE OF THE LARGEST THEATRE COLLECTIONS IN AMERICA.
PLAQUE ERECTED 1962 BY
THE NEW YORK COMMUNITY TRUST

84
Plaza Hotel
Fifth Avenue and 59th Street
Manhattan

LANDMARKS OF NEW YORK
THE PLAZA HOTEL
DESIGNED BY HENRY J. HARDENBERGH IN FRENCH RENAISSANCE STYLE, THE PLAZA OPENED ITS DOORS ON OCTOBER 1, 1907. AMONG ORIGINAL RESIDENTS WERE MEMBERS OF THE GOULD, HARRIMAN AND VANDERBILT FAMILIES. AN EARLIER PLAZA HOTEL OPENED AT THIS LOCATION IN 1890 AND WAS DEMOLISHED IN 1905 TO MAKE WAY FOR THE PRESENT STRUCTURE.
PLAQUE ERECTED 1963 BY
THE NEW YORK COMMUNITY TRUST

85
Pulitzer Memorial Fountain
Fifth Avenue and 58th Street, Grand Army Plaza
Manhattan

LANDMARKS OF NEW YORK
PULITZER MEMORIAL FOUNTAIN
GIVEN TO THE CITY IN 1916 BY THE ESTATE OF JOSEPH PULITZER, PUBLISHER OF THE NEW YORK WORLD. THIS "FOUNTAIN OF ABUNDANCE" WAS THE WORK OF CARRÈRE AND HASTINGS AS ARCHITECTS AND KARL BITTER AS SCULPTOR. AFTER BITTER'S DEATH IN 1915 THE SCULPTURE WAS COMPLETED BY HIS ASSOCIATES.
PLAQUE ERECTED 1965 BY
THE NEW YORK COMMUNITY TRUST

86
Regis High School
55 East 84th Street (Park Avenue)
Manhattan

"HERITAGE OF NEW YORK"
REGIS HIGH SCHOOL
DESIGNED IN CLASSIC ECLECTIC STYLE BY MAGINNIS AND WALSH AND COMPLETED IN 1917. THIS STRUCTURE WAS BUILT FOR THE SOCIETY OF JESUS. THE FACADE'S DECORATIVE DETAILS INCORPORATE GREEK, ROMAN AND RENAISSANCE MOTIFS.
PLAQUE ERECTED 1966 BY
THE NEW YORK COMMUNITY TRUST

PIETAS · CHRISTIANA · EREXIT

87

President Franklin D. Roosevelt Residence

47 East 65th Street (Park Avenue)
Manhattan

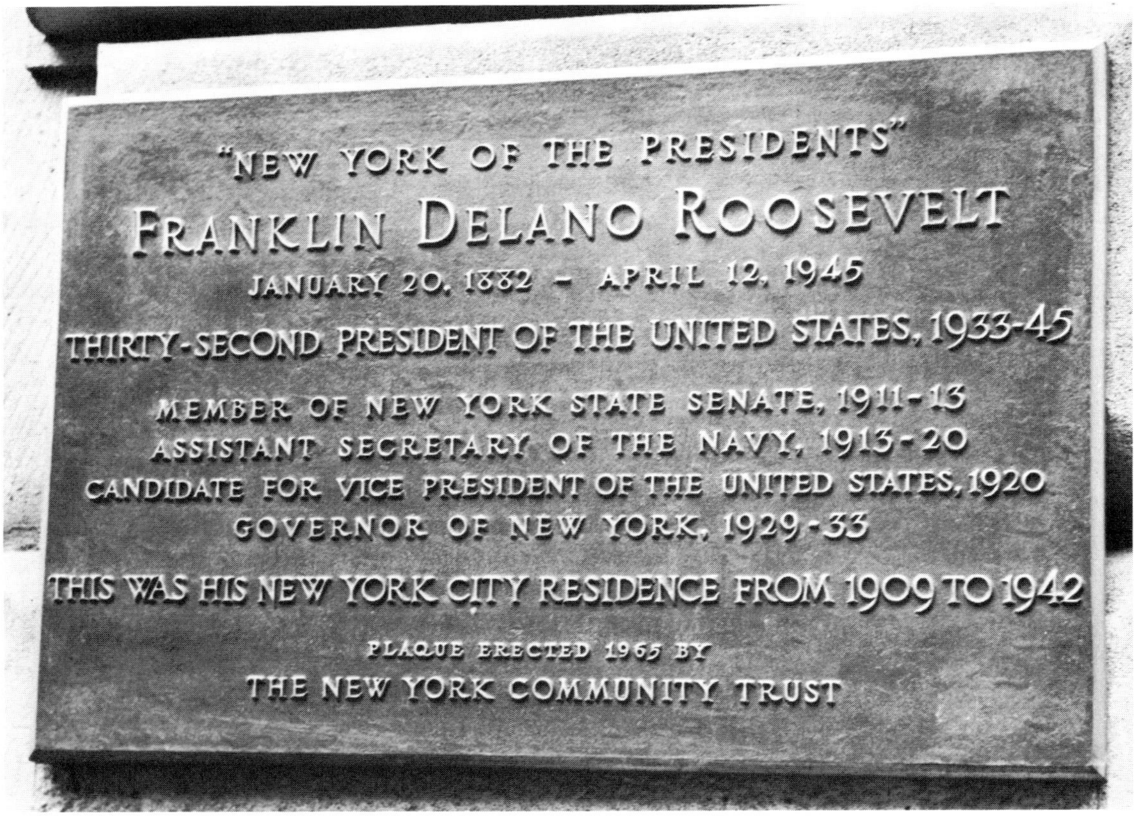
"NEW YORK OF THE PRESIDENTS"
FRANKLIN DELANO ROOSEVELT
JANUARY 20, 1882 – APRIL 12, 1945
THIRTY-SECOND PRESIDENT OF THE UNITED STATES, 1933-45
MEMBER OF NEW YORK STATE SENATE, 1911-13
ASSISTANT SECRETARY OF THE NAVY, 1913-20
CANDIDATE FOR VICE PRESIDENT OF THE UNITED STATES, 1920
GOVERNOR OF NEW YORK, 1929-33
THIS WAS HIS NEW YORK CITY RESIDENCE FROM 1909 TO 1942
PLAQUE ERECTED 1965 BY
THE NEW YORK COMMUNITY TRUST

88
Theodore Roosevelt Birthplace
28 East 20th Street (Broadway)
Manhattan

LANDMARKS OF NEW YORK
THEODORE ROOSEVELT BIRTHPLACE
PRESIDENT THEODORE ROOSEVELT WAS BORN HERE ON OCTOBER 27, 1858, AND LIVED HERE UNTIL HE WAS 15. THE HOUSE, A TYPICAL BROWNSTONE OF THE 1840'S, WAS RESTORED IN 1923 AND OPENED AS A MUSEUM
PLAQUE ERECTED 1962 BY
THE NEW YORK COMMUNITY TRUST

89

St. Augustine's Chapel (Episcopal)

292 Henry Street (Montgomery Street)

Manhattan

LANDMARKS OF NEW YORK
ST. AUGUSTINE'S CHAPEL
KNOWN ORIGINALLY AS ALL SAINTS CHURCH, THIS BUILDING WAS CONSECRATED BY BISHOP JOHN HENRY HOBART IN 1828. THE RECESSED CHANCEL AND SANCTUARY WERE ADDED IN 1848. WHEN ALL SAINTS BECAME A CHAPEL OF TRINITY CHURCH IN 1949 ITS NAME WAS CHANGED TO ST. AUGUSTINE'S, PERPETUATING THE TITLE OF TRINITY'S FORMER CHAPEL AND MISSION HOUSE ON EAST HOUSTON STREET.
PLAQUE ERECTED 1963 BY
THE NEW YORK COMMUNITY TRUST

90
St. James' Church (R.C.)
28 James Street (Madison Street)
Manhattan

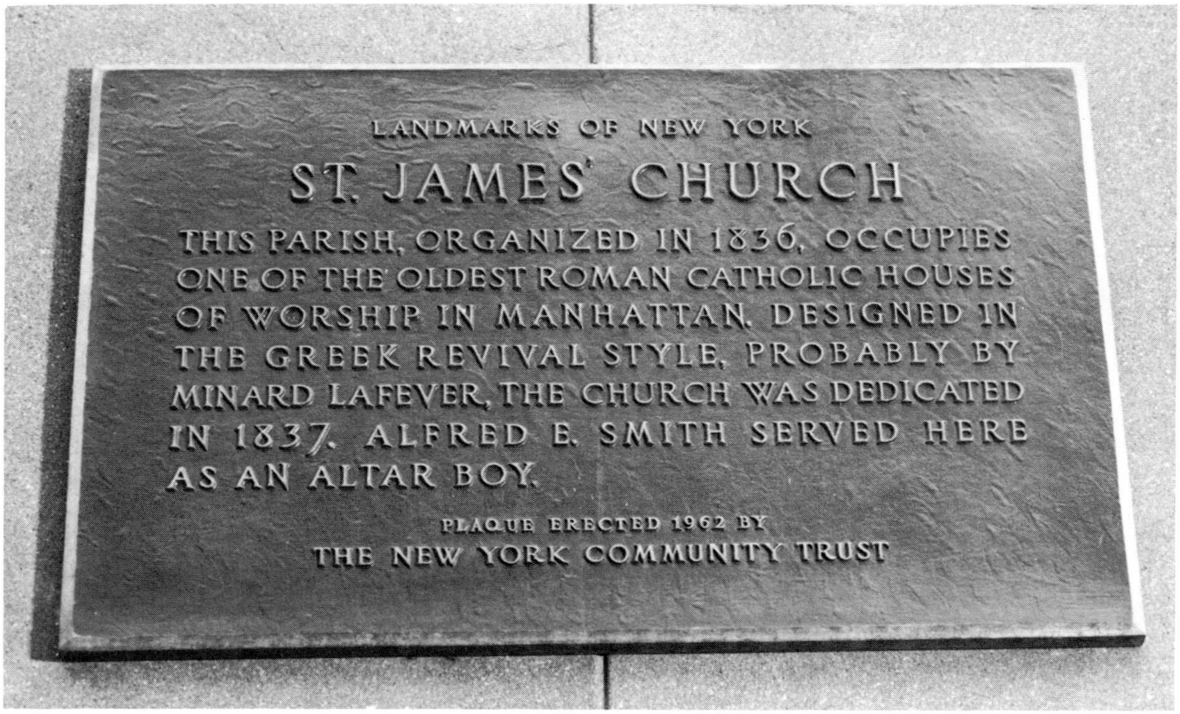
LANDMARKS OF NEW YORK
ST. JAMES' CHURCH
THIS PARISH, ORGANIZED IN 1836, OCCUPIES ONE OF THE OLDEST ROMAN CATHOLIC HOUSES OF WORSHIP IN MANHATTAN. DESIGNED IN THE GREEK REVIVAL STYLE, PROBABLY BY MINARD LAFEVER, THE CHURCH WAS DEDICATED IN 1837. ALFRED E. SMITH SERVED HERE AS AN ALTAR BOY.
PLAQUE ERECTED 1962 BY
THE NEW YORK COMMUNITY TRUST

91

St. John's Evangelical Lutheran Church

81 Christopher Street (Bleecker Street), Greenwich Village
Manhattan

LANDMARKS OF NEW YORK
ST. JOHN'S EVANGELICAL LUTHERAN CHURCH
THIS CHURCH IN MODIFIED FEDERAL STYLE WAS BUILT IN 1821 AS THE EIGHTH PRESBYTERIAN CHURCH. FROM 1842 UNTIL 1856 IT WAS THE HOUSE OF WORSHIP FOR THE ST. MATTHEW'S PROTESTANT EPISCOPAL PARISH, BECOMING ST. JOHN'S EVANGELICAL LUTHERAN CHURCH IN 1858.
PLAQUE ERECTED 1965 BY
THE NEW YORK COMMUNITY TRUST

St JOHANNES ACADEMIE

1855

92

St. Joseph's Church (R.C.)

371 Sixth Avenue (Washington Place), Greenwich Village

Manhattan

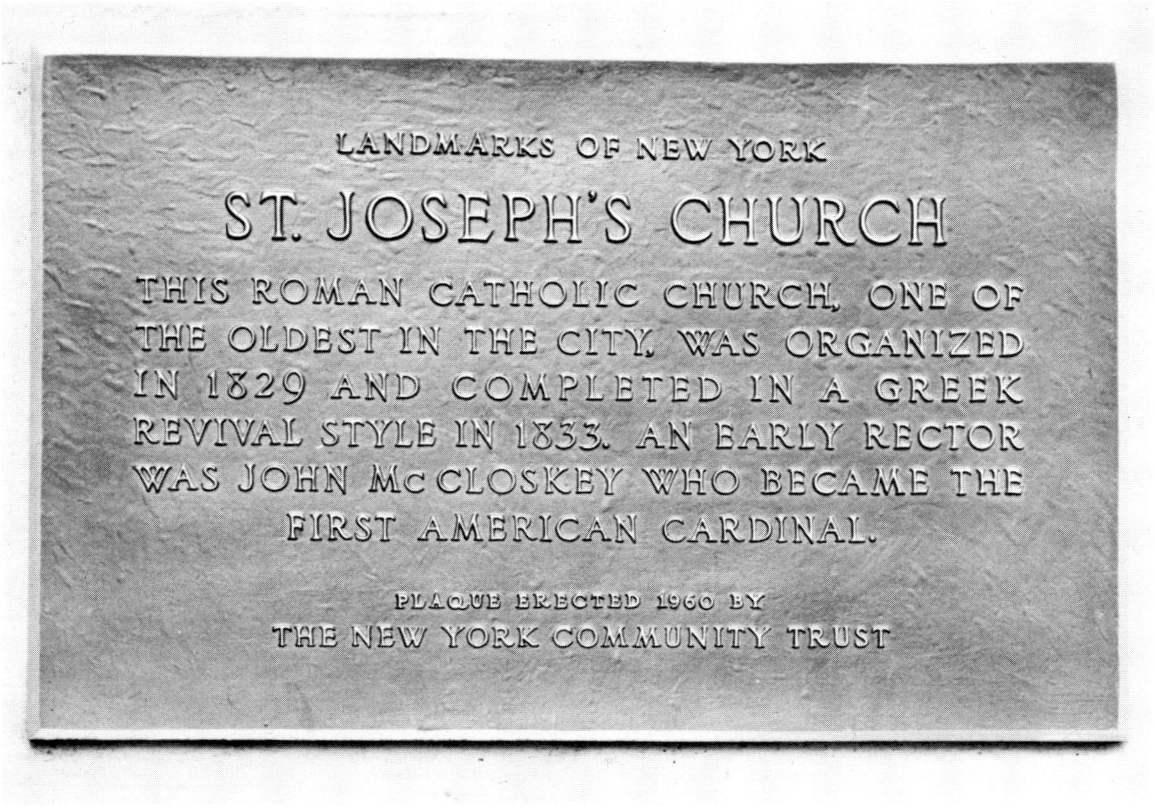
LANDMARKS OF NEW YORK
ST. JOSEPH'S CHURCH
THIS ROMAN CATHOLIC CHURCH, ONE OF THE OLDEST IN THE CITY, WAS ORGANIZED IN 1829 AND COMPLETED IN A GREEK REVIVAL STYLE IN 1833. AN EARLY RECTOR WAS JOHN McCLOSKEY WHO BECAME THE FIRST AMERICAN CARDINAL.
PLAQUE ERECTED 1960 BY
THE NEW YORK COMMUNITY TRUST

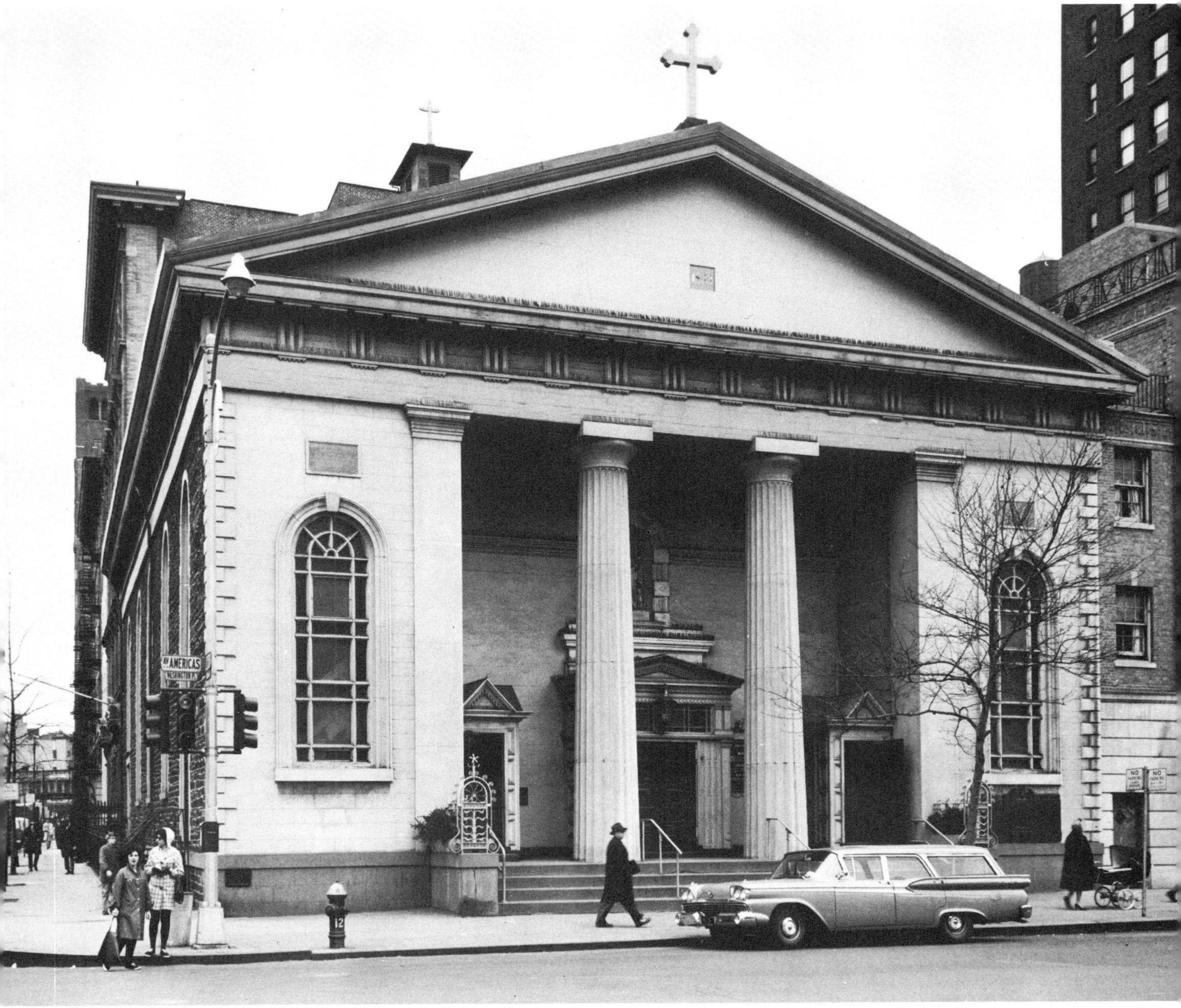
AMERICAS
12

93
St. Luke's Chapel (Episcopal)

487 Hudson Street (Christopher Street), Greenwich Village
Manhattan

LANDMARKS OF NEW YORK
ST. LUKE'S CHAPEL
THIS THIRD OLDEST EXISTING CHURCH EDIFICE IN MANHATTAN WAS BUILT IN 1821 ON FARMLAND DONATED BY TRINITY PARISH TO THE INDEPENDENT PARISH OF ST. LUKE'S CHURCH, OF WHICH CLEMENT C. MOORE WAS A FOUNDER AND FIRST SENIOR WARDEN. WHEN THAT CONGREGATION MOVED UPTOWN, THE LAND WAS BOUGHT BACK AND THE STRUCTURE BECAME ST. LUKE'S CHAPEL OF TRINITY PARISH IN 1892.
PLAQUE ERECTED 1960 BY
THE NEW YORK COMMUNITY TRUST

94

St. Nicholas Historic District

plaque on 2370 Seventh Avenue (138th Street), Harlem
West 138th and West 139th Streets between Seventh and Eighth Avenues
Manhattan

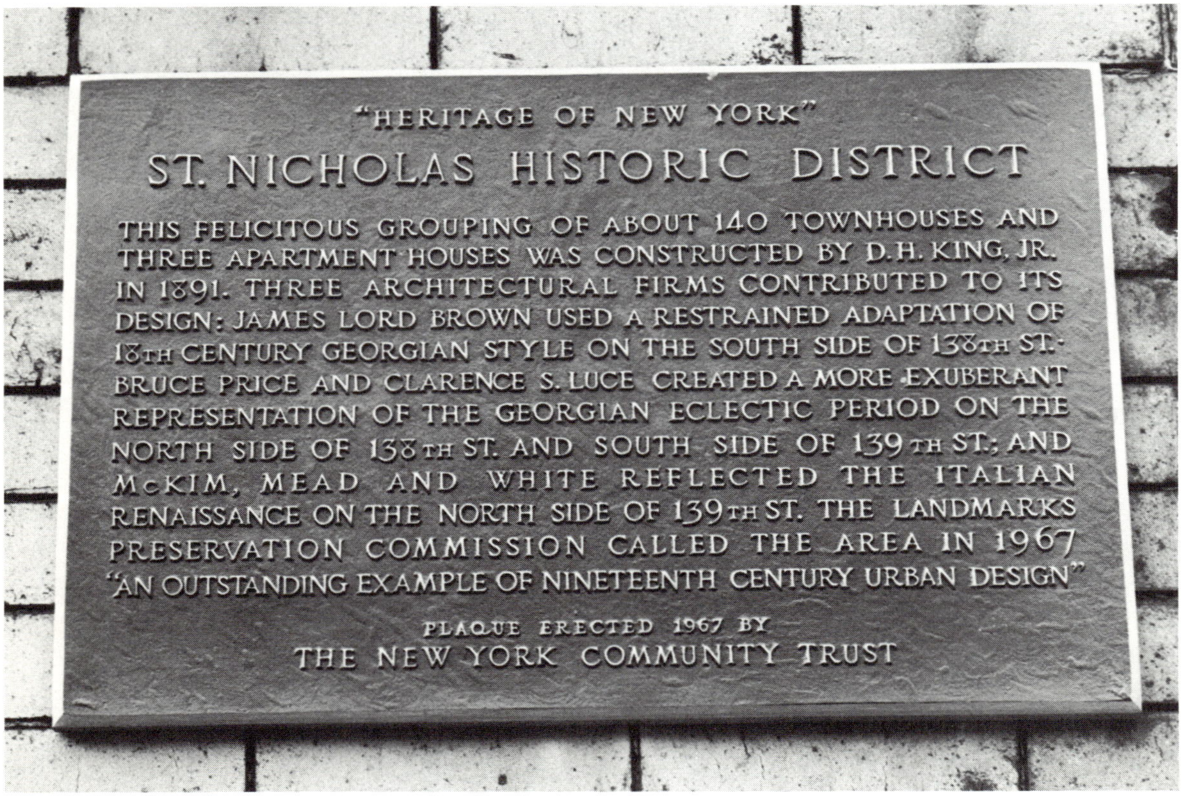
"HERITAGE OF NEW YORK"
ST. NICHOLAS HISTORIC DISTRICT
THIS FELICITOUS GROUPING OF ABOUT 140 TOWNHOUSES AND
THREE APARTMENT HOUSES WAS CONSTRUCTED BY D.H. KING, JR.
IN 1891. THREE ARCHITECTURAL FIRMS CONTRIBUTED TO ITS
DESIGN: JAMES LORD BROWN USED A RESTRAINED ADAPTATION OF
18TH CENTURY GEORGIAN STYLE ON THE SOUTH SIDE OF 138TH ST.;
BRUCE PRICE AND CLARENCE S. LUCE CREATED A MORE EXUBERANT
REPRESENTATION OF THE GEORGIAN ECLECTIC PERIOD ON THE
NORTH SIDE OF 138TH ST. AND SOUTH SIDE OF 139TH ST.; AND
McKIM, MEAD AND WHITE REFLECTED THE ITALIAN
RENAISSANCE ON THE NORTH SIDE OF 139TH ST. THE LANDMARKS
PRESERVATION COMMISSION CALLED THE AREA IN 1967
"AN OUTSTANDING EXAMPLE OF NINETEENTH CENTURY URBAN DESIGN"
PLAQUE ERECTED 1967 BY
THE NEW YORK COMMUNITY TRUST

BEAUTY SALON
CONTRACTORS

95

St. Paul's Chapel (Episcopal)

Broadway, Fulton and Vesey Streets

Manhattan

LANDMARKS OF NEW YORK
ST. PAUL'S CHAPEL
THIS FAMOUS EXAMPLE OF GEORGIAN ARCHITECTURE, BUILT 1764-1766, WITH SPIRE AND PORTICO ADDED 1794-1796, IS THE ONLY CHURCH STRUCTURE SURVIVING THE COLONIAL ERA OF NEW YORK CITY. THE DESIGN BY THOMAS MCBEAN CLOSELY FOLLOWED THAT OF ST. MARTIN-IN-THE-FIELDS BY JAMES GIBBS. PRESIDENT WASHINGTON WAS A REGULAR ATTENDANT FOLLOWING HIS INAUGURATION IN 1789 WHEN NEW YORK WAS THE NATIONAL CAPITAL.
PLAQUE ERECTED 1957 BY
THE NEW YORK COMMUNITY TRUST

PARK ROW
ANN ST.
ANN ST.
PARK RO
ONE-WAY
NO
PARKING
8 AM TO 6 PM
MON THRU FRI.
DEPT OF TRAFFIC

96

St. Peter's Episcopal Church

344 West 20th Street (9th Avenue), Chelsea
Manhattan

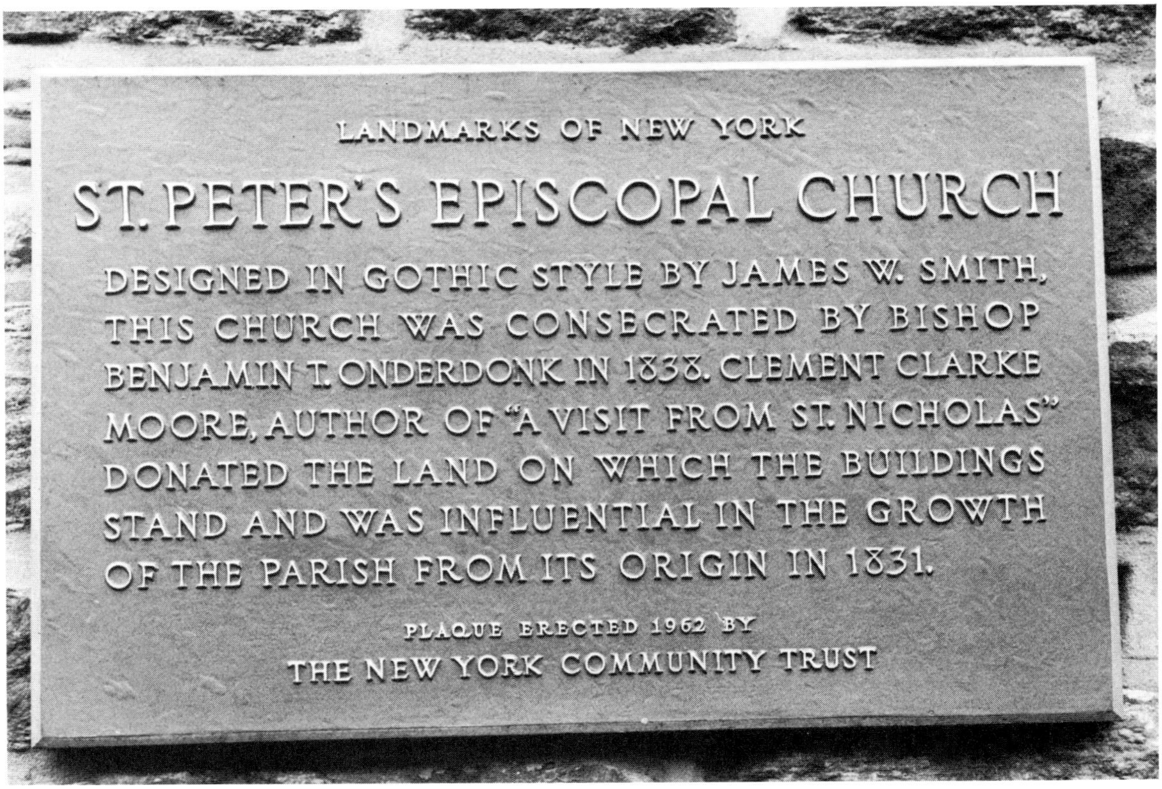
LANDMARKS OF NEW YORK
ST. PETER'S EPISCOPAL CHURCH
DESIGNED IN GOTHIC STYLE BY JAMES W. SMITH, THIS CHURCH WAS CONSECRATED BY BISHOP BENJAMIN T. ONDERDONK IN 1838. CLEMENT CLARKE MOORE, AUTHOR OF "A VISIT FROM ST. NICHOLAS" DONATED THE LAND ON WHICH THE BUILDINGS STAND AND WAS INFLUENTIAL IN THE GROWTH OF THE PARISH FROM ITS ORIGIN IN 1831.
PLAQUE ERECTED 1962 BY
THE NEW YORK COMMUNITY TRUST

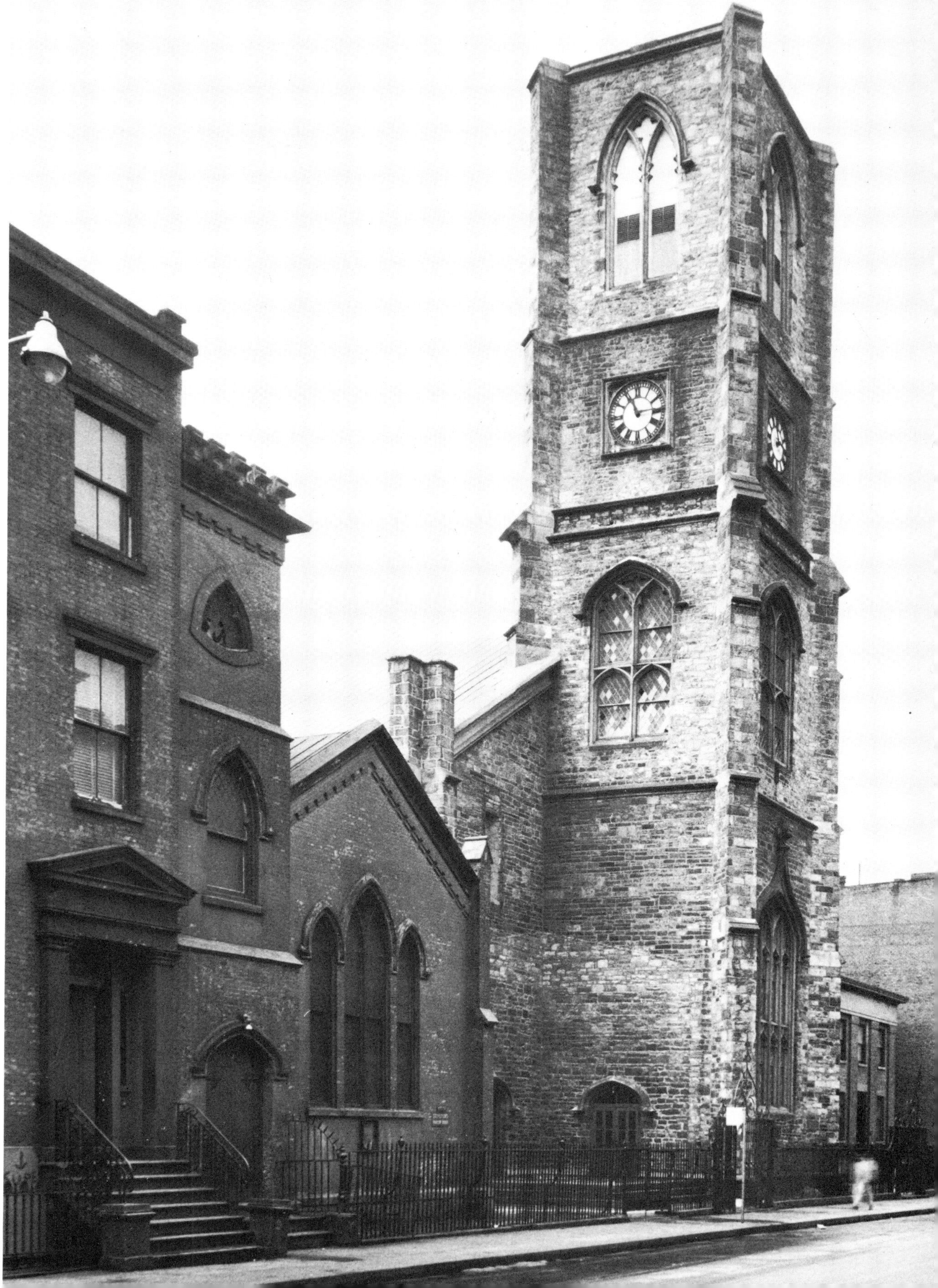

97
St. Regis Hotel
Fifth Avenue and 55th Street
Manhattan

LANDMARKS OF NEW YORK
ST. REGIS HOTEL
WHEN COMPLETED IN 1904, THIS WAS THE HIGHEST HOTEL BUILDING IN NEW YORK. DESIGNED BY TROWBRIDGE & LIVINGSTON AND CONSTRUCTED BY MARC EIDLITZ & SON, IT WAS CONCEIVED AND OWNED BY COLONEL JOHN JACOB ASTOR, WHOSE SON VINCENT ASTOR ENLARGED THE ORIGINAL STRUCTURE IN 1928.
PLAQUE ERECTED 1965 BY
THE NEW YORK COMMUNITY TRUST

NO STANDING
8AM-1PM 5PM-7PM
NO PARKING
8AM-7PM

98
St. Thomas Church (P.E.)
Fifth Avenue and 53rd Street
Manhattan

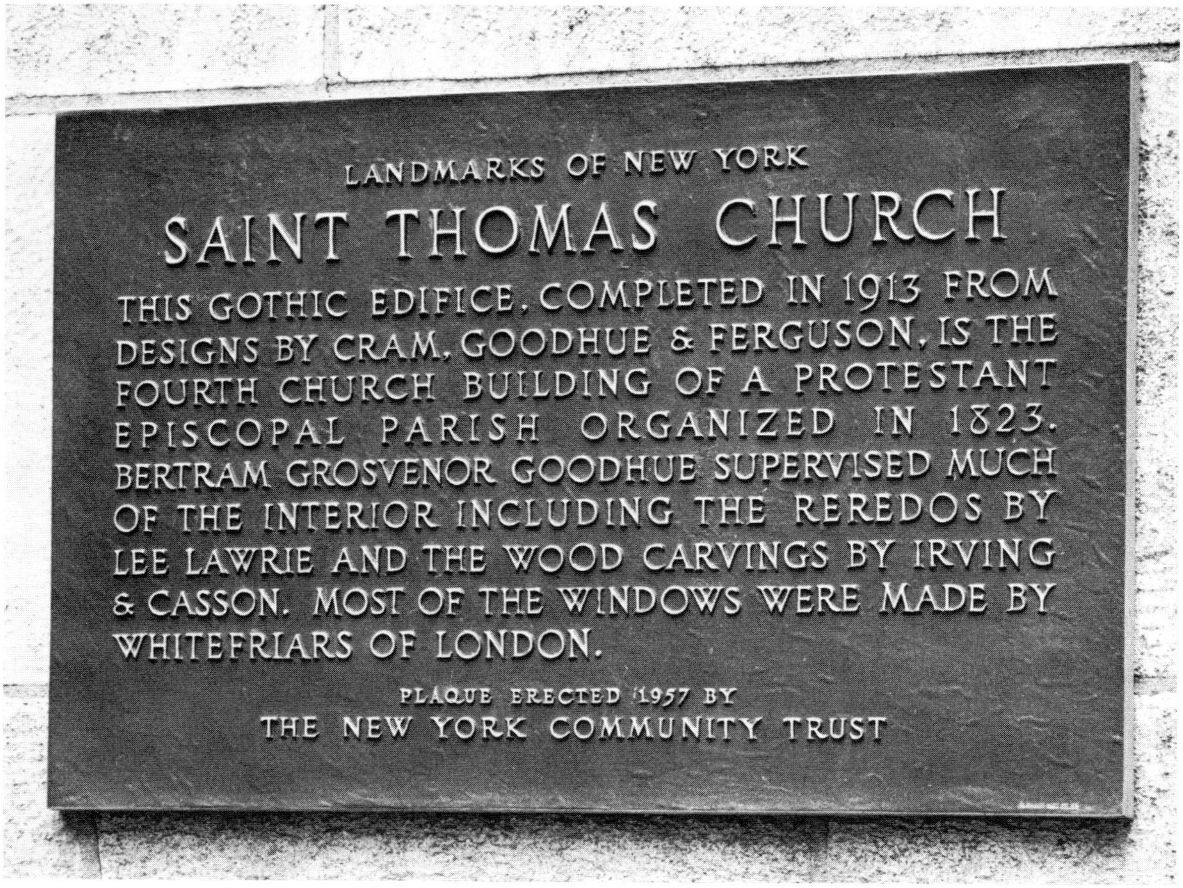
LANDMARKS OF NEW YORK
SAINT THOMAS CHURCH
THIS GOTHIC EDIFICE, COMPLETED IN 1913 FROM DESIGNS BY CRAM, GOODHUE & FERGUSON, IS THE FOURTH CHURCH BUILDING OF A PROTESTANT EPISCOPAL PARISH ORGANIZED IN 1823. BERTRAM GROSVENOR GOODHUE SUPERVISED MUCH OF THE INTERIOR INCLUDING THE REREDOS BY LEE LAWRIE AND THE WOOD CARVINGS BY IRVING & CASSON. MOST OF THE WINDOWS WERE MADE BY WHITEFRIARS OF LONDON.
PLAQUE ERECTED 1957 BY
THE NEW YORK COMMUNITY TRUST

NO PARKING
8AM — 7PM

99
St. Vincent Ferrer Church (R.C.)
Lexington Avenue and 66th Street
Manhattan

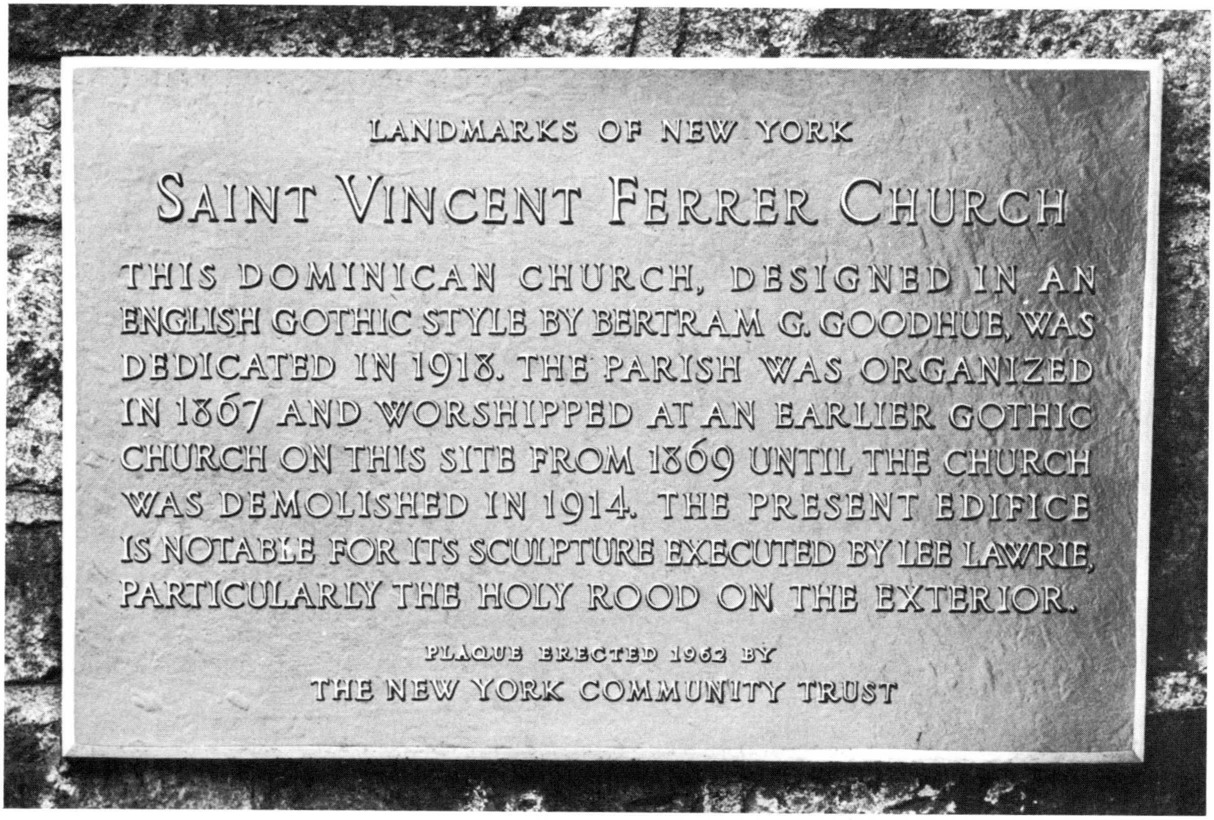
LANDMARKS OF NEW YORK
SAINT VINCENT FERRER CHURCH
THIS DOMINICAN CHURCH, DESIGNED IN AN ENGLISH GOTHIC STYLE BY BERTRAM G. GOODHUE, WAS DEDICATED IN 1918. THE PARISH WAS ORGANIZED IN 1867 AND WORSHIPPED AT AN EARLIER GOTHIC CHURCH ON THIS SITE FROM 1869 UNTIL THE CHURCH WAS DEMOLISHED IN 1914. THE PRESENT EDIFICE IS NOTABLE FOR ITS SCULPTURE EXECUTED BY LEE LAWRIE, PARTICULARLY THE HOLY ROOD ON THE EXTERIOR.
PLAQUE ERECTED 1962 BY
THE NEW YORK COMMUNITY TRUST

100
Salmagundi Club
47 Fifth Avenue (10th Street), Greenwich Village
Manhattan

LANDMARKS OF NEW YORK
THE SALMAGUNDI CLUB
THE SALMAGUNDI CLUB, ORIGINATING IN 1871 AS A SKETCH CLASS IN JONATHAN SCOTT HARTLEY'S STUDIO, PURCHASED THIS MID-NINETEENTH CENTURY BROWNSTONE HOUSE IN 1917 AS ITS FIRST PERMANENT HOME. IT WAS CITED IN 1957 FOR ITS ARCHITECTURAL DISTINCTION BY THE SOCIETY OF ARCHITECTURAL HISTORIANS AND THE MUNICIPAL ART SOCIETY.
PLAQUE ERECTED 1958 BY
THE NEW YORK COMMUNITY TRUST

101
Scribner Building
597 Fifth Avenue (48th Street)
Manhattan

LANDMARKS OF NEW YORK
SCRIBNER BUILDING
THIS BUILDING, THE SEVENTH HOME OF THE SCRIBNER FIRM SINCE ITS FOUNDING IN 1846, WAS DESIGNED BY ERNEST FLAGG, THE ARCHITECT OF THE SINGER BUILDING, AND COMPLETED IN 1913. FLAGG'S ADEPTNESS WITH GLASS FAÇADES WAS BASED ON TRAINING RECEIVED AT THE ECOLE DES BEAUX ARTS.
PLAQUE ERECTED 1961 BY
THE NEW YORK COMMUNITY TRUST

SONS
PUBLISHERS
AND
BOOKSELLERS
FOUNDED 1846
CHARLES SCRIBNER'S SONS
ALASKA AIRLINES
FIFTH AVENUE COACH LINES

102
Serbian Cathedral Church of St. Sava (Orthodox)
16-20 West 26th Street (Broadway)
Manhattan

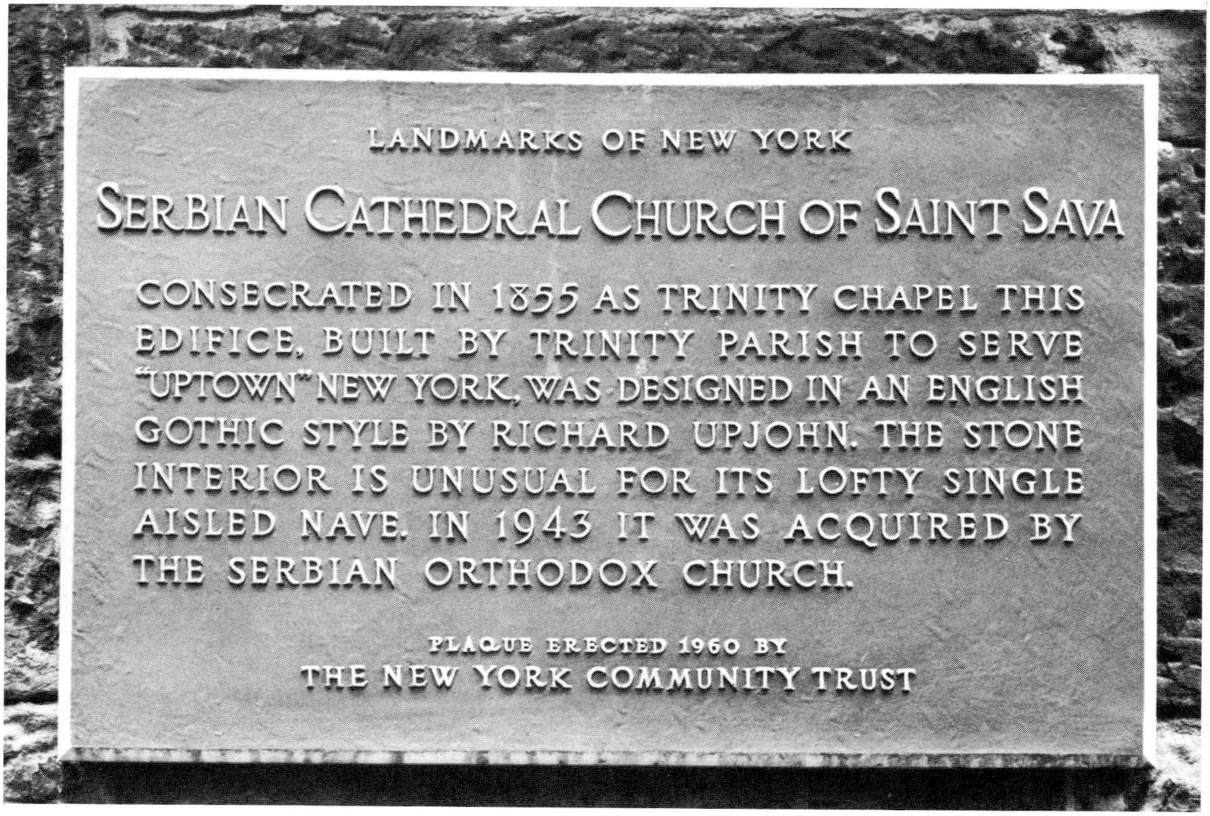
LANDMARKS OF NEW YORK
SERBIAN CATHEDRAL CHURCH OF SAINT SAVA
CONSECRATED IN 1855 AS TRINITY CHAPEL THIS EDIFICE, BUILT BY TRINITY PARISH TO SERVE "UPTOWN" NEW YORK, WAS DESIGNED IN AN ENGLISH GOTHIC STYLE BY RICHARD UPJOHN. THE STONE INTERIOR IS UNUSUAL FOR ITS LOFTY SINGLE AISLED NAVE. IN 1943 IT WAS ACQUIRED BY THE SERBIAN ORTHODOX CHURCH.
PLAQUE ERECTED 1960 BY
THE NEW YORK COMMUNITY TRUST

103
Seventh Regiment Armory
643 Park Avenue (66th Street)
Manhattan

LANDMARKS OF NEW YORK
SEVENTH REGIMENT ARMORY
DESIGNED BY CHARLES W. CLINTON FROM THE
ORIGINAL PLANS OF COLONEL EMMONS CLARK.
THIS STRUCTURE WAS OPENED IN 1880.
LOUIS C. TIFFANY DIRECTED THE DECORATION
OF THE INTERIOR. ENLARGEMENTS WERE MADE
IN 1911, WHEN A CENTRAL TOWER WAS REMOVED
AND AGAIN IN 1931.
PLAQUE ERECTED 1959 BY
THE NEW YORK COMMUNITY TRUST

104
Spring Street Presbyterian Church
Spring and Varick Streets [demolished]
Manhattan

LANDMARKS OF NEW YORK
SPRING STREET PRESBYTERIAN CHURCH
THIS EDIFICE IN GREEK REVIVAL STYLE, COMPLETED IN 1836, REPLACED A SHINGLED FRAME CHURCH BUILT ON FARMLAND PURCHASED FROM TRINITY CORPORATION AND DEDICATED IN 1811.
PLAQUE ERECTED 1960 BY
THE NEW YORK COMMUNITY TRUST

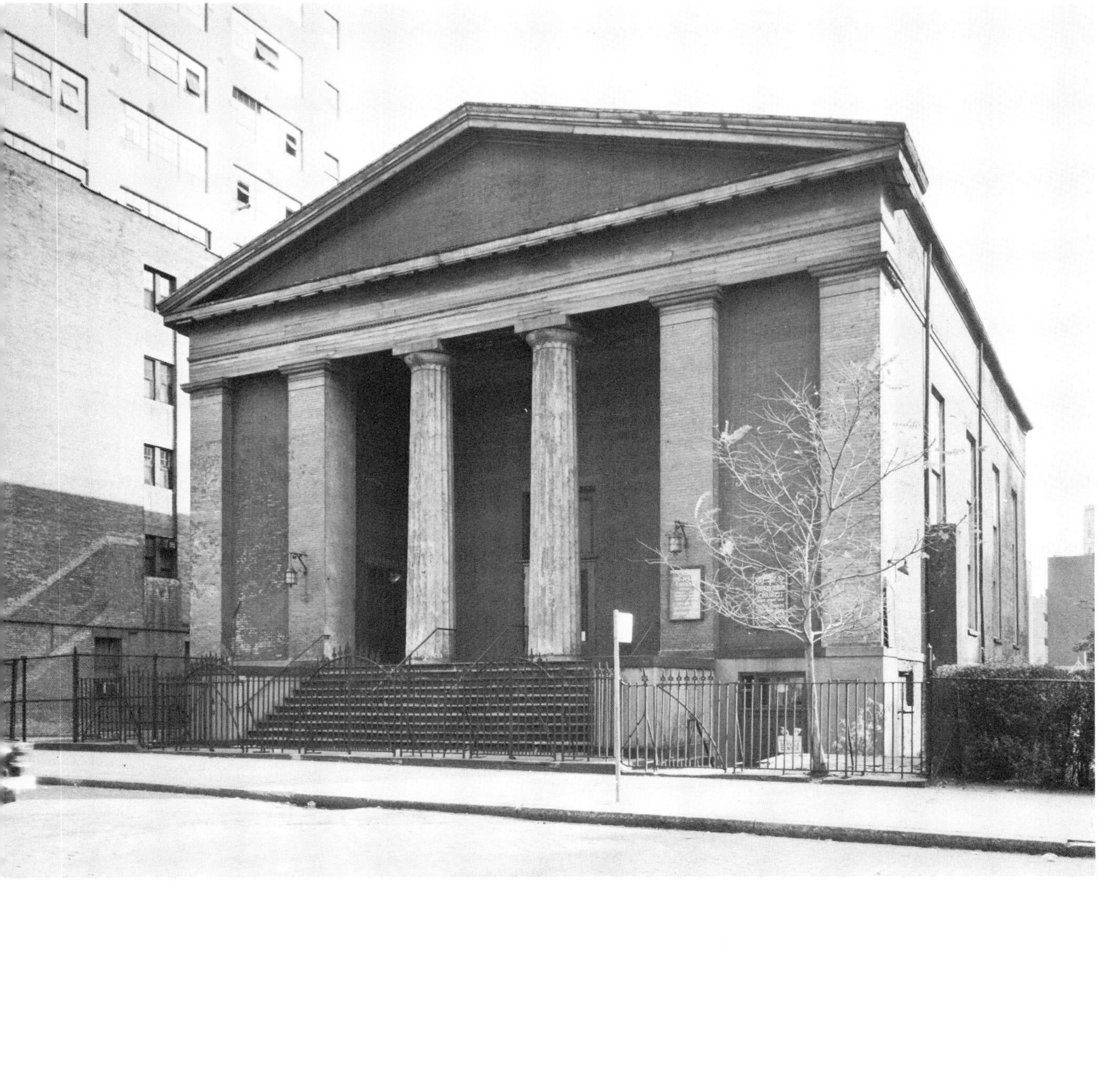

105
Temple Emanu-El (Reform)
Fifth Avenue and 65th Street
Manhattan

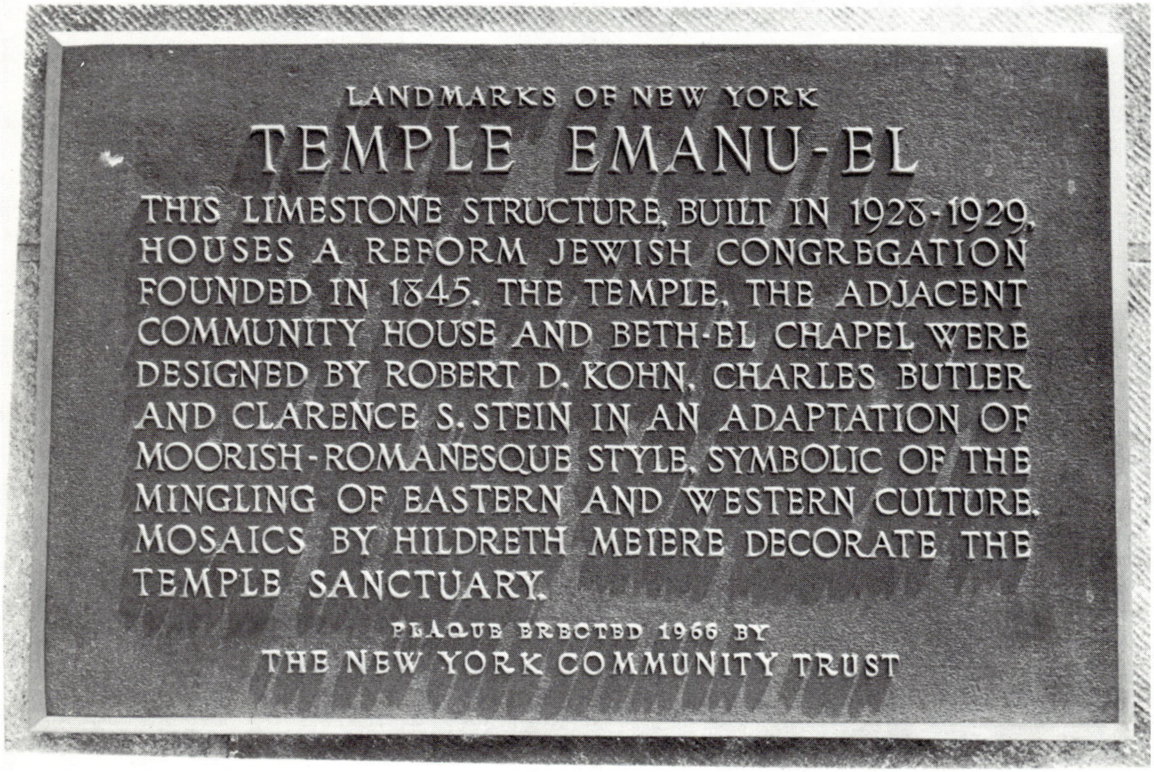
LANDMARKS OF NEW YORK
TEMPLE EMANU-EL
THIS LIMESTONE STRUCTURE, BUILT IN 1928-1929, HOUSES A REFORM JEWISH CONGREGATION FOUNDED IN 1845. THE TEMPLE, THE ADJACENT COMMUNITY HOUSE AND BETH-EL CHAPEL WERE DESIGNED BY ROBERT D. KOHN, CHARLES BUTLER AND CLARENCE S. STEIN IN AN ADAPTATION OF MOORISH-ROMANESQUE STYLE, SYMBOLIC OF THE MINGLING OF EASTERN AND WESTERN CULTURE. MOSAICS BY HILDRETH MEIERE DECORATE THE TEMPLE SANCTUARY.
PLAQUE ERECTED 1966 BY
THE NEW YORK COMMUNITY TRUST

NO
PARKING
SECTION
B
LOVE TH

106
Tiffany and Company Stables
140 East 41st Street (Lexington Avenue) [demolished]
Manhattan

LANDMARKS OF NEW YORK
FORMER STABLES OF
TIFFANY & COMPANY
DESIGNED BY MC KIM, MEAD & WHITE
ON A PALLADIAN MOTIVE, THIS STRUCTURE,
BUILT BY C.T. WILLS IN 1904,
ORIGINALLY STABLED HORSES AND, LATER,
ELECTRIC TRUCKS.
PLAQUE ERECTED 1957 BY
THE NEW YORK COMMUNITY TRUST

GARAGE
TIFFANY & COMPANY
DRIVEWAY
NO
PARKING
DRIVEWAY
NO
PARKING

107

Times Tower (rebuilt as Allied Chemical Tower)

Times Square and 42nd Street

Manhattan

LANDMARKS OF NEW YORK
TIMES TOWER
THIS BUILDING, FROM WHICH TIMES SQUARE
DERIVES ITS NAME, WAS BUILT BY
ADOLPH S. OCHS
FROM PLANS BY EIDLITZ AND MCKENZIE.
IT SERVED AS THE HOME OF
THE NEW YORK TIMES
FROM 1905 UNTIL 1913.
PLAQUE ERECTED 1957 BY
THE NEW YORK COMMUNITY TRUST

STATE
HOTEL
ASTOR
CLARIDGE
LOEW'S STATE
ST LOUIS BLUES
PEARL EARTHA NAT KING
BAILEY KITT COLE
BARTON'S
HOWARD JOHNSON'S
SOUTH PACIFIC
THE MUSIC MAN
LOOK HOMEWARD, ANGEL
ALL BEEF FRANKFURTERS
PENS-PENCILS
Hi-Fi TV

108

Treadwell Farm Historic District

plaque on 208 East 62nd Street
East 61st and East 62nd Streets between Second and Third Avenues
Manhattan

"HERITAGE OF NEW YORK"
TREADWELL FARM HISTORIC DISTRICT
THIS "HISTORIC DISTRICT" ALONG EAST 61ST AND EAST 62ND STREETS BETWEEN SECOND AND THIRD AVENUES IS THE ORIGINAL SITE OF A FARM PURCHASED BY ADAM TREADWELL AND STEPHEN THORNE JR. FROM HEIRS OF PETER VAN ZANDT AT AN AUCTION IN THE TONTINE COFFEE HOUSE IN 1815. AT MR. THORNE'S DEATH IN 1830 HIS HALF WAS BOUGHT BY MR. TREADWELL. MOST OF THE PRESENT HOUSES WERE CONSTRUCTED BETWEEN 1868 AND 1876, WITH THEIR CONTINUED RESIDENTIAL CHARACTER PLEDGED BY COVENANTS. THE AREA WAS DESIGNATED AN HISTORIC DISTRICT IN 1967.
PLAQUE ERECTED 1968 BY
THE NEW YORK COMMUNITY TRUST

109
Trinity Church (Episcopal)
Broadway at Wall Street
Manhattan

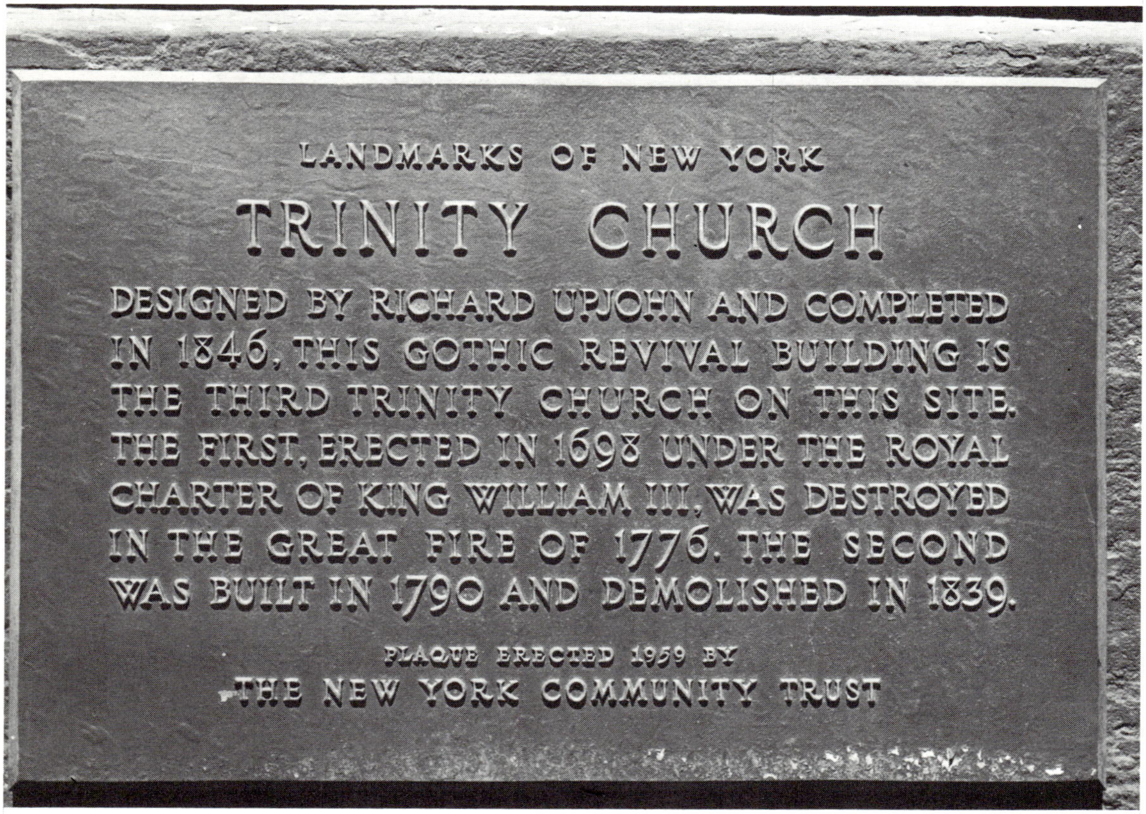
LANDMARKS OF NEW YORK
TRINITY CHURCH
DESIGNED BY RICHARD UPJOHN AND COMPLETED IN 1846, THIS GOTHIC REVIVAL BUILDING IS THE THIRD TRINITY CHURCH ON THIS SITE. THE FIRST, ERECTED IN 1698 UNDER THE ROYAL CHARTER OF KING WILLIAM III, WAS DESTROYED IN THE GREAT FIRE OF 1776. THE SECOND WAS BUILT IN 1790 AND DEMOLISHED IN 1839.
PLAQUE ERECTED 1959 BY
THE NEW YORK COMMUNITY TRUST

110
United States Custom House
Bowling Green, State and Whitehall Streets
Manhattan

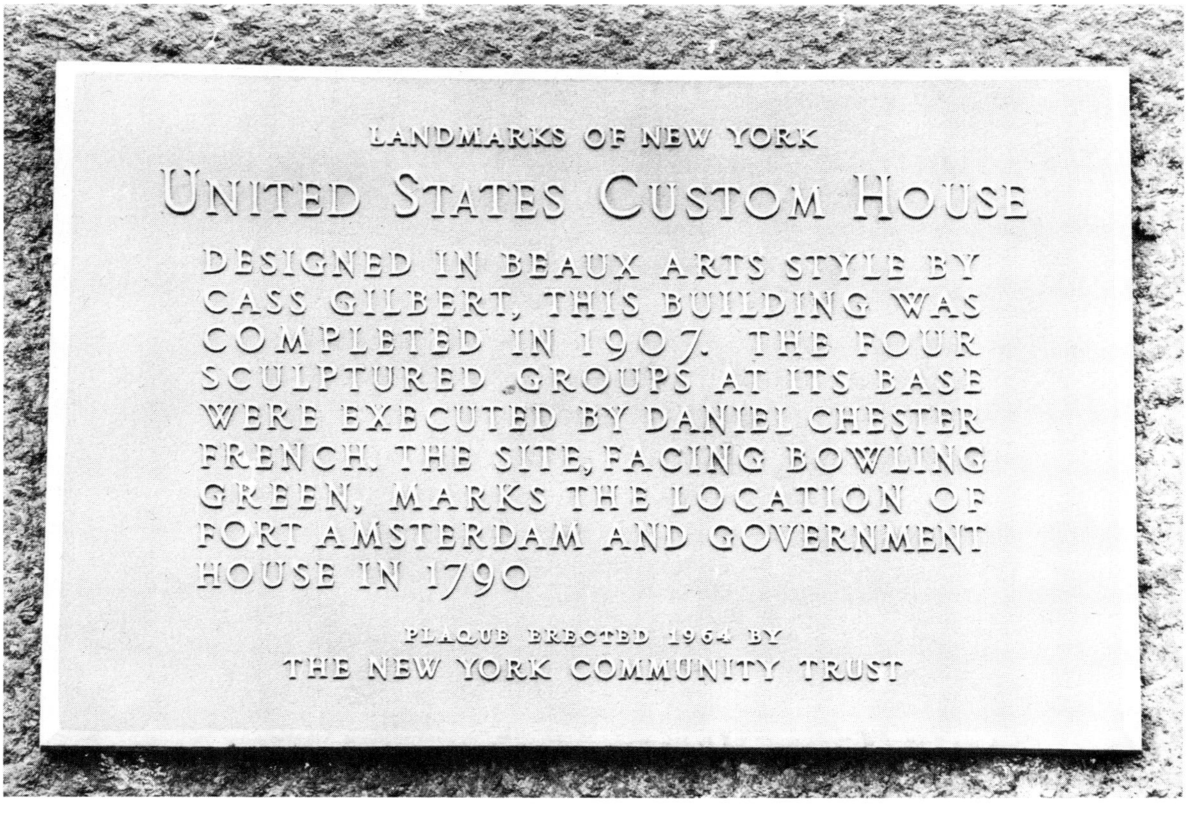
LANDMARKS OF NEW YORK
UNITED STATES CUSTOM HOUSE
DESIGNED IN BEAUX ARTS STYLE BY CASS GILBERT, THIS BUILDING WAS COMPLETED IN 1907. THE FOUR SCULPTURED GROUPS AT ITS BASE WERE EXECUTED BY DANIEL CHESTER FRENCH. THE SITE, FACING BOWLING GREEN, MARKS THE LOCATION OF FORT AMSTERDAM AND GOVERNMENT HOUSE IN 1790
PLAQUE ERECTED 1964 BY
THE NEW YORK COMMUNITY TRUST

111
University Club
Fifth Avenue and 54th Street
Manhattan

LANDMARKS OF NEW YORK
THE UNIVERSITY CLUB
THIS BUILDING, INSPIRED BY
PALACE ARCHITECTURE
OF THE ITALIAN RENAISSANCE,
WAS DESIGNED BY
MC KIM, MEAD & WHITE
AND WAS COMPLETED IN 1899.
PLAQUE ERECTED 1957 BY
THE NEW YORK COMMUNITY TRUST

5TH AV
E.54 ST
5TH AV
NO PARKING

112
Villard Mansion
Madison Avenue between 50th and 51st Streets
Manhattan

LANDMARKS OF NEW YORK
VILLARD MANSION
THIS BLOCK OF SIX TOWN HOUSES, REMINISCENT OF THE PALAZZO DELLA CANCELLERIA IN ROME, WAS COMPLETED IN 1885 FROM DESIGNS OF McKIM, MEAD AND WHITE FOR THE JOURNALIST AND RAILROAD FINANCIER, HENRY VILLARD, AND A GROUP OF HIS FRIENDS. NUMBER 451, THE VILLARD RESIDENCE, LATER THE HOME OF WHITELAW REID, PUBLISHER AND DIPLOMAT, IS THE ADMINISTRATIVE CENTER FOR THE ROMAN CATHOLIC ARCHDIOCESE OF NEW YORK ALONG WITH NUMBERS 453-455 AS WELL AS 24 AND 30 EAST 51 STREET. RANDOM HOUSE, BOOK PUBLISHERS, ACQUIRED NUMBER 457 FROM JOSEPH P. KENNEDY IN 1946. STANFORD WHITE COLLABORATED WITH AUGUSTUS SAINT-GAUDENS IN DESIGNING THE CLOCK FOR THE VILLARD STAIRWELL.
PLAQUE ERECTED 1966 BY
THE NEW YORK COMMUNITY TRUST

113
Vincent Office Building (later School of Education, Fordham University)
302 Broadway (Duane Street) [demolished]
Manhattan

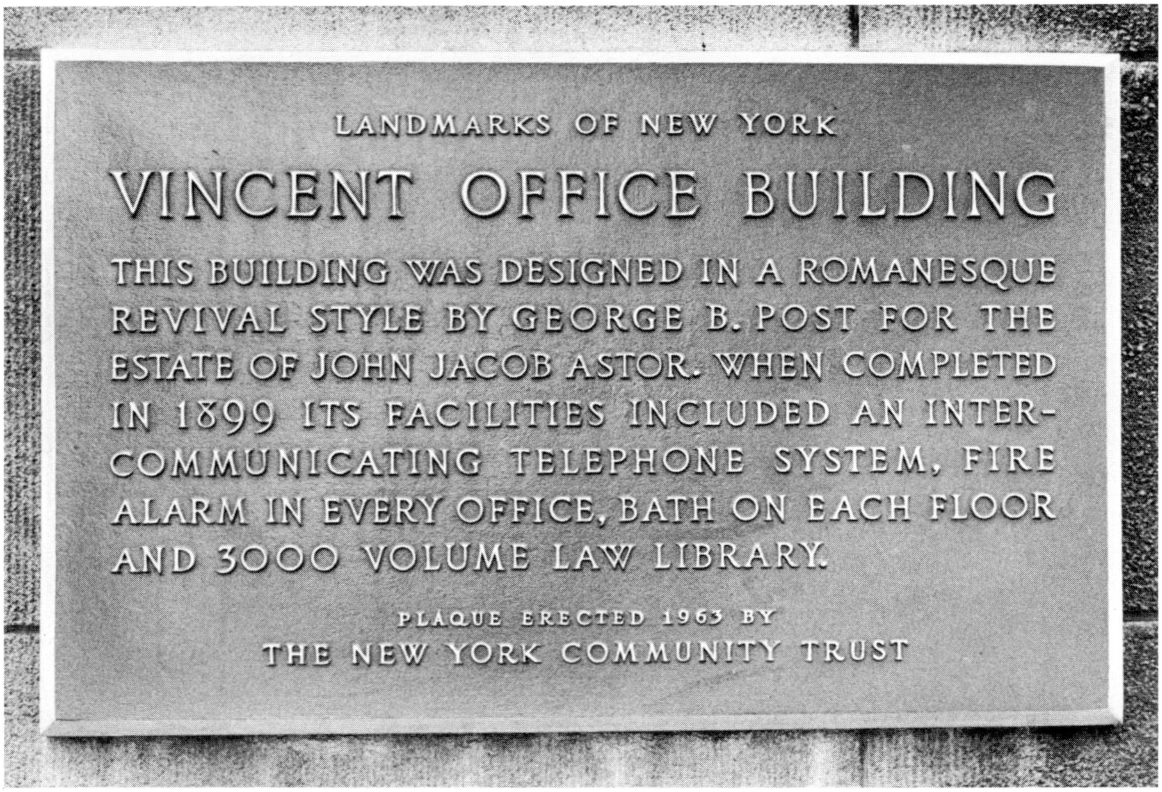

LANDMARKS OF NEW YORK
VINCENT OFFICE BUILDING
THIS BUILDING WAS DESIGNED IN A ROMANESQUE REVIVAL STYLE BY GEORGE B. POST FOR THE ESTATE OF JOHN JACOB ASTOR. WHEN COMPLETED IN 1899 ITS FACILITIES INCLUDED AN INTER-COMMUNICATING TELEPHONE SYSTEM, FIRE ALARM IN EVERY OFFICE, BATH ON EACH FLOOR AND 3000 VOLUME LAW LIBRARY.
PLAQUE ERECTED 1963 BY
THE NEW YORK COMMUNITY TRUST

FORDHAM UNIVERSITY

114
Wall of New Amsterdam (site)
plaque on 1 Wall Street (Broadway)
Manhattan

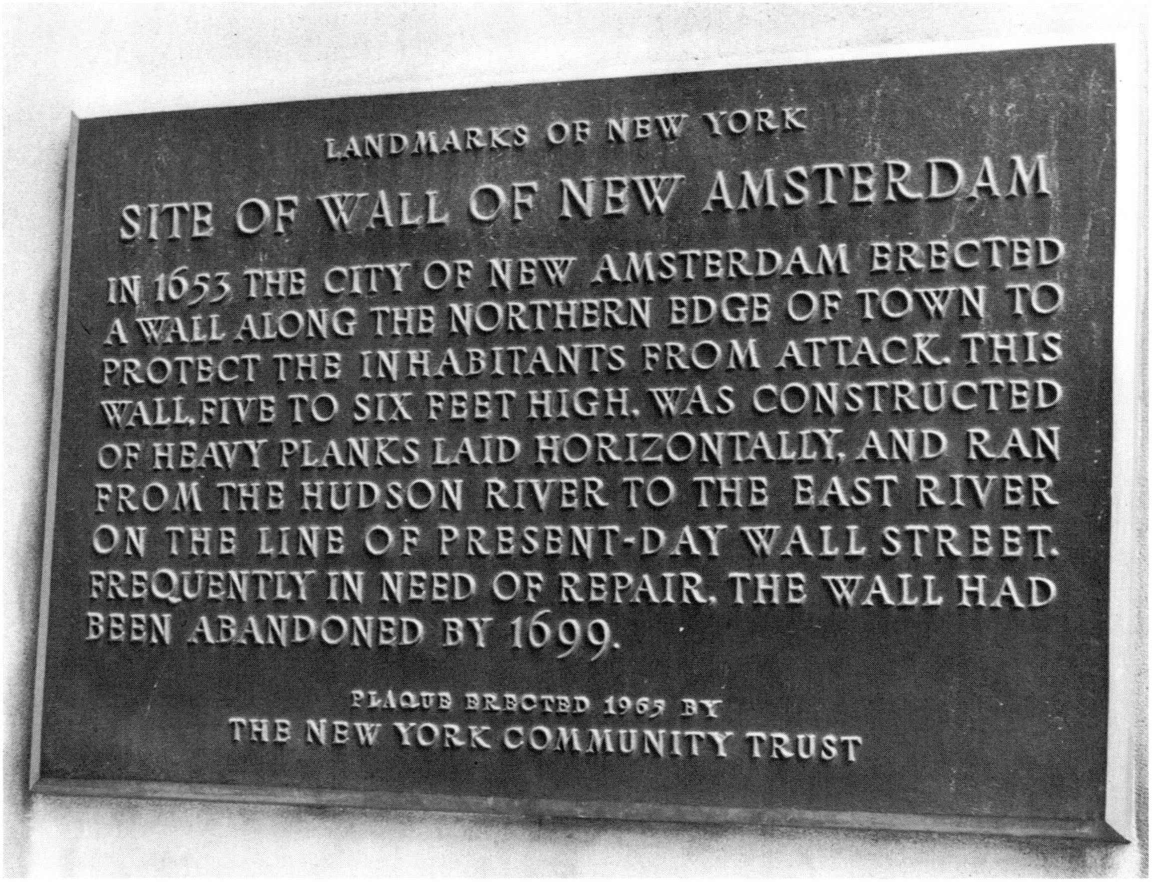
LANDMARKS OF NEW YORK
SITE OF WALL OF NEW AMSTERDAM
IN 1653 THE CITY OF NEW AMSTERDAM ERECTED A WALL ALONG THE NORTHERN EDGE OF TOWN TO PROTECT THE INHABITANTS FROM ATTACK. THIS WALL, FIVE TO SIX FEET HIGH, WAS CONSTRUCTED OF HEAVY PLANKS LAID HORIZONTALLY, AND RAN FROM THE HUDSON RIVER TO THE EAST RIVER ON THE LINE OF PRESENT-DAY WALL STREET. FREQUENTLY IN NEED OF REPAIR, THE WALL HAD BEEN ABANDONED BY 1699.
PLAQUE ERECTED 1965 BY
THE NEW YORK COMMUNITY TRUST

1673

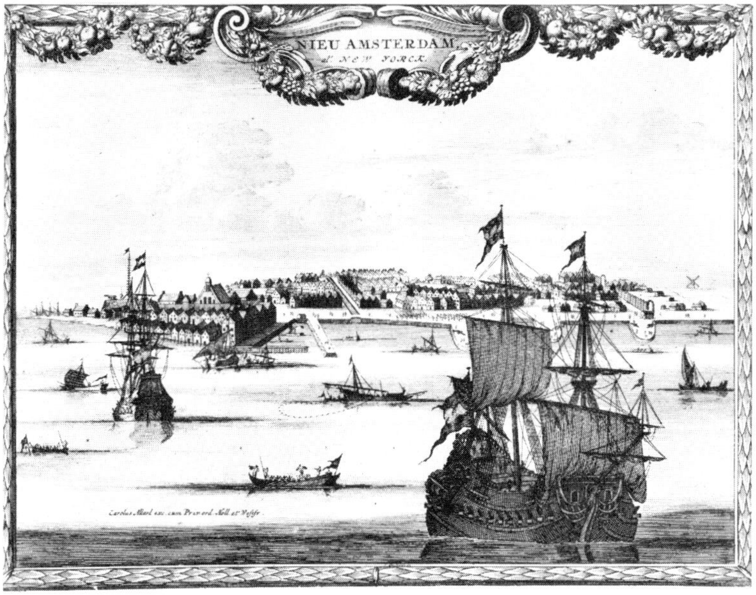
NIEU AMSTERDAM,
at NEW YORCK.

1660

115
No. 22 Washington Square North
near Fifth Avenue, Greenwich Village
Manhattan

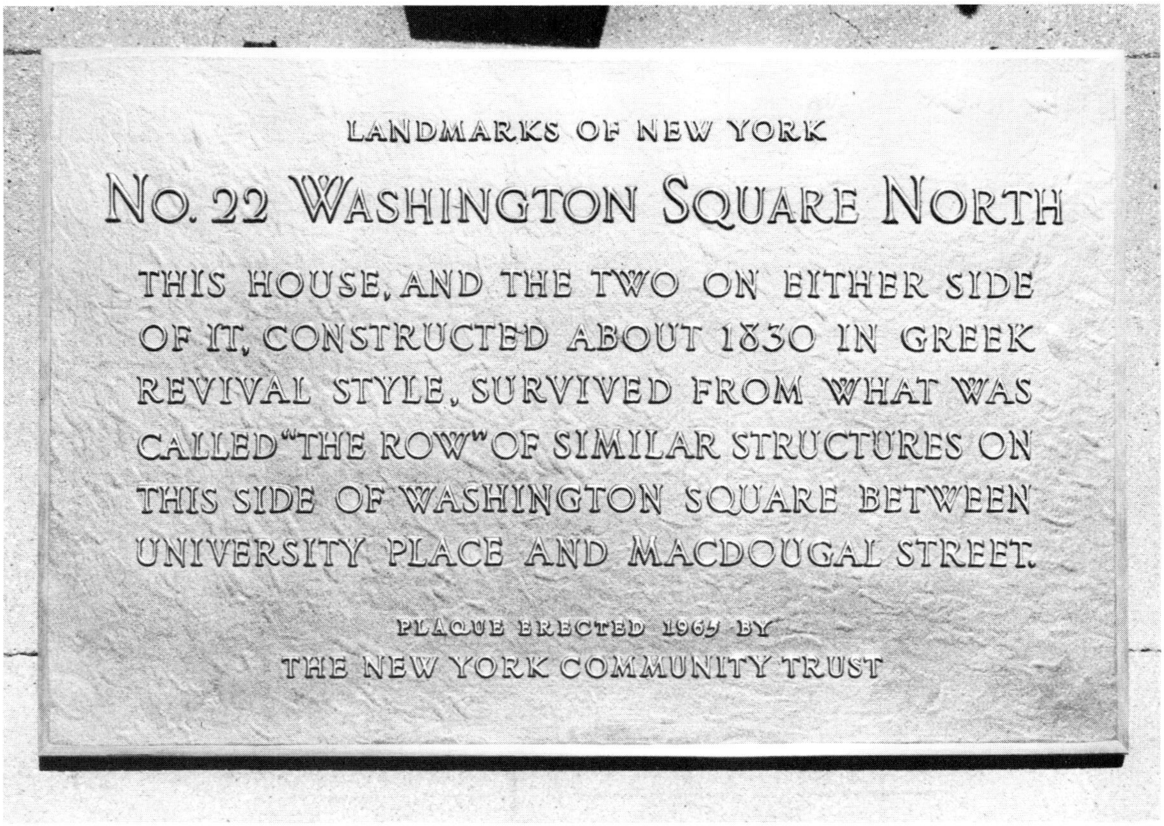
LANDMARKS OF NEW YORK
NO. 22 WASHINGTON SQUARE NORTH
THIS HOUSE, AND THE TWO ON EITHER SIDE OF IT, CONSTRUCTED ABOUT 1830 IN GREEK REVIVAL STYLE, SURVIVED FROM WHAT WAS CALLED "THE ROW" OF SIMILAR STRUCTURES ON THIS SIDE OF WASHINGTON SQUARE BETWEEN UNIVERSITY PLACE AND MACDOUGAL STREET.
PLAQUE ERECTED 1965 BY
THE NEW YORK COMMUNITY TRUST

116

Watson House (now Church of Our Lady of the Rosary [R.C.])

7 State Street (South Ferry)

Manhattan

LANDMARKS OF NEW YORK
WATSON HOUSE
THIS STRUCTURE, NOW THE ROMAN CATHOLIC CHURCH OF OUR LADY OF THE ROSARY, WAS DESIGNED BY JOHN MC COMB IN FEDERAL STYLE AND BUILT ABOUT 1800 WHEN MANY OTHER MANSIONS OCCUPIED THIS THEN FASHIONABLE THOROUGHFARE. OF PARTICULAR ARCHITECTURAL INTEREST IS ITS COLONNADE THAT CURVES WITH THE LINE OF THE STREET.
PLAQUE ERECTED 1958 BY
THE NEW YORK COMMUNITY TRUST

8 STATE ST

117

West End Collegiate Church and Collegiate School (Reformed Protestant Dutch)

241 West 77th Street (West End Avenue)

Manhattan

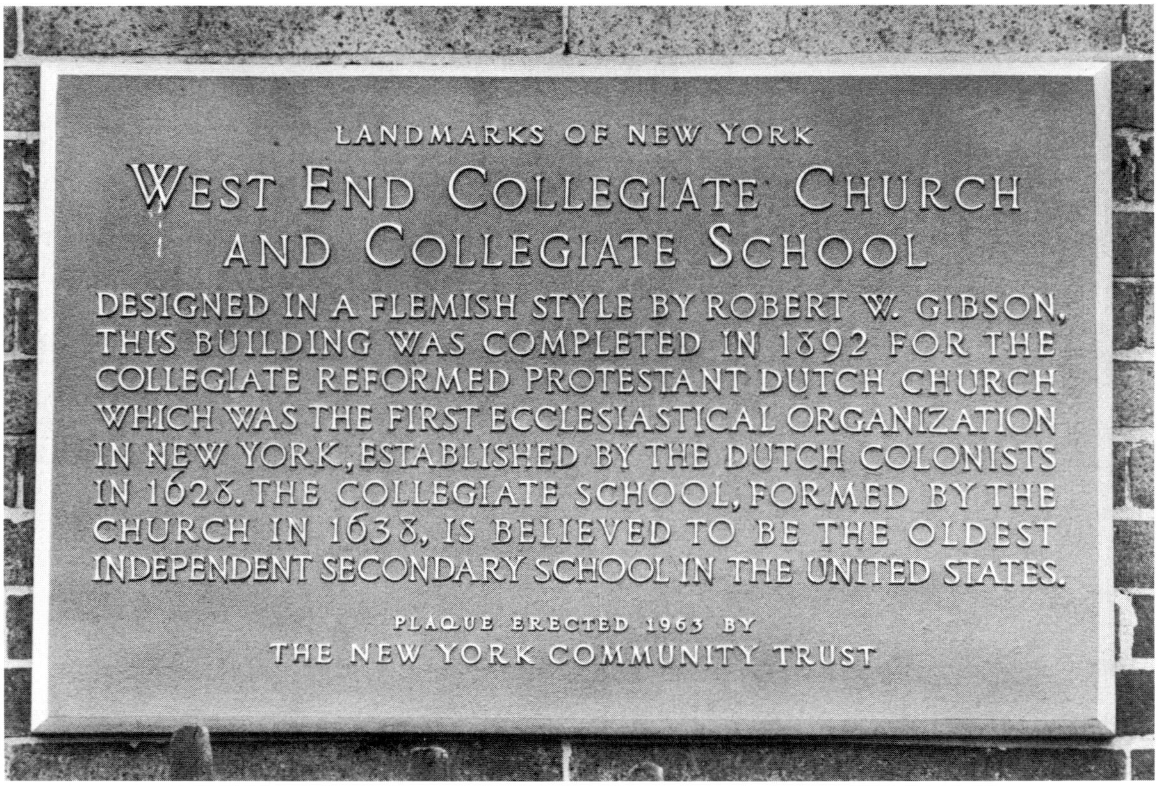
LANDMARKS OF NEW YORK
WEST END COLLEGIATE CHURCH AND COLLEGIATE SCHOOL
DESIGNED IN A FLEMISH STYLE BY ROBERT W. GIBSON, THIS BUILDING WAS COMPLETED IN 1892 FOR THE COLLEGIATE REFORMED PROTESTANT DUTCH CHURCH WHICH WAS THE FIRST ECCLESIASTICAL ORGANIZATION IN NEW YORK, ESTABLISHED BY THE DUTCH COLONISTS IN 1628. THE COLLEGIATE SCHOOL, FORMED BY THE CHURCH IN 1638, IS BELIEVED TO BE THE OLDEST INDEPENDENT SECONDARY SCHOOL IN THE UNITED STATES.
PLAQUE ERECTED 1963 BY
THE NEW YORK COMMUNITY TRUST

118
Woolworth Building
Broadway between Barclay Street and Park Place, City Hall
Manhattan

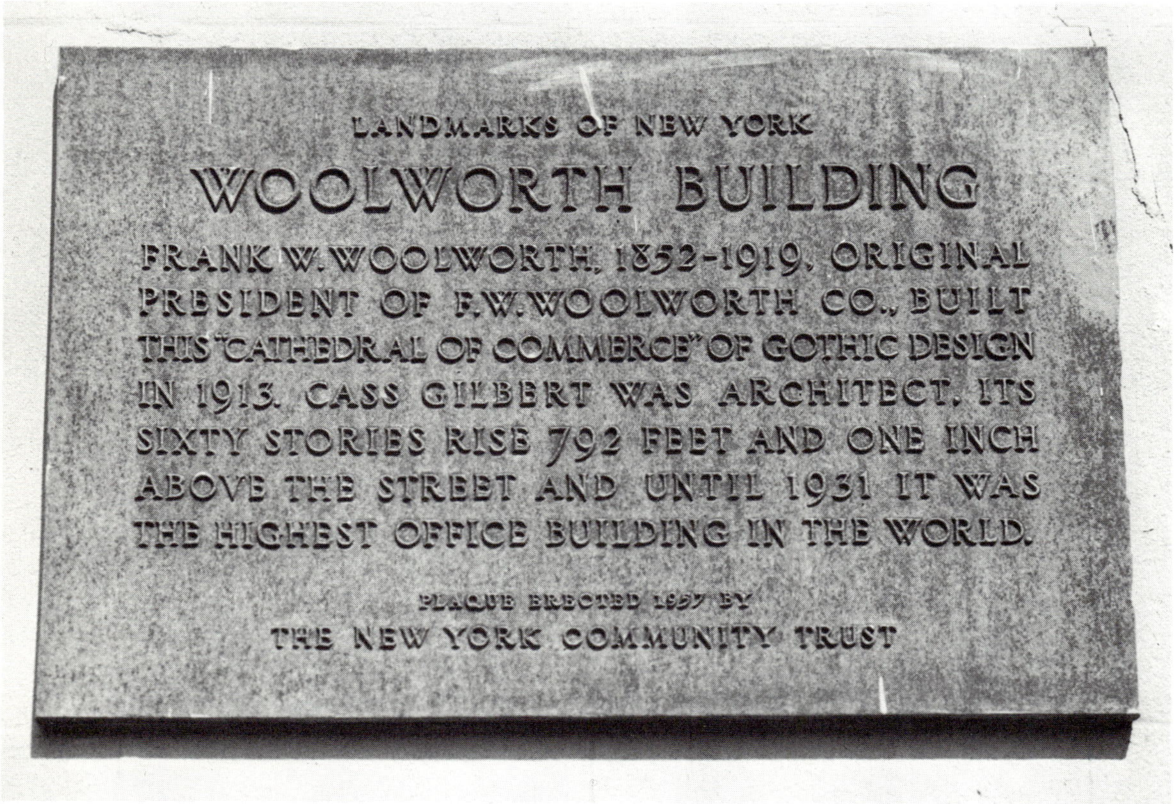
LANDMARKS OF NEW YORK
WOOLWORTH BUILDING
FRANK W. WOOLWORTH, 1852-1919, ORIGINAL PRESIDENT OF F.W. WOOLWORTH CO., BUILT THIS "CATHEDRAL OF COMMERCE" OF GOTHIC DESIGN IN 1913. CASS GILBERT WAS ARCHITECT. ITS SIXTY STORIES RISE 792 FEET AND ONE INCH ABOVE THE STREET AND UNTIL 1931 IT WAS THE HIGHEST OFFICE BUILDING IN THE WORLD.
PLAQUE ERECTED 1957 BY
THE NEW YORK COMMUNITY TRUST

PRINTING HOUSE
SQUARE

119
Yivo Institute for Jewish Research (former William Starr Miller Residence)
1048 Fifth Avenue (86th Street)
Manhattan

LANDMARKS OF NEW YORK
YIVO INSTITUTE FOR JEWISH RESEARCH
DESIGNED BY CARRÈRE & HASTINGS ABOUT 1914
AS A RESIDENCE FOR WILLIAM STARR MILLER,
THIS BUILDING OF BRICK AND LIMESTONE RESEMBLES
A FRENCH CHATEAU OF THE LOUIS XIII PERIOD.
IN 1944 IT BECAME THE HOME OF MRS. CORNELIUS
VANDERBILT. AFTER HER DEATH IN 1953 THE
PROPERTY WAS PURCHASED BY THE YIVO INSTITUTE
FOR JEWISH RESEARCH, FOUNDED IN 1925.
PLAQUE ERECTED 1960 BY
THE NEW YORK COMMUNITY TRUST

THE
ADAMS
E.86ST

Brooklyn

BROOKLYN

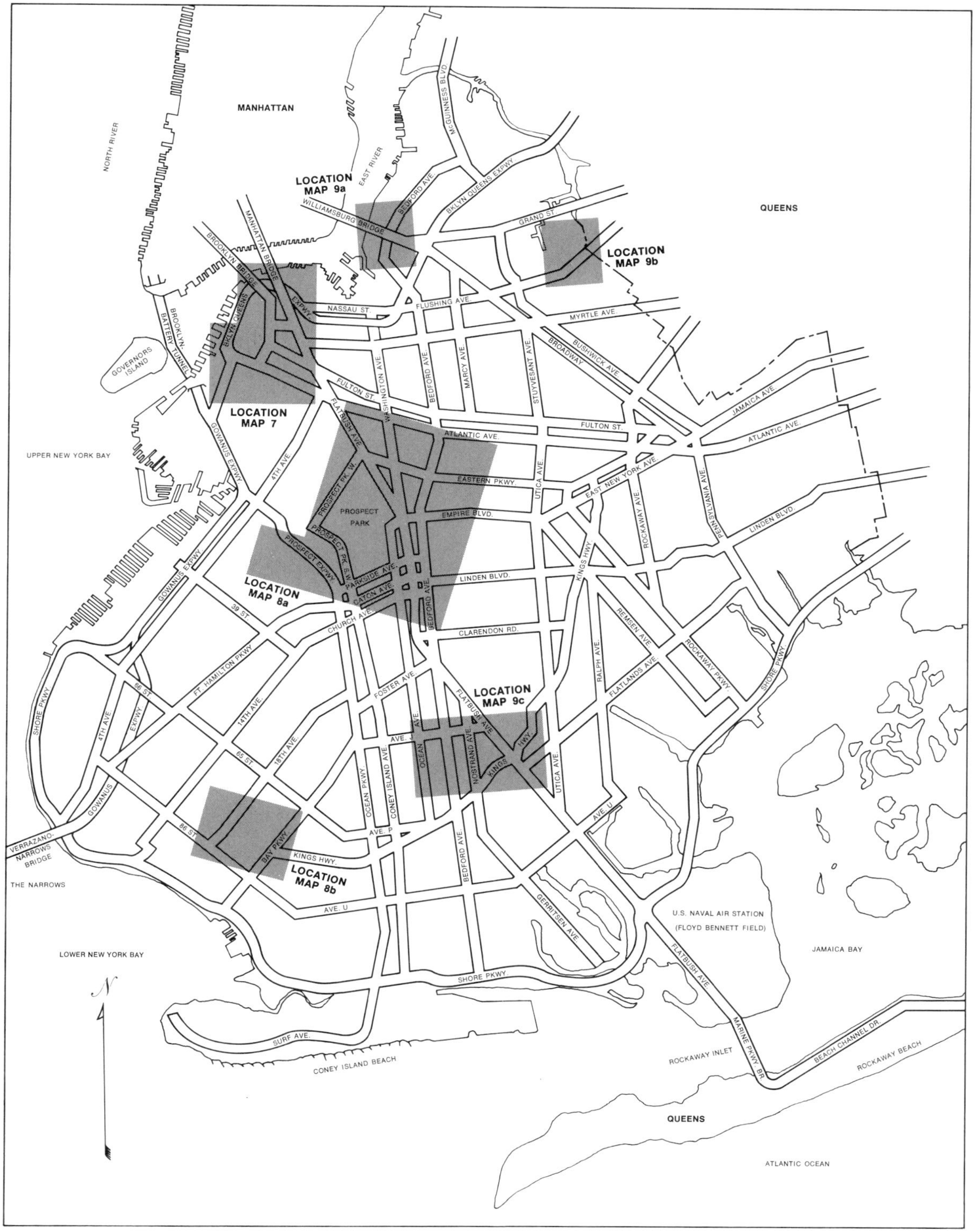

MANHATTAN
NORTH RIVER
EAST RIVER
LOCATION MAP 9a
WILLIAMSBURG BRIDGE
BEDFORD AVE.
McGUINNESS BLVD.
BKLYN QUEENS EXPWY.
QUEENS
GRAND ST.
LOCATION MAP 9b
MANHATTAN BRIDGE
BROOKLYN BRIDGE
NASSAU ST.
FLUSHING AVE.
MYRTLE AVE.
BROOKLYN-BATTERY TUNNEL
GOVERNORS ISLAND
BKLYN QUEENS EXPWY.
BUSHWICK AVE.
BROADWAY
WASHINGTON AVE.
BEDFORD AVE.
MARCY AVE.
STUYVESANT AVE.
FULTON ST.
JAMAICA AVE.
LOCATION MAP 7
FLATBUSH AVE.
ATLANTIC AVE.
FULTON ST.
ATLANTIC AVE.
UPPER NEW YORK BAY
GOWANUS EXPWY.
4TH AVE.
PROSPECT PK. W.
EASTERN PKWY.
UTICA AVE.
EAST NEW YORK AVE.
PENNSYLVANIA AVE.
PROSPECT PARK
EMPIRE BLVD.
ROCKAWAY AVE.
LINDEN BLVD.
PROSPECT EXPWY.
PROSPECT PK. S.W.
PARKSIDE AVE.
KINGS HWY.
LINDEN BLVD.
LOCATION MAP 8a
CATON AVE.
39 ST.
CHURCH AVE.
BEDFORD AVE.
REMSEN AVE.
CLARENDON RD.
RALPH AVE.
ROCKAWAY PKWY.
SHORE PKWY.
FT. HAMILTON PKWY.
FLATLANDS AVE.
56 ST.
FOSTER AVE.
LOCATION MAP 9c
FLATBUSH AVE.
SHORE PKWY.
4TH AVE.
EXPWY.
14TH AVE.
65 ST.
18TH AVE.
OCEAN AVE.
NOSTRAND AVE.
KINGS HWY.
UTICA AVE.
OCEAN PKWY.
CONEY ISLAND AVE.
AVE. U
GOWANUS
86 ST.
AVE. P
BAY PKWY.
KINGS HWY.
BEDFORD AVE.
VERRAZANO-NARROWS BRIDGE
LOCATION MAP 8b
THE NARROWS
AVE. U
GERRITSEN AVE.
U.S. NAVAL AIR STATION
(FLOYD BENNETT FIELD)
LOWER NEW YORK BAY
JAMAICA BAY
FLATBUSH AVE.
SHORE PKWY.
N
SURF AVE.
MARINE PKWY. BR.
BEACH CHANNEL DR.
ROCKAWAY INLET
ROCKAWAY BEACH
CONEY ISLAND BEACH
QUEENS
ATLANTIC OCEAN

120
Brooklyn Borough Hall
Fulton and Court Streets
Brooklyn

LANDMARKS OF NEW YORK
BROOKLYN BOROUGH HALL
THIS EDIFICE, DESIGNED BY GAMALIEL KING AND COMPLETED IN 1849, WAS ORIGINALLY THE CITY HALL OF BROOKLYN. IT NOW CONTAINS THE OFFICES OF THE BOROUGH PRESIDENT AND HIS STAFF. BROOKLYN, INCORPORATED AS A CITY IN 1834, BECAME A BOROUGH OF GREATER NEW YORK IN 1898.
PLAQUE ERECTED 1959 BY
THE NEW YORK COMMUNITY TRUST

121
Brooklyn Botanic Garden, Administration Building
1000 Washington Avenue (Crown Street), Prospect Park East
Brooklyn

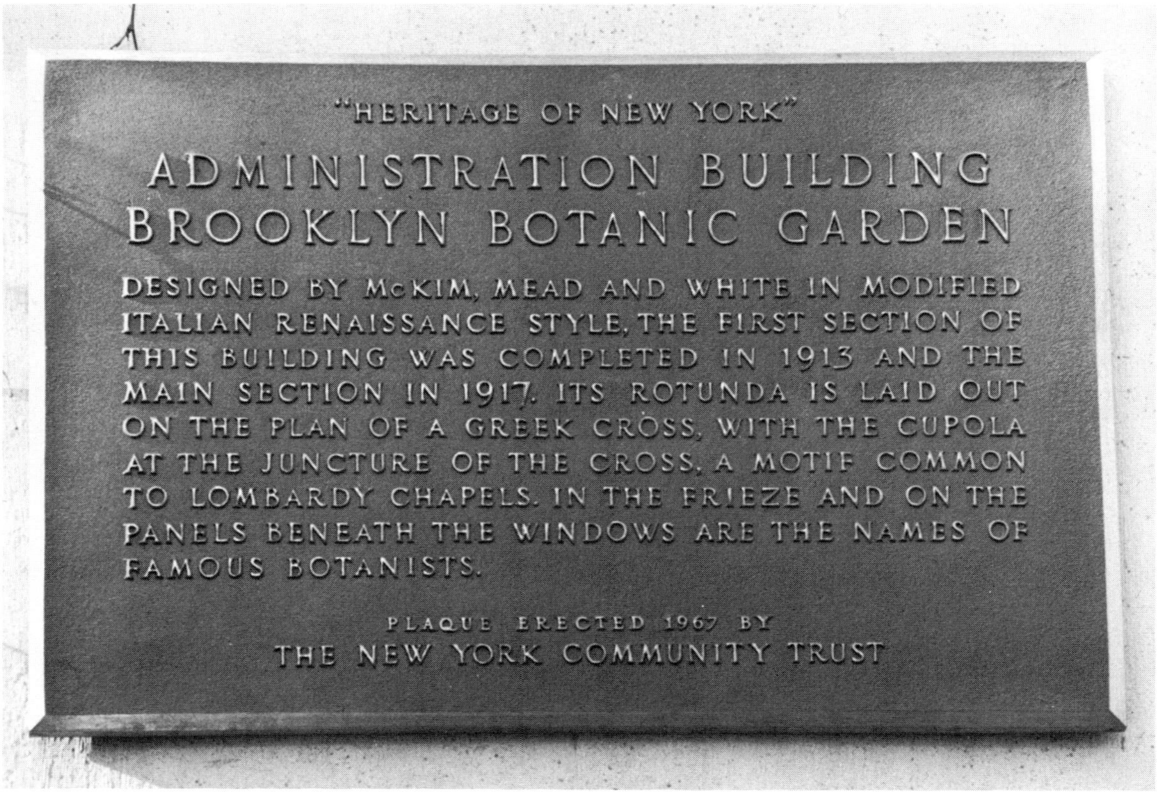
"HERITAGE OF NEW YORK"
ADMINISTRATION BUILDING
BROOKLYN BOTANIC GARDEN
DESIGNED BY McKIM, MEAD AND WHITE IN MODIFIED ITALIAN RENAISSANCE STYLE, THE FIRST SECTION OF THIS BUILDING WAS COMPLETED IN 1913 AND THE MAIN SECTION IN 1917. ITS ROTUNDA IS LAID OUT ON THE PLAN OF A GREEK CROSS, WITH THE CUPOLA AT THE JUNCTURE OF THE CROSS, A MOTIF COMMON TO LOMBARDY CHAPELS. IN THE FRIEZE AND ON THE PANELS BENEATH THE WINDOWS ARE THE NAMES OF FAMOUS BOTANISTS.
PLAQUE ERECTED 1967 BY
THE NEW YORK COMMUNITY TRUST

122

Brooklyn Children's Museum (former "Spanish Adams House")

Brooklyn Avenue and Park Place [demolished]

Brooklyn

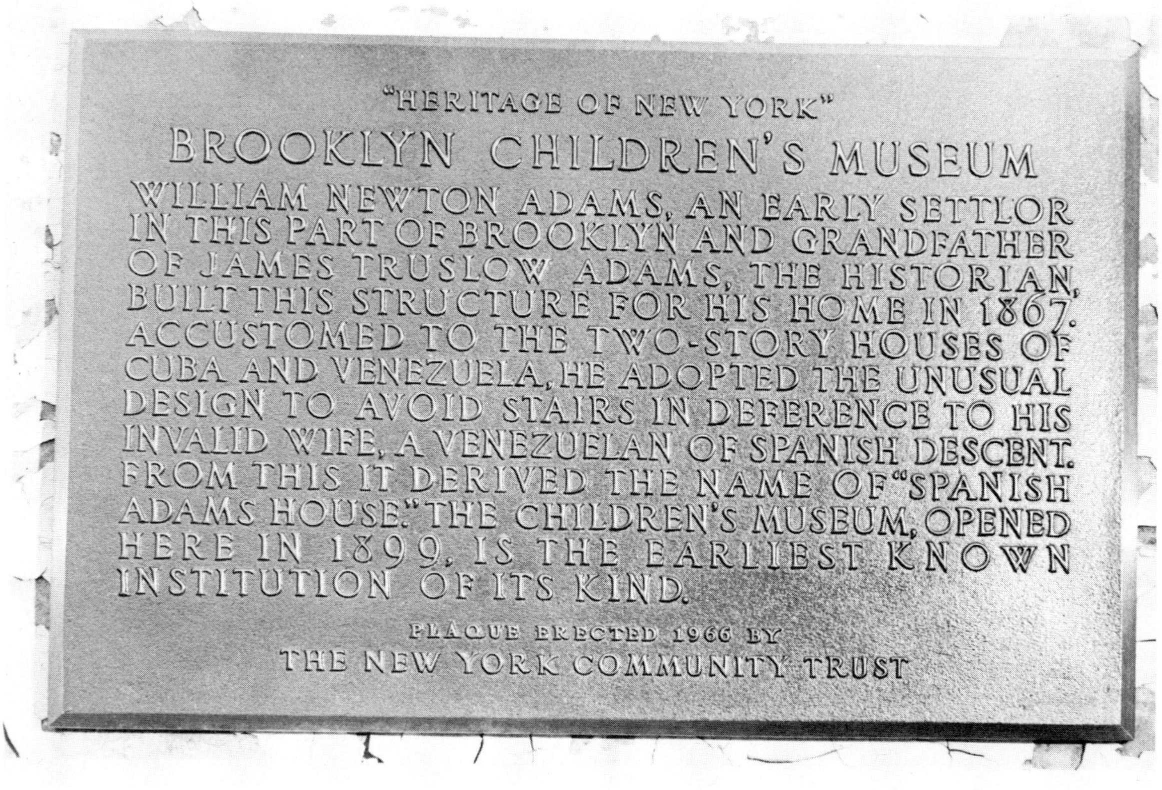
"HERITAGE OF NEW YORK"
BROOKLYN CHILDREN'S MUSEUM
WILLIAM NEWTON ADAMS, AN EARLY SETTLOR IN THIS PART OF BROOKLYN AND GRANDFATHER OF JAMES TRUSLOW ADAMS, THE HISTORIAN, BUILT THIS STRUCTURE FOR HIS HOME IN 1867. ACCUSTOMED TO THE TWO-STORY HOUSES OF CUBA AND VENEZUELA, HE ADOPTED THE UNUSUAL DESIGN TO AVOID STAIRS IN DEFERENCE TO HIS INVALID WIFE, A VENEZUELAN OF SPANISH DESCENT. FROM THIS IT DERIVED THE NAME OF "SPANISH ADAMS HOUSE." THE CHILDREN'S MUSEUM, OPENED HERE IN 1899, IS THE EARLIEST KNOWN INSTITUTION OF ITS KIND.
PLAQUE ERECTED 1966 BY
THE NEW YORK COMMUNITY TRUST

123
Brooklyn Ethical Culture School (former Henry C. Hulbert Residence)
49-50 Prospect Park W. (2nd Street), Park Slope
Brooklyn

LANDMARKS OF NEW YORK
THIS STRUCTURE OF RENAISSANCE STYLE, DESIGNED BY MONTROSE W. MORRIS, WAS BUILT IN 1881-83 FOR HENRY C. HULBERT, PAPER MERCHANT, AND ACQUIRED IN 1928 BY THE BROOKLYN ETHICAL CULTURE SCHOOL. IT WAS CITED IN 1957 BY THE SOCIETY OF ARCHITECTURAL HISTORIANS AND THE MUNICIPAL ART SOCIETY FOR ITS ARCHITECTURAL SIGNIFICANCE.
PLAQUE ERECTED 1958 BY
THE NEW YORK COMMUNITY TRUST

124
Brooklyn Municipal Building
Fulton and Court Streets
Brooklyn

"HERITAGE OF NEW YORK"
BROOKLYN MUNICIPAL BUILDING
McKENZIE, VOORHEES AND GMELIN DESIGNED THIS STRUCTURE IN A MODIFIED ROMAN ECLECTIC STYLE. THE INTERIOR MARBLE WAS QUARRIED IN TENNESSEE AND VERMONT, THE GRANITE FOR ITS BASE IN DEER ISLAND, MAINE, AND MOST OF ITS LIMESTONE FACADE IN INDIANA. THIS BUILDING WAS OPENED IN 1926. IT LATER HOUSED MOST OF THE DEPARTMENTS OF THE BOROUGH GOVERNMENT.
PLAQUE ERECTED 1967 BY
THE NEW YORK COMMUNITY TRUST

125
Brooklyn Museum
Eastern Parkway and Washington Avenue, Prospect Park N.E.
Brooklyn

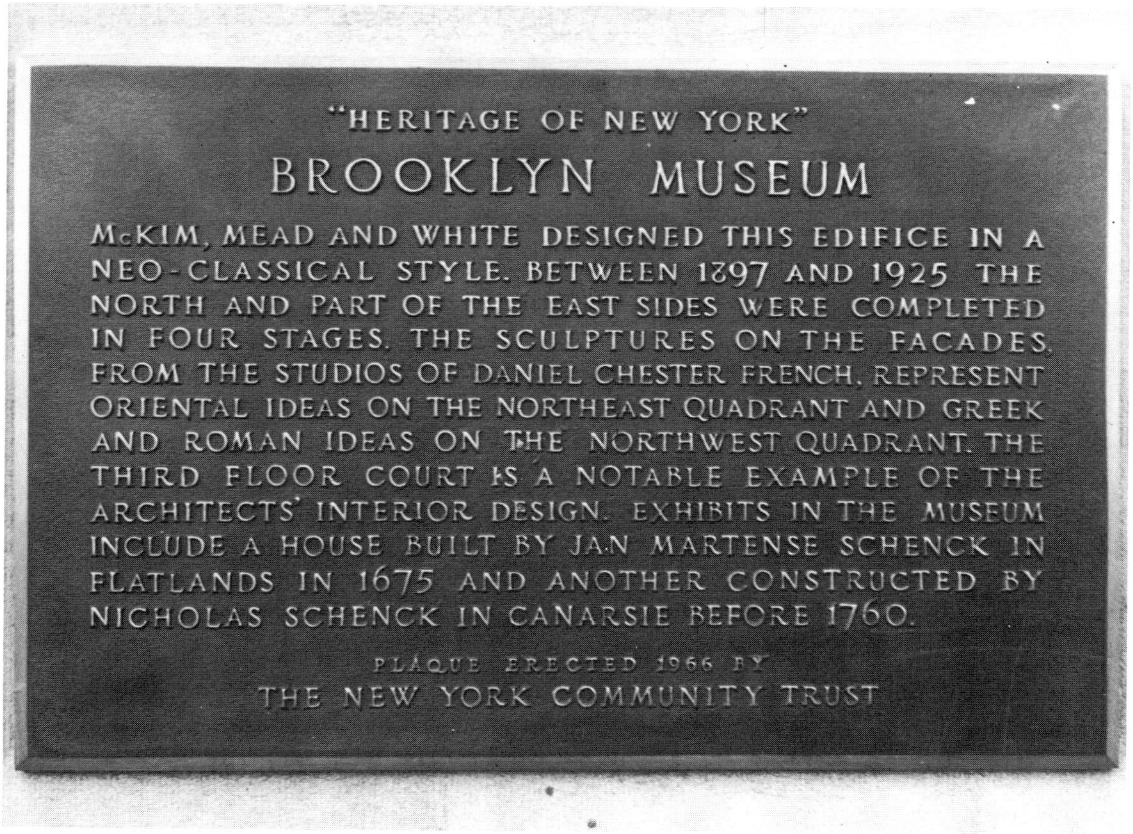
"HERITAGE OF NEW YORK"
BROOKLYN MUSEUM
McKIM, MEAD AND WHITE DESIGNED THIS EDIFICE IN A NEO-CLASSICAL STYLE. BETWEEN 1897 AND 1925 THE NORTH AND PART OF THE EAST SIDES WERE COMPLETED IN FOUR STAGES. THE SCULPTURES ON THE FACADES, FROM THE STUDIOS OF DANIEL CHESTER FRENCH, REPRESENT ORIENTAL IDEAS ON THE NORTHEAST QUADRANT AND GREEK AND ROMAN IDEAS ON THE NORTHWEST QUADRANT. THE THIRD FLOOR COURT IS A NOTABLE EXAMPLE OF THE ARCHITECTS' INTERIOR DESIGN. EXHIBITS IN THE MUSEUM INCLUDE A HOUSE BUILT BY JAN MARTENSE SCHENCK IN FLATLANDS IN 1675 AND ANOTHER CONSTRUCTED BY NICHOLAS SCHENCK IN CANARSIE BEFORE 1760.
PLAQUE ERECTED 1966 BY
THE NEW YORK COMMUNITY TRUST

126
Christ Church (P.E.)
Clinton and Kane Streets, Cobble Hill
Brooklyn

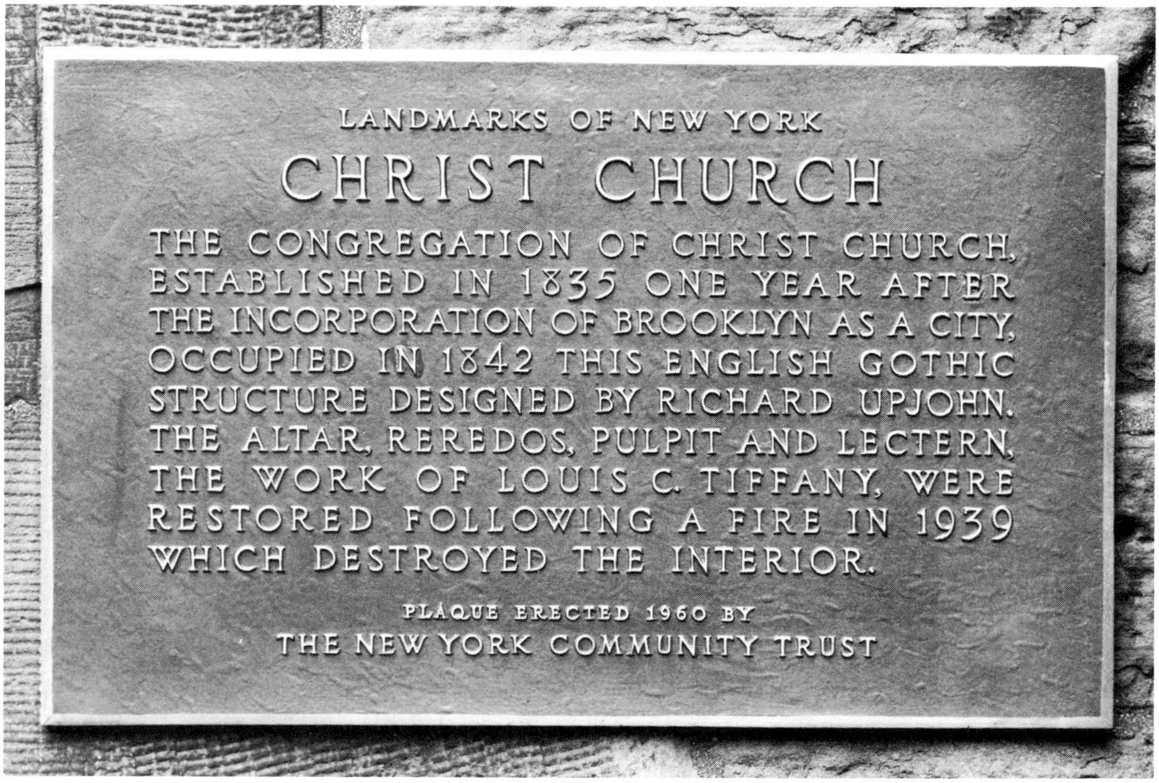
LANDMARKS OF NEW YORK
CHRIST CHURCH
THE CONGREGATION OF CHRIST CHURCH, ESTABLISHED IN 1835 ONE YEAR AFTER THE INCORPORATION OF BROOKLYN AS A CITY, OCCUPIED IN 1842 THIS ENGLISH GOTHIC STRUCTURE DESIGNED BY RICHARD UPJOHN. THE ALTAR, REREDOS, PULPIT AND LECTERN, THE WORK OF LOUIS C. TIFFANY, WERE RESTORED FOLLOWING A FIRE IN 1939 WHICH DESTROYED THE INTERIOR.
PLAQUE ERECTED 1960 BY
THE NEW YORK COMMUNITY TRUST

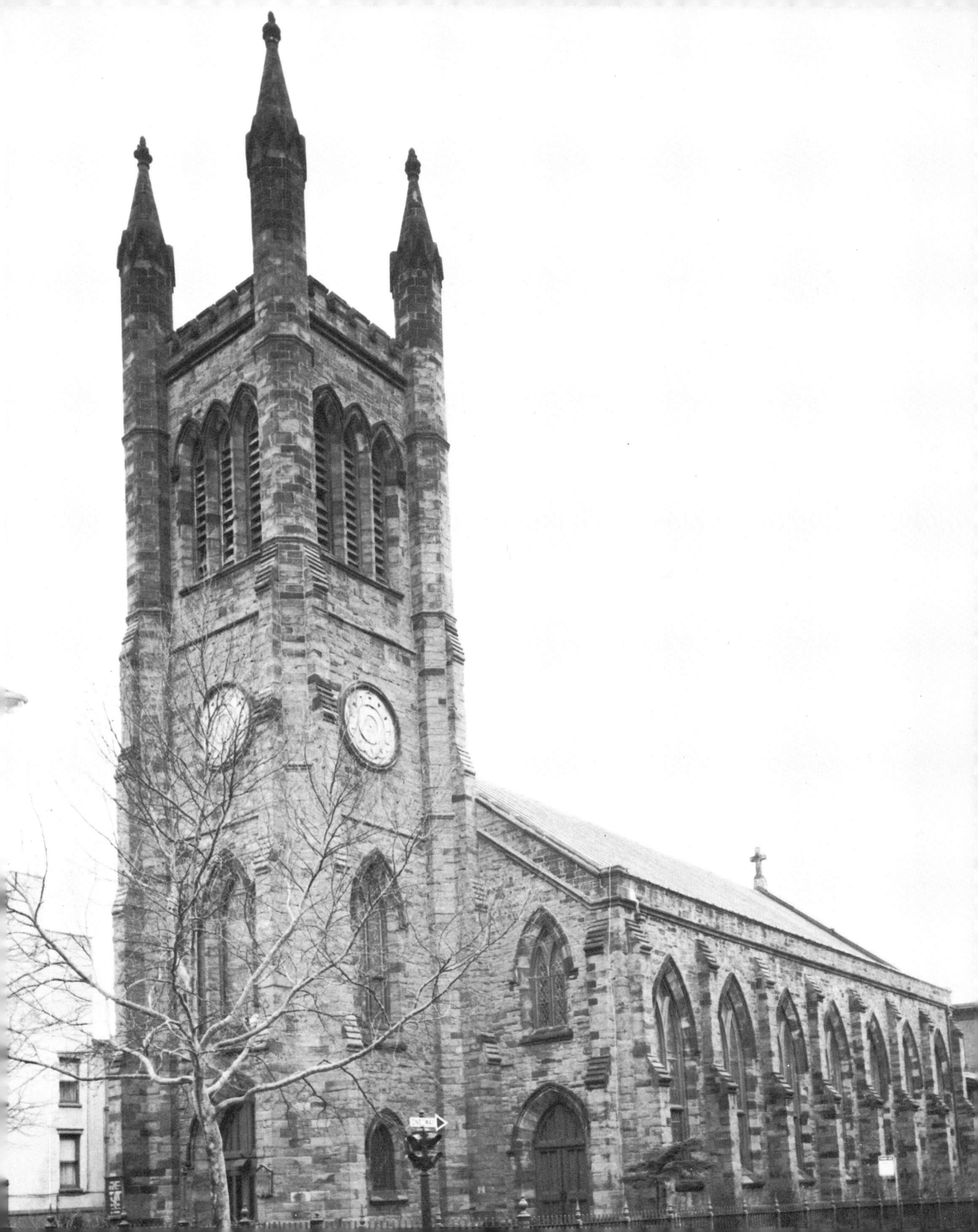

127
Church of the Saviour (First Unitarian Church)
Pierrepont Street and Monroe Place, Brooklyn Heights
Brooklyn

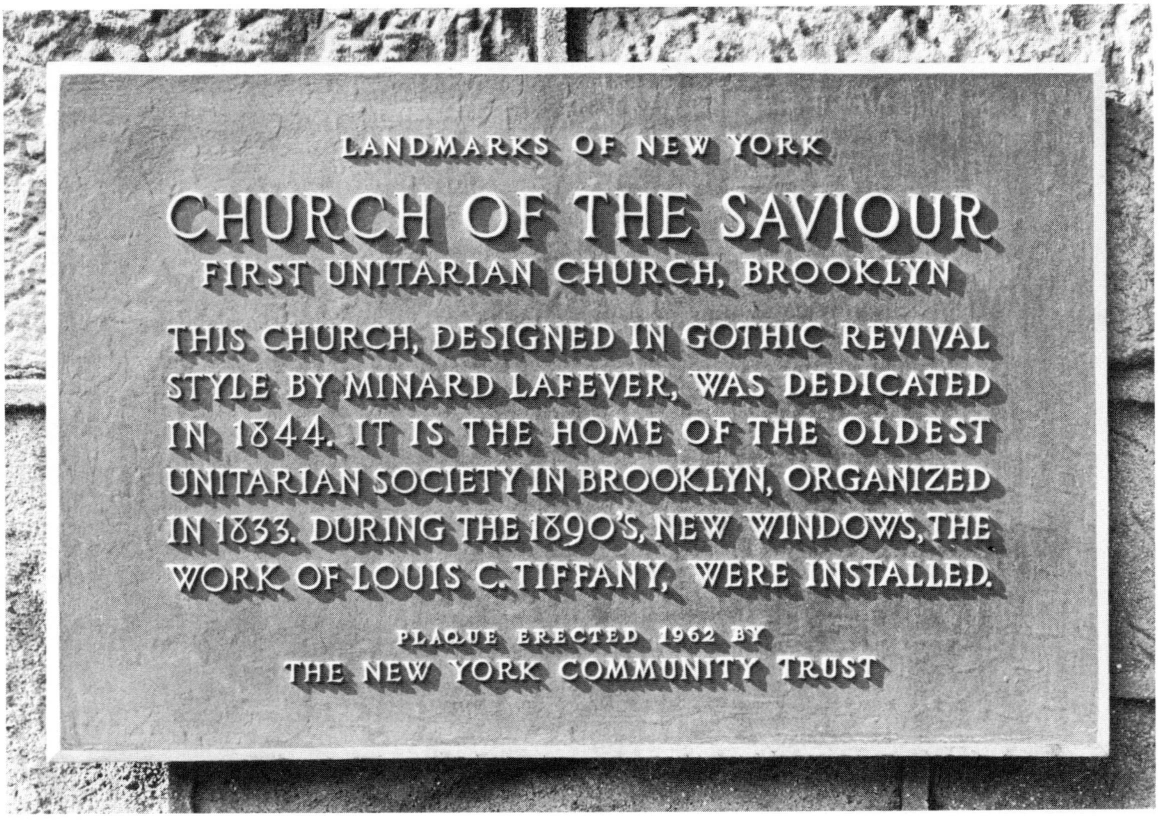

LANDMARKS OF NEW YORK
CHURCH OF THE SAVIOUR
FIRST UNITARIAN CHURCH, BROOKLYN
THIS CHURCH, DESIGNED IN GOTHIC REVIVAL
STYLE BY MINARD LAFEVER, WAS DEDICATED
IN 1844. IT IS THE HOME OF THE OLDEST
UNITARIAN SOCIETY IN BROOKLYN, ORGANIZED
IN 1833. DURING THE 1890'S, NEW WINDOWS, THE
WORK OF LOUIS C. TIFFANY, WERE INSTALLED.
PLAQUE ERECTED 1962 BY
THE NEW YORK COMMUNITY TRUST

NO
PARKING

128
Dutch Reformed Church of Flatlands
Kings Highway and East 40th Street
Brooklyn

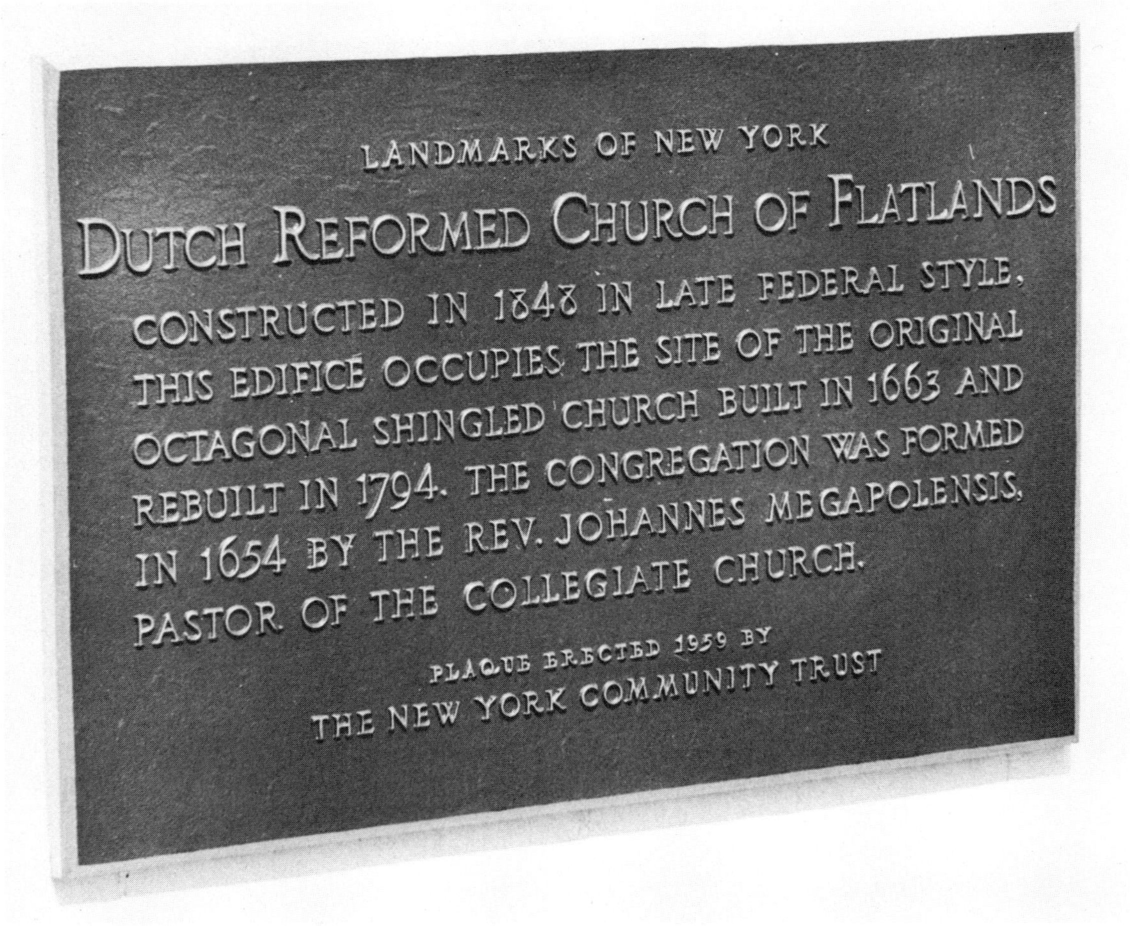
LANDMARKS OF NEW YORK
DUTCH REFORMED CHURCH OF FLATLANDS
CONSTRUCTED IN 1848 IN LATE FEDERAL STYLE, THIS EDIFICE OCCUPIES THE SITE OF THE ORIGINAL OCTAGONAL SHINGLED CHURCH BUILT IN 1663 AND REBUILT IN 1794. THE CONGREGATION WAS FORMED IN 1654 BY THE REV. JOHANNES MEGAPOLENSIS, PASTOR OF THE COLLEGIATE CHURCH.
PLAQUE ERECTED 1959 BY
THE NEW YORK COMMUNITY TRUST

129
Erasmus Hall
Flatbush and Church Avenues
Brooklyn

LANDMARKS OF NEW YORK
ERASMUS HALL
THE ORIGINAL ACADEMY ON THIS SITE WAS
FOUNDED BY THE DUTCH REFORMED CHURCH
AND BUILT BY CHURCH MEMBERS IN 1786.
LARGELY OF MATERIAL FURNISHED BY
NEIGHBORING FARMERS. ALEXANDER HAMILTON.
JOHN JAY AND AARON BURR CONTRIBUTED TO
ITS CONSTRUCTION FUND. OPENED IN 1787
IT WAS THE FIRST SECONDARY SCHOOL
CHARTERED BY NEW YORK STATE REGENTS.
AND IN 1896 IT BECAME ERASMUS HALL
HIGH SCHOOL WHEN GIVEN TO THE CITY
BY THE CHURCH.
PLAQUE ERECTED 1957 BY
THE NEW YORK COMMUNITY TRUST

130

Green-Wood Cemetery Gates

Fifth Avenue and 25th Street, Park Slope
Brooklyn

LANDMARKS OF NEW YORK
GREEN-WOOD CEMETERY GATES
DESIGNED BY RICHARD M. UPJOHN IN GOTHIC REVIVAL STYLE, THIS MAIN ENTRANCE TO GREEN-WOOD CEMETERY WAS BUILT IN 1861 OF BELLEVILLE BROWNSTONE. THE SCULPTURED GROUPS DEPICTING BIBLICAL SCENES OVER THE GATEWAYS ARE THE WORK OF JOHN M. MOFFITT.
PLAQUE ERECTED 1958 BY
THE NEW YORK COMMUNITY TRUST

131

No. 131 Hicks Street (Henry C. Bowen Residence)

near Clark Street, Brooklyn Heights

Brooklyn

"HERITAGE OF NEW YORK"
131 HICKS STREET
BUILT SHORTLY BEFORE 1850, THIS TOWN HOUSE IS ONE OF THE FEW REMAINING EXAMPLES OF THE GOTHIC REVIVAL DESIGN POPULAR IN MID-19TH CENTURY. THE TUDOR-ARCHED DOORWAY AND ELABORATE CORNICES, ENTABLATURES AND CAST-IRON RAILINGS ARE CHARACTERISTIC OF THIS STYLE APPLIED TO THE ROW HOUSE.
PLAQUE ERECTED 1966 BY
THE NEW YORK COMMUNITY TRUST

132

Hotel Margaret

97 Columbia Heights (Orange Street), Brooklyn Heights
Brooklyn

LANDMARKS OF NEW YORK
HOTEL MARGARET
DESIGNED IN A ROMANESQUE STYLE BY FRANK FREEMAN, THIS BUILDING WAS ERECTED FOR CHARLES ARBUCKLE IN 1889. ITS RESIDENTS HAVE INCLUDED THE ETCHER JOSEPH PENNELL AND NOVELISTS SIGRID UNDSET AND LILLIAN SMITH.
PLAQUE ERECTED 1962 BY
THE NEW YORK COMMUNITY TRUST

HOTEL MARGAR
ONE WAY

133
Kings County Savings Bank
135 Broadway (Bedford Avenue), Williamsburg
Brooklyn

LANDMARKS OF NEW YORK
THE KINGS COUNTY SAVINGS BANK
COMPLETED IN 1868, THIS BUILDING OF
DORCHESTER STONE WAS DESIGNED IN
VICTORIAN STYLE BY WILLIAM H. WILLCOX.
IT WAS CITED FOR ARCHITECTURAL DISTINCTION
BY THE MUNICIPAL ART SOCIETY IN 1957.
THIS PLAQUE IS PRESENTED ON THE OCCASION
OF THE BANK'S CENTENNIAL.
PLAQUE ERECTED 1960 BY
THE NEW YORK COMMUNITY TRUST

BROADWAY FOOD SHOP
HARDWARE
SUPPLIES FOR
PAINTERS JANITORS FACTORIES MASONS
PAINT
INTEREST
DO NOT ENTER
NO RIGHT TURN

134
Lefferts Homestead
Prospect Park E. near Flatbush Avenue and Empire Boulevard
Brooklyn

LANDMARKS OF NEW YORK
LEFFERTS HOMESTEAD
THIS HOUSE, A NOTABLE EXAMPLE OF LATE DUTCH COLONIAL STYLE, WAS REBUILT IN 1777 BY LIEUTENANT PETER LEFFERTS AFTER PARTIAL DESTRUCTION BY FIRE DURING THE BATTLE OF LONG ISLAND. IN 1918 IT WAS PRESENTED TO THE CITY BY HIS DESCENDANTS AND MOVED HERE FROM ITS ORIGINAL LOCATION AT 563 FLATBUSH AVENUE. THE INTERIOR IS UNDER THE CARE OF THE FORT GREENE CHAPTER, DAUGHTERS OF THE AMERICAN REVOLUTION.
PLAQUE ERECTED 1960 BY
THE NEW YORK COMMUNITY TRUST

135
Litchfield Mansion
Prospect Park near Prospect Park West and 5th Street
Brooklyn

LANDMARKS OF NEW YORK
LITCHFIELD MANSION
THIS ITALIANATE VILLA, "RIDGEWOOD," WAS CON-
STRUCTED IN 1855 FOR RAILROAD PIONEER
EDWIN C. LITCHFIELD FROM PLANS BY ALEXANDER
JACKSON DAVIS. FAMED FOR ITS RICH INTERIORS,
IT WAS A CENTER OF BROOKLYN SOCIAL LIFE FOR
MANY YEARS. THE CITY OF BROOKLYN ACQUIRED
THE MANSION AND ITS GROUNDS IN 1869. SINCE 1892
IT HAS HOUSED THE BROOKLYN PARK HEADQUARTERS.
PLAQUE ERECTED 1958 BY
THE NEW YORK COMMUNITY TRUST

136
Long Island Historical Society
128 Pierrepont Street (Clinton Street)
Brooklyn

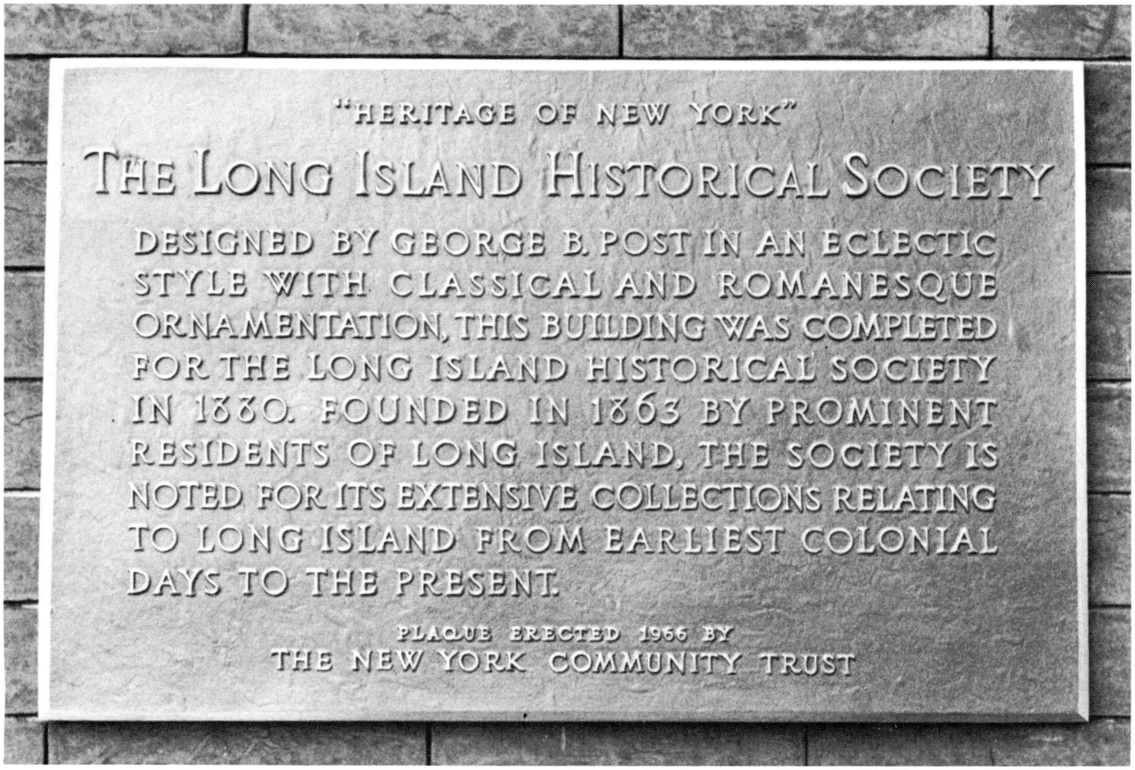
"HERITAGE OF NEW YORK"
THE LONG ISLAND HISTORICAL SOCIETY
DESIGNED BY GEORGE B. POST IN AN ECLECTIC STYLE WITH CLASSICAL AND ROMANESQUE ORNAMENTATION, THIS BUILDING WAS COMPLETED FOR THE LONG ISLAND HISTORICAL SOCIETY IN 1880. FOUNDED IN 1863 BY PROMINENT RESIDENTS OF LONG ISLAND, THE SOCIETY IS NOTED FOR ITS EXTENSIVE COLLECTIONS RELATING TO LONG ISLAND FROM EARLIEST COLONIAL DAYS TO THE PRESENT.
PLAQUE ERECTED 1966 BY
THE NEW YORK COMMUNITY TRUST

workbench

137
Manufacturers Hanover Trust Company
177 Montague Street (Clinton Street)
Brooklyn

LANDMARKS OF NEW YORK
MANUFACTURERS HANOVER TRUST COMPANY
DESIGNED IN MODIFIED ITALIAN RENAISSANCE STYLE BY YORK & SAWYER, THIS GRANITE AND LIMESTONE STRUCTURE WAS COMPLETED IN 1915 FOR BROOKLYN TRUST COMPANY, CHARTERED IN 1866. THAT INSTITUTION BECAME IN 1950 PART OF MANUFACTURERS TRUST COMPANY WHICH ELEVEN YEARS LATER MERGED WITH THE HANOVER BANK.
PLAQUE ERECTED 1962 BY
THE NEW YORK COMMUNITY TRUST

MANUFACTURERS
HANOVER TRUST
FIRST NATIONAL CITY BANK
7up

138
Montauk Club
Eighth Avenue and Lincoln Place, Grand Army Plaza
Brooklyn

LANDMARKS OF NEW YORK
MONTAUK CLUB
THIS BUILDING, COMPLETED IN 1891 FOR THE MONTAUK CLUB, WAS MODELLED BY FRANCIS H. KIMBALL AFTER THE CA'D'ORO IN VENICE. THE FRIEZE ABOVE THE THIRD-STORY WINDOWS REPRESENTS EXPLOITS OF THE MONTAUK INDIANS.
PLAQUE ERECTED 1958 BY
THE NEW YORK COMMUNITY TRUST

139
New Utrecht Reformed Church
18th Avenue and 83rd Street
Brooklyn

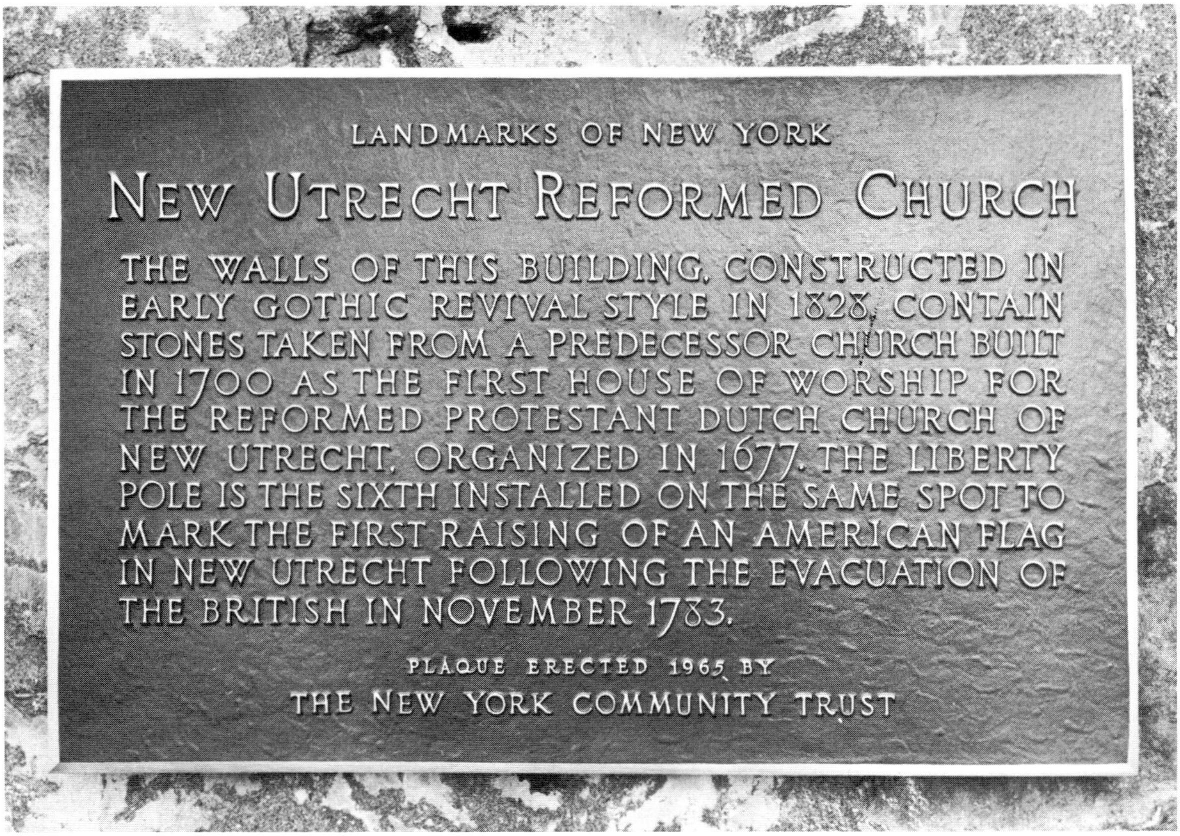
LANDMARKS OF NEW YORK
NEW UTRECHT REFORMED CHURCH
THE WALLS OF THIS BUILDING, CONSTRUCTED IN EARLY GOTHIC REVIVAL STYLE IN 1828, CONTAIN STONES TAKEN FROM A PREDECESSOR CHURCH BUILT IN 1700 AS THE FIRST HOUSE OF WORSHIP FOR THE REFORMED PROTESTANT DUTCH CHURCH OF NEW UTRECHT, ORGANIZED IN 1677. THE LIBERTY POLE IS THE SIXTH INSTALLED ON THE SAME SPOT TO MARK THE FIRST RAISING OF AN AMERICAN FLAG IN NEW UTRECHT FOLLOWING THE EVACUATION OF THE BRITISH IN NOVEMBER 1783.
PLAQUE ERECTED 1965 BY
THE NEW YORK COMMUNITY TRUST

140

Our Lady of Lebanon R.C. Church (Maronite Rite)

113 Remsen Street (Henry Street), Brooklyn Heights
Brooklyn

LANDMARKS OF NEW YORK
OUR LADY OF LEBANON R.C. CHURCH
MARONITE RITE
DESIGNED IN EARLY ROMANESQUE REVIVAL STYLE BY RICHARD UPJOHN, THIS STRUCTURE WAS DEDICATED IN 1846 AS THE CONGREGATIONAL CHURCH OF THE PILGRIMS, WHICH PARISH UNITED WITH THE PLYMOUTH CHURCH IN 1934. TEN YEARS LATER, THIS PROPERTY WAS ACQUIRED BY THE ROMAN CATHOLIC CHURCH OF OUR LADY OF LEBANON.
PLAQUE ERECTED 1965 BY
THE NEW YORK COMMUNITY TRUST

141
Packer Collegiate Institute
170 Joralemon Street (Court Street), Brooklyn Heights
Brooklyn

LANDMARKS OF NEW YORK
THE PACKER COLLEGIATE INSTITUTE
ON THE SITE OF THE BROOKLYN FEMALE
ACADEMY, DESTROYED BY FIRE IN 1852, THIS
EDIFICE WAS OPENED IN 1854, A GIFT
FROM THE WIDOW OF WILLIAM S. PACKER
COMMEMORATING HIS ACTIVE INTEREST IN
WOMEN'S EDUCATION. THE MAIN BUILDING
IN VICTORIAN GOTHIC STYLE WAS ONE OF
THE LAST DESIGNED BY MINARD LAFEVER.
PLAQUE ERECTED 1958 BY
THE NEW YORK COMMUNITY TRUST

142

Plymouth Church of the Pilgrims (Congregational)

Orange and Hicks Streets, Brooklyn Heights

Brooklyn

LANDMARKS OF NEW YORK
PLYMOUTH CHURCH OF THE PILGRIMS
FOUNDED IN 1847 AS PLYMOUTH CHURCH AND BUILT IN 1849 FROM DESIGNS BY J. C. WELLS, THIS CONGREGATIONAL CHURCH BECAME A CENTER OF ANTI-SLAVERY SENTIMENT PRECEDING THE CIVIL WAR. HENRY WARD BEECHER WAS ITS FIRST MINISTER, 1847-1887. ABRAHAM LINCOLN WORSHIPED HERE TWICE IN 1860. A FRAGMENT OF PLYMOUTH ROCK IS IN AN ADJOINING ARCADE. IN 1934 IT WAS UNITED WITH CHURCH OF THE PILGRIMS, FOUNDED IN 1844.
PLAQUE ERECTED 1961 BY
THE NEW YORK COMMUNITY TRUST

PLYMOUTH CHURCH

143
Prospect Park (Soldiers and Sailors Memorial Arch)
Grand Army Plaza
Brooklyn

LANDMARKS OF NEW YORK
PROSPECT PARK
AUTHORIZED IN 1860, THE DEVELOPMENT OF THE PARK WAS DELAYED UNTIL AFTER THE CIVIL WAR. IN 1866 FREDERICK LAW OLMSTED AND CALVERT VAUX, THE DESIGNERS OF CENTRAL PARK, WERE ENGAGED AS LANDSCAPE ARCHITECTS AND THIS PARK IS OFTEN CONSIDERED THEIR MASTERPIECE. COMPLETED IN 1873, IT HAS EVER SINCE BEEN ONE OF THE MAJOR URBAN PARKS OF THE NATION
PLAQUE ERECTED 1965 BY
THE NEW YORK COMMUNITY TRUST

TO·THE·DEFENDERS·OF·THE·UNION·1861·1865

144

St. Ann's Church (Episcopal)

131 Clinton Street (Livingston Street), Brooklyn Heights
Brooklyn

LANDMARKS OF NEW YORK
ST. ANN'S CHURCH
THIS EPISCOPAL PARISH, ORGANIZED IN 1784, IS THE OLDEST OF ITS DENOMINATION IN BROOKLYN. FIVE OF ITS RECTORS HAVE BECOME BISHOPS. THE PRESENT VICTORIAN GOTHIC CHURCH, OPENED FOR SERVICES IN 1869, WAS DESIGNED BY JAMES RENWICK, JR.
PLAQUE ERECTED 1963 BY
THE NEW YORK COMMUNITY TRUST

AITKEN PL
ONE WAY
ONE WAY

145
Schenck-Wyckoff House
1325 Flushing Avenue (Johnson Avenue) [demolished]
Brooklyn

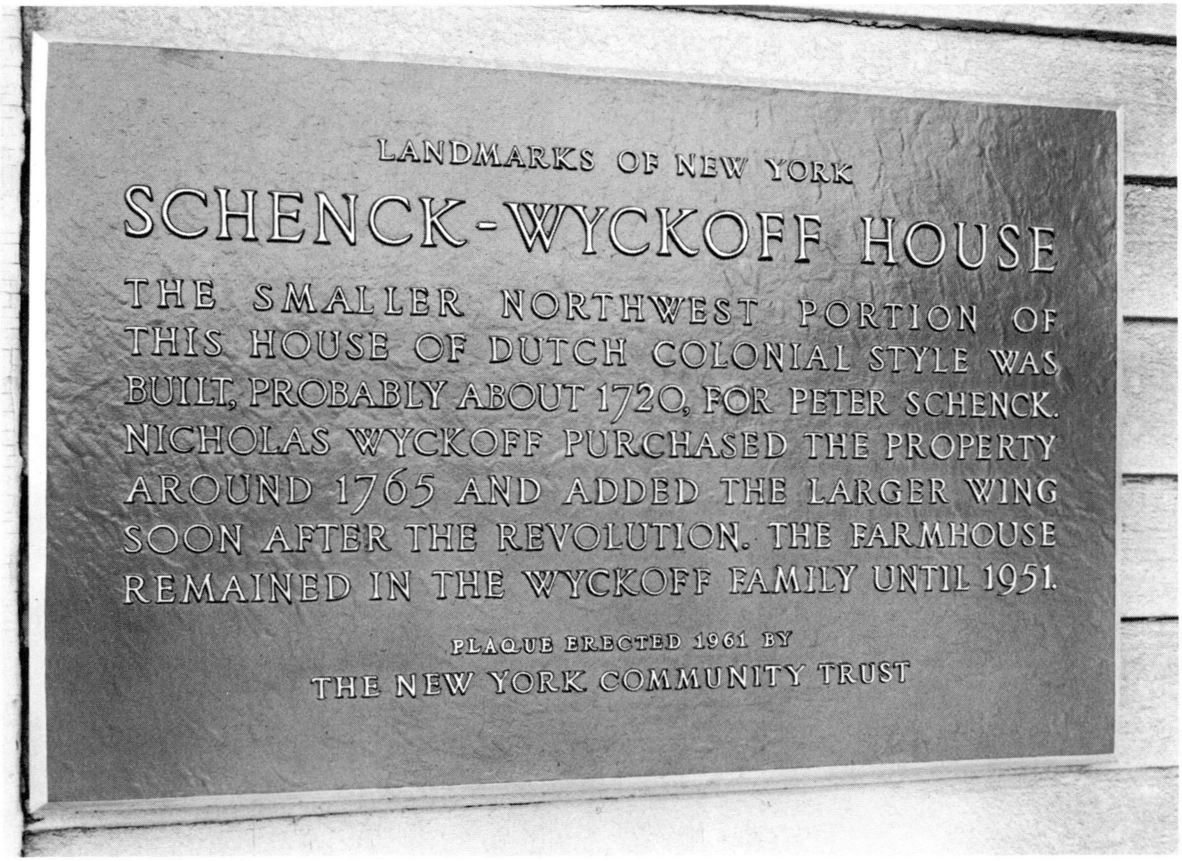
LANDMARKS OF NEW YORK
SCHENCK-WYCKOFF HOUSE
THE SMALLER NORTHWEST PORTION OF THIS HOUSE OF DUTCH COLONIAL STYLE WAS BUILT, PROBABLY ABOUT 1720, FOR PETER SCHENCK. NICHOLAS WYCKOFF PURCHASED THE PROPERTY AROUND 1765 AND ADDED THE LARGER WING SOON AFTER THE REVOLUTION. THE FARMHOUSE REMAINED IN THE WYCKOFF FAMILY UNTIL 1951.
PLAQUE ERECTED 1961 BY
THE NEW YORK COMMUNITY TRUST

146
United States Post Office (Brooklyn G.P.O.)
271 Washington Street (Tillary Street)
Brooklyn

LANDMARKS OF NEW YORK
UNITED STATES POST OFFICE
THE OLDER SECTION OF THIS ROMANESQUE REVIVAL BUILDING WAS BEGUN IN 1885 AND COMPLETED IN 1892. THE PLANS OF MIFFLIN E. BELL, THE ORIGINAL ARCHITECT, WERE MODIFIED BY WILLIAM E. FRERET, HIS SUCCESSOR AS SUPERVISING ARCHITECT OF THE TREASURY DEPARTMENT, WHILE THE BUILDING WAS UNDER CONSTRUCTION. THE ADDITION WAS BEGUN IN 1930 AND FINISHED THREE YEARS LATER.
PLAQUE ERECTED 1963 BY
THE NEW YORK COMMUNITY TRUST

147

Johannes Van Nuyse House

1041 East 22nd Street (Avenue J), Flatbush

Brooklyn

LANDMARKS OF NEW YORK
JOHANNES VAN NUYSE HOUSE
IN THIS DUTCH COLONIAL HOUSE, BUILT ABOUT 1800 BY JOHANNES VAN NUYSE, THE WOODWORK AND OVAL WINDOW IN THE HALL ARE FEDERAL IN STYLE. OTHER INTERIOR DETAIL IS LATE XIX CENTURY. AFTER 1916 THE HOUSE WAS MOVED HERE FROM ITS ORIGINAL SITE ON FLATLANDS PLAIN. THE ENTRANCE PORTICO WAS ADDED WHEN THE HOUSE WAS RESTORED IN 1952
PLAQUE ERECTED 1965 BY
THE NEW YORK COMMUNITY TRUST

148
Joost Van Nuyse House
1128-30 East 34th Street (Flatbush Avenue), Flatbush
Brooklyn

LANDMARKS OF NEW YORK
JOOST VAN NUYSE HOUSE
THE SMALLER SECTION OF THIS HOUSE WAS PROBABLY BUILT ABOUT 1744 BY JOOST VAN NUYSE, A DESCENDANT OF AUCKE JANSEN WHO IMMIGRATED TO NEW AMSTERDAM IN 1651. IN 1793 THE PROPERTY WAS SOLD TO WILHEMUS STOOTHOFF AND WAS SUBSEQUENTLY TENANTED BY ROBERT MAGAW, DITMAS COE AND OTHERS. THE HOUSE WAS MOVED TO ITS PRESENT LOCATION AROUND 1923.
PLAQUE ERECTED 1965 BY
THE NEW YORK COMMUNITY TRUST

149

Robert White House

57 Willow Street (Orange Street), Brooklyn Heights
Brooklyn

"HERITAGE OF NEW YORK"
ROBERT WHITE HOUSE
FIRST OCCUPIED BY THE MERCHANT ROBERT WHITE THIS HOUSE BUILT BEFORE 1825, IS A WELL-PRESERVED SMALL-SCALE EXAMPLE OF SIMPLIFIED FEDERAL DESIGN. NOTABLE ARE THE FLEMISH-BOND BRICKWORK, TOOLED STONE LINTELS ABOVE THE OPENINGS ON THE FRONT AND SIDE, THE KEY MOTIF IN THE FRIEZE, AND THE TREATMENT OF THE DORMERS. THE ORIGINAL SIZE OF THE FIRST STORY WINDOWS IS INDICATED BY THE BLIND WINDOWS ON THE SIDE. THE IRONWORK, ENTRANCE AND STOOP ARE LATE NINETEENTH CENTURY CHANGES.
PLAQUE ERECTED 1966 BY
THE NEW YORK COMMUNITY TRUST

ORANGE ST
WILLOW ST

150
Williamsburg Savings Bank
175 Broadway (Driggs Avenue), Williamsburg
Brooklyn

LANDMARKS OF NEW YORK
THE WILLIAMSBURGH SAVINGS BANK
DESIGNED BY GEORGE B. POST IN RENAISSANCE STYLE, THIS BUILDING WAS COMPLETED IN 1875 TWENTY-FOUR YEARS AFTER THE BANK RECEIVED ITS CHARTER. ALTHOUGH THREE EXTENSIONS HAVE BEEN ADDED, THE BASIC ARCHITECTURE HAS NOT BEEN ALTERED.
PLAQUE ERECTED 1960 BY
THE NEW YORK COMMUNITY TRUST

WILLIAMSBURGH SAVINGS BANK

151
Nos. 2-8 Willow Place
near Joralemon Street, Brooklyn Heights
Brooklyn

"HERITAGE OF NEW YORK"
2-8 WILLOW PLACE
THESE DUPLEXES WERE BUILT IN THE GOTHIC REVIVAL STYLE ABOUT 1847. NOTABLE FEATURES INCLUDE COUPLED PORCHES WITH THEIR CLUSTERED COLONNETTES AND DIAMOND-PANED SIDE LIGHTS AND TRANSOMS IN THE ENTRANCES. THE ORIGINAL WINDOW TREATMENT BETWEEN THE SECOND AND THIRD STORIES, WHERE RECESSED PANELS WITH THEIR CHEVRON PATTERNS LEND A VERTICAL EMPHASIS TO THE DESIGN, FORESHADOWS THE SPANDREL ARRANGEMENT LATER EMPLOYED ON HIGH BUILDINGS.
PLAQUE ERECTED 1966 BY
THE NEW YORK COMMUNITY TRUST

152
Nos. 155-157-159 Willow Street
near Pierrepont Street, Brooklyn Heights
Brooklyn

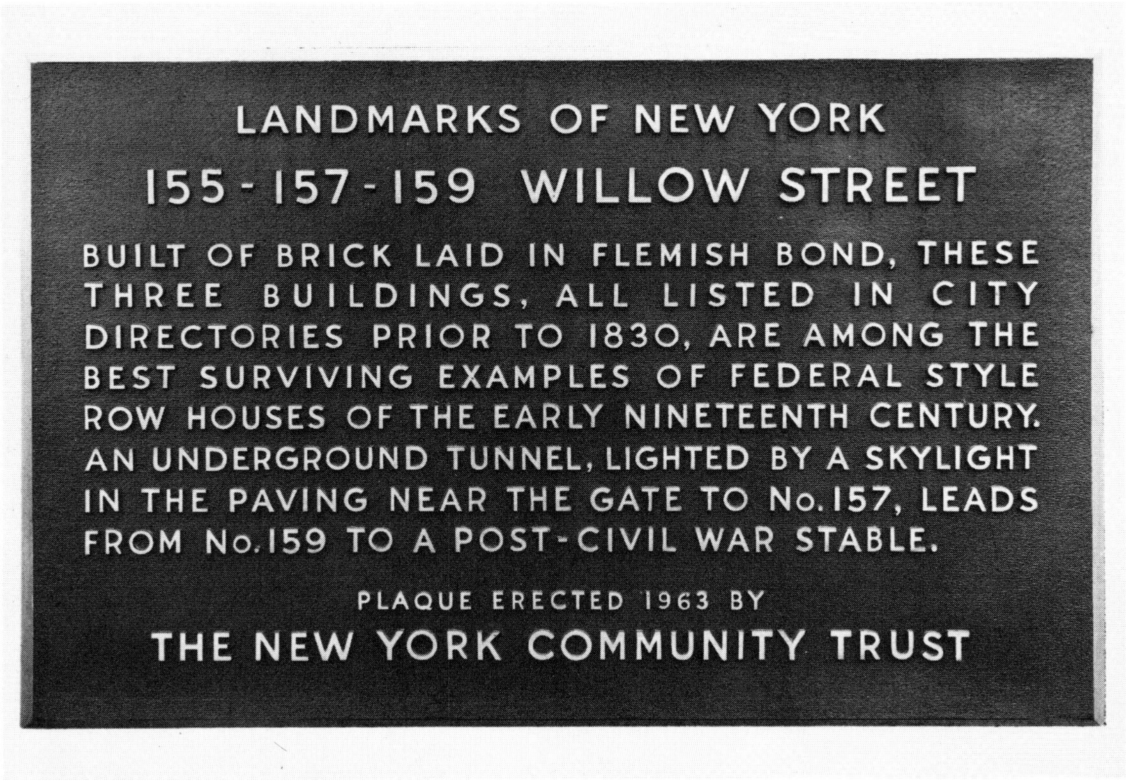
LANDMARKS OF NEW YORK
155-157-159 WILLOW STREET
BUILT OF BRICK LAID IN FLEMISH BOND, THESE THREE BUILDINGS, ALL LISTED IN CITY DIRECTORIES PRIOR TO 1830, ARE AMONG THE BEST SURVIVING EXAMPLES OF FEDERAL STYLE ROW HOUSES OF THE EARLY NINETEENTH CENTURY. AN UNDERGROUND TUNNEL, LIGHTED BY A SKYLIGHT IN THE PAVING NEAR THE GATE TO No. 157, LEADS FROM No. 159 TO A POST-CIVIL WAR STABLE.
PLAQUE ERECTED 1963 BY
THE NEW YORK COMMUNITY TRUST

153
The Willows
37 Willow Street (Cranberry Street), Brooklyn Heights
Brooklyn

"HERITAGE OF NEW YORK"
THE WILLOWS
A. F. NORRIS WAS THE ARCHITECT OF THIS EARLY EXAMPLE OF A BUILDING DESIGNED AS AN APARTMENT HOUSE AND CONSTRUCTED IN 1886. THE HIGH BAY WINDOW, WITH ITS CLASSICAL SWAYS AND SMALL BROKEN PEDIMENT, IS TYPICAL OF THE QUEEN ANNE STYLE POPULAR AT THE TIME.
PLAQUE ERECTED 1966 BY
THE NEW YORK COMMUNITY TRUST

The Bronx

THE BRONX

YONKERS
MT. VERNON
HART ISLAND
CITY ISLAND ROAD
CITY ISLAND
NORTH RIVER
RIVERDALE AVE.
BROADWAY
VAN CORTLANDT PARK
HENRY HUDSON PKWY
MOSHOLU PKWY
JEROME AVE.
E. 233 ST.
BRONX RIVER EXPWY.
WHITE PLAINS RD
BOSTON RD.
NEW ENGLAND THRUWAY
HUTCHINSON RIVER
HUTCHINSON RIVER PKWY.
PELHAM BAY PARK
SHORE RD
ORCHARD BEACH
LOCATION MAP 10a
GUN HILL RD.
WEBSTER AVE.
LACONIA AVE.
EASTCHESTER RD.
W. 230 ST.
MAJOR DEEGAN EXPWY.
KINGSBRIDGE RD.
ALLERTON AVE.
BRONX PARK
MANHATTAN
GRAND BLVD and CONCOURSE
W. FORDHAM RD.
E. FORDHAM RD.
BRONX & PELHAM PKWY
WILLIAMSBRIDGE RD.
EASTCHESTER BAY
CITY ISLAND (See inset above)
LOCATION MAP 10b
HARLEM RIVER
SOUTHERN BLVD.
LOCATION MAP 10c
WESTCHESTER AVE.
E. TREMONT AVE.
CROSS BRONX EXPWY.
CASTLE HILL AVE.
BRUCKNER BLVD.
THROGS NECK EXPWY.
SHERIDAN EXPWY.
E. 161 ST.
E. 163 ST.
SOUND VIEW AVE.
WESTCHESTER CREEK
BRONX RIVER
E. 149 ST.
MELROSE AVE.
HUNTS POINT AVE.
EAST RIVER
BRONX-WHITESTONE BRIDGE
LOCATION MAP 10d
THIRD AVE.
WILLIS AVE.
E. 138 ST.
BRUCKNER EXPWY.
QUEENS
RIKERS ISLAND

154
Christ Church (Episcopal)

Henry Hudson Parkway East at West 252nd Street, Riverdale
Bronx

LANDMARKS OF NEW YORK
CHRIST CHURCH
THIS EPISCOPAL CHURCH, DESIGNED BY RICHARD UPJOHN & COMPANY IN RURAL GOTHIC STYLE, WAS CONSECRATED IN 1866. THE CHANCEL WINDOWS WERE EXECUTED BY THE ENGLISH ARTIST, WILLIAM WAILES.
PLAQUE ERECTED 1960 BY
THE NEW YORK COMMUNITY TRUST

155
Fonthill Castle
Elizabeth Seton Library, College of Mt. St. Vincent-on Hudson
Bronx

LANDMARKS OF NEW YORK
FONTHILL CASTLE
BUILT FOR EDWIN FORREST THE ACTOR BY THOMAS L. SMITH IN 1849, THIS HOUSE WITH NORMAN AND GOTHIC ELEMENTS WAS PURCHASED IN 1856 BY THE SISTERS OF CHARITY OF ST. VINCENT DE PAUL AND IS NOW THE ELIZABETH SETON LIBRARY OF THE COLLEGE OF MOUNT ST. VINCENT. THE HIGHEST OF ITS SIX GRANITE TOWERS RISES TO 70 FEET. SOME STRUCTURAL DETAILS WERE PROBABLY INSPIRED BY FONTHILL ABBEY IN ENGLAND.
PLAQUE ERECTED 1965 BY
THE NEW YORK COMMUNITY TRUST

LIBRARY

156
Fordham University Church (R.C.)
Rose Hill Campus, near East Fordham Road and Webster Avenue
Bronx

"HERITAGE OF NEW YORK"
CHURCH OF OUR LADY, MEDIATRIX OF ALL GRACES
FORDHAM UNIVERSITY CHURCH
THE NAVE AND THE LOWER PORTION OF THE TOWER OVER THE NARTHEX OF THIS EDIFICE COMPRISE THE ORIGINAL GOTHIC STYLE CHURCH BUILT IN 1845. THE TRANSEPTS, CHANCEL AND CROSSING, WITH THE ELABORATE LANTERN SURMOUNTING ITS OCTAGONAL ROOF, WERE ADDED IN 1929. THE HIGH ALTAR WAS UNTIL 1942, THE MAIN ALTAR OF ST. PATRICK'S CATHEDRAL, NEW YORK, WHEN IT WAS GIVEN TO THE UNIVERSITY BY CARDINAL SPELLMAN.
PLAQUE ERECTED 1966 BY
THE NEW YORK COMMUNITY TRUST

157

President John F. Kennedy Residence

5040 Independence Avenue (West 252nd Street), Riverdale

Bronx

"NEW YORK OF THE PRESIDENTS"
JOHN FITZGERALD KENNEDY
MAY 29, 1917 - NOVEMBER 22, 1963
THIRTY-FIFTH PRESIDENT OF THE UNITED STATES, 1961-63
REPRESENTATIVE FROM MASSACHUSETTS, 1947-53
SENATOR FROM MASSACHUSETTS, 1953-60
LIVED HERE BETWEEN 1926 AND 1928, ATTENDING
THE NEARBY RIVERDALE COUNTRY SCHOOL
PLAQUE ERECTED 1965 BY
THE NEW YORK COMMUNITY TRUST

158
Poe Cottage
Grand Concourse and Kingsbridge Road, Fordham
Bronx

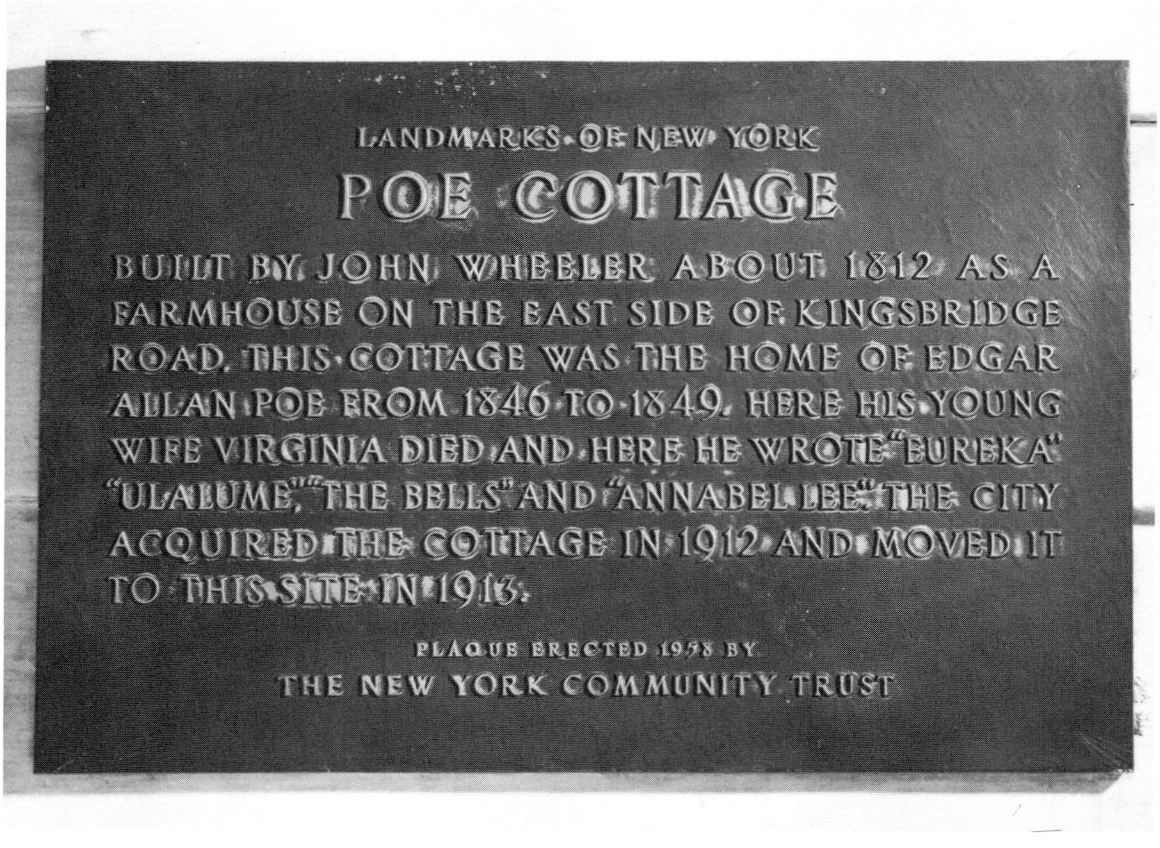
LANDMARKS OF NEW YORK
POE COTTAGE
BUILT BY JOHN WHEELER ABOUT 1812 AS A FARMHOUSE ON THE EAST SIDE OF KINGSBRIDGE ROAD, THIS COTTAGE WAS THE HOME OF EDGAR ALLAN POE FROM 1846 TO 1849. HERE HIS YOUNG WIFE VIRGINIA DIED AND HERE HE WROTE "EUREKA" "ULALUME," "THE BELLS" AND "ANNABEL LEE." THE CITY ACQUIRED THE COTTAGE IN 1912 AND MOVED IT TO THIS SITE IN 1913.
PLAQUE ERECTED 1958 BY
THE NEW YORK COMMUNITY TRUST

POE COTTAGE
CLOSED

159
Riverdale Presbyterian Church
4765 Henry Hudson Parkway West (West 247th Street)
Bronx

LANDMARKS OF NEW YORK
RIVERDALE PRESBYTERIAN CHURCH
DESIGNED IN AN ENGLISH GOTHIC STYLE
BY JAMES RENWICK, ARCHITECT OF
ST. PATRICK'S CATHEDRAL, THIS CHURCH
WAS BUILT IN 1863, FUNDS HAVING BEEN
CONTRIBUTED BY RESIDENTS OF RIVERDALE
INCLUDING WILLIAM E. DODGE, JR.,
JOSEPH DELAFIELD, ROBERT COLGATE
AND JOHN MOTT. THE CHURCH STRUCTURE
WAS ENLARGED AND REMODELED IN 1936
FROM A DESIGN BY DWIGHT JAMES BAUM.
PLAQUE ERECTED 1963 BY
THE NEW YORK COMMUNITY TRUST

ONE WAY

160
St. Ann's Church of Morrisania (Episcopal)
295 St. Ann's Avenue (East 140th Street)
Bronx

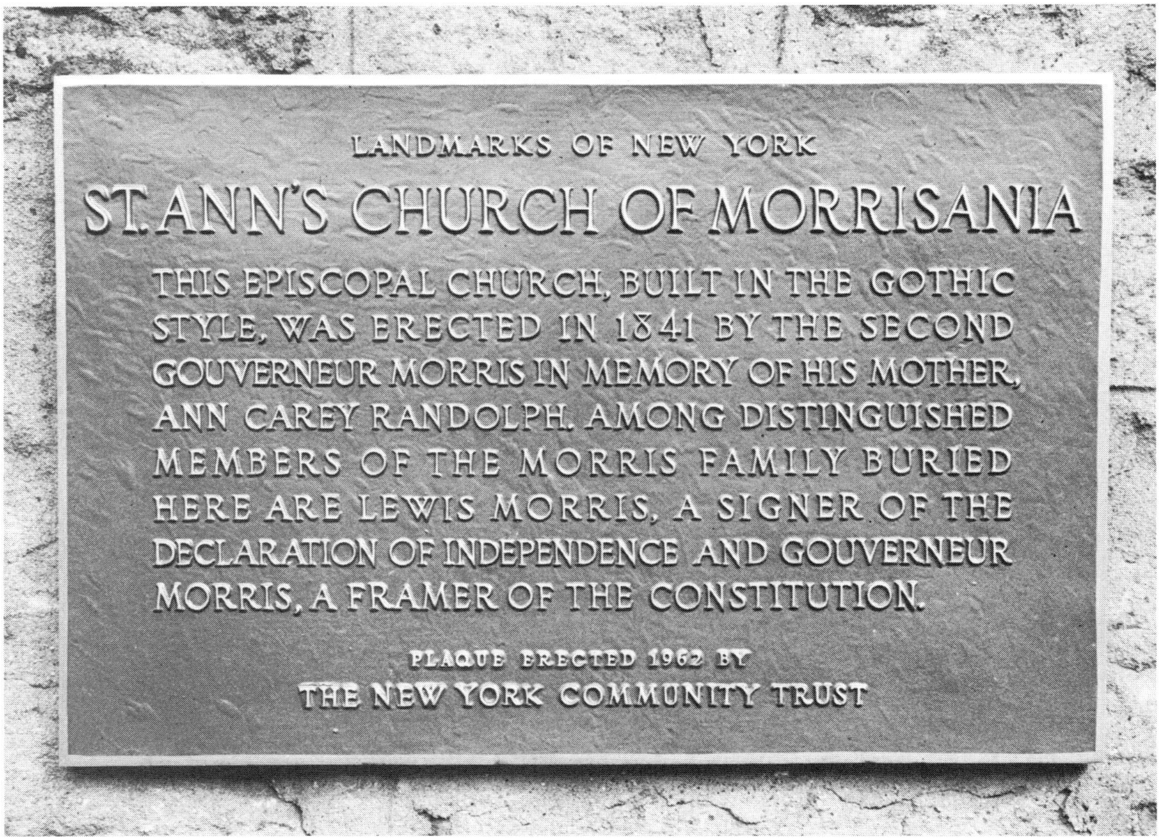
LANDMARKS OF NEW YORK
ST. ANN'S CHURCH OF MORRISANIA
THIS EPISCOPAL CHURCH, BUILT IN THE GOTHIC STYLE, WAS ERECTED IN 1841 BY THE SECOND GOUVERNEUR MORRIS IN MEMORY OF HIS MOTHER, ANN CAREY RANDOLPH. AMONG DISTINGUISHED MEMBERS OF THE MORRIS FAMILY BURIED HERE ARE LEWIS MORRIS, A SIGNER OF THE DECLARATION OF INDEPENDENCE AND GOUVERNEUR MORRIS, A FRAMER OF THE CONSTITUTION.
PLAQUE ERECTED 1962 BY
THE NEW YORK COMMUNITY TRUST

161
St. James Church (P.E.)
Jerome Avenue and 190th Street, Fordham
Bronx

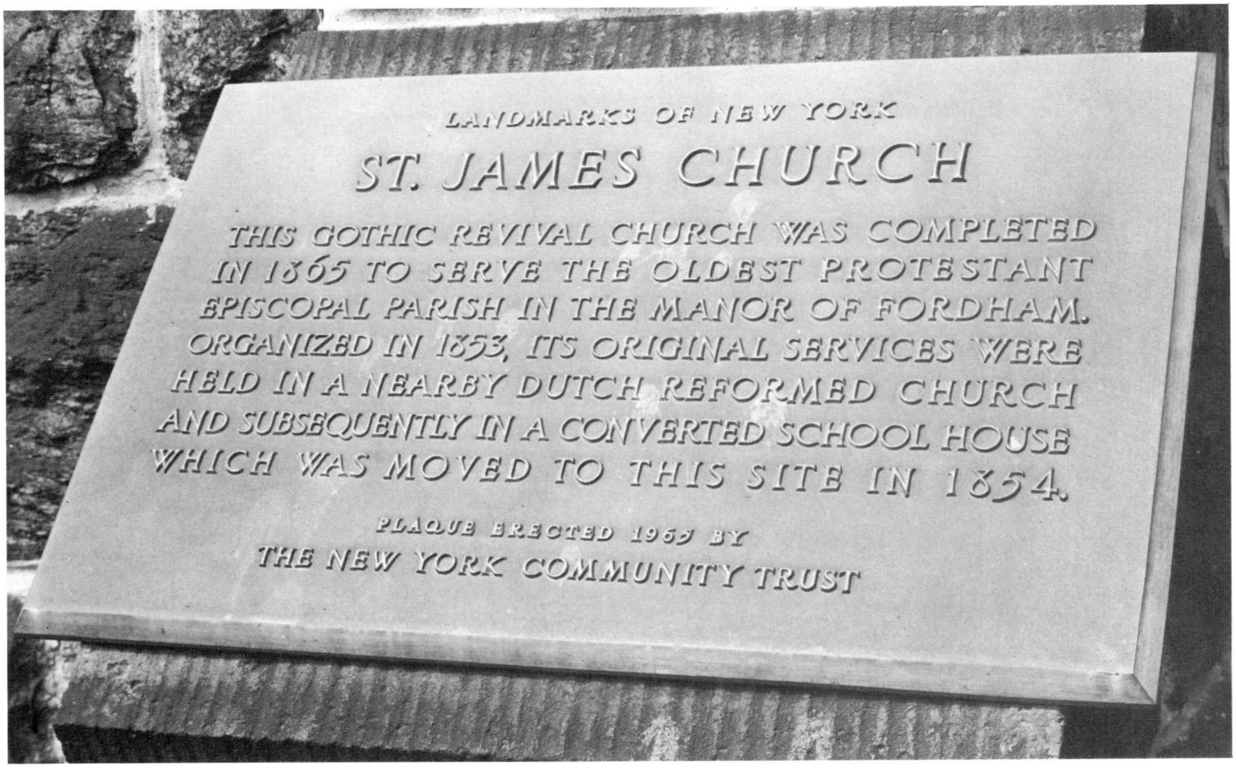
LANDMARKS OF NEW YORK
ST. JAMES CHURCH
THIS GOTHIC REVIVAL CHURCH WAS COMPLETED IN 1865 TO SERVE THE OLDEST PROTESTANT EPISCOPAL PARISH IN THE MANOR OF FORDHAM. ORGANIZED IN 1853, ITS ORIGINAL SERVICES WERE HELD IN A NEARBY DUTCH REFORMED CHURCH AND SUBSEQUENTLY IN A CONVERTED SCHOOL HOUSE WHICH WAS MOVED TO THIS SITE IN 1854.
PLAQUE ERECTED 1965 BY
THE NEW YORK COMMUNITY TRUST

162
St. Peter's Church, Westchester (P.E.)
2500 Westchester Avenue (St. Peter's Avenue), Westchester Square
Bronx

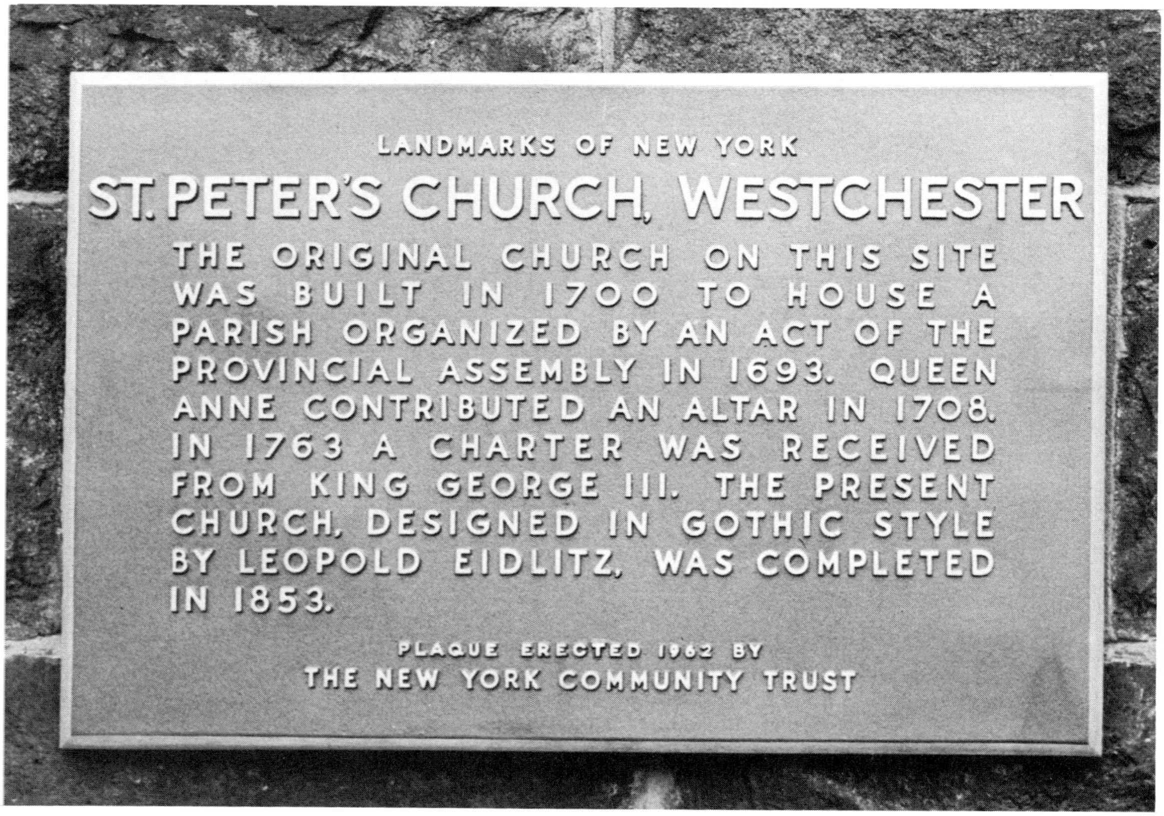
LANDMARKS OF NEW YORK
ST. PETER'S CHURCH, WESTCHESTER
THE ORIGINAL CHURCH ON THIS SITE WAS BUILT IN 1700 TO HOUSE A PARISH ORGANIZED BY AN ACT OF THE PROVINCIAL ASSEMBLY IN 1693. QUEEN ANNE CONTRIBUTED AN ALTAR IN 1708. IN 1763 A CHARTER WAS RECEIVED FROM KING GEORGE III. THE PRESENT CHURCH, DESIGNED IN GOTHIC STYLE BY LEOPOLD EIDLITZ, WAS COMPLETED IN 1853.
PLAQUE ERECTED 1962 BY
THE NEW YORK COMMUNITY TRUST

163

Wave Hill

645 West 252nd Street (Independence Avenue), Riverdale
Bronx

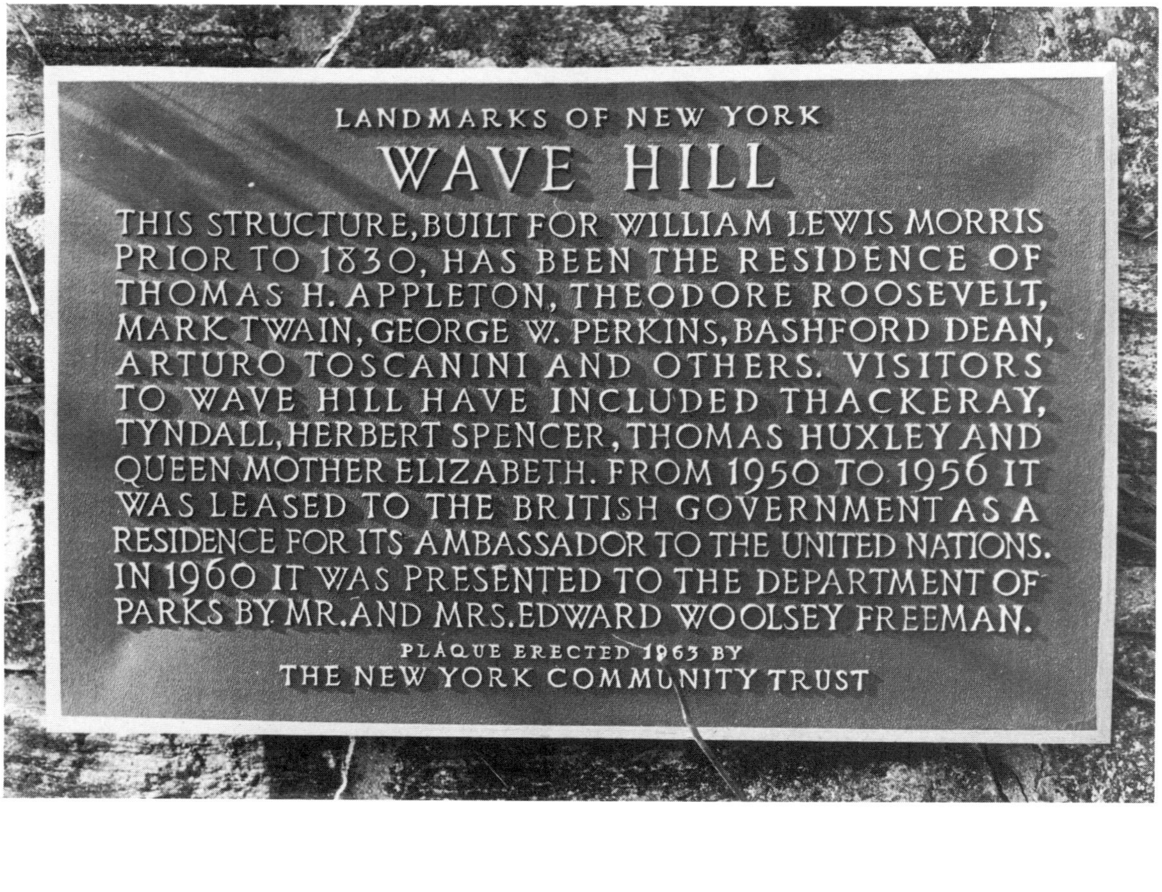
LANDMARKS OF NEW YORK
WAVE HILL
THIS STRUCTURE, BUILT FOR WILLIAM LEWIS MORRIS PRIOR TO 1830, HAS BEEN THE RESIDENCE OF THOMAS H. APPLETON, THEODORE ROOSEVELT, MARK TWAIN, GEORGE W. PERKINS, BASHFORD DEAN, ARTURO TOSCANINI AND OTHERS. VISITORS TO WAVE HILL HAVE INCLUDED THACKERAY, TYNDALL, HERBERT SPENCER, THOMAS HUXLEY AND QUEEN MOTHER ELIZABETH. FROM 1950 TO 1956 IT WAS LEASED TO THE BRITISH GOVERNMENT AS A RESIDENCE FOR ITS AMBASSADOR TO THE UNITED NATIONS. IN 1960 IT WAS PRESENTED TO THE DEPARTMENT OF PARKS BY MR. AND MRS. EDWARD WOOLSEY FREEMAN.
PLAQUE ERECTED 1963 BY
THE NEW YORK COMMUNITY TRUST

STATEN ISLAND (SOUTH HALF)

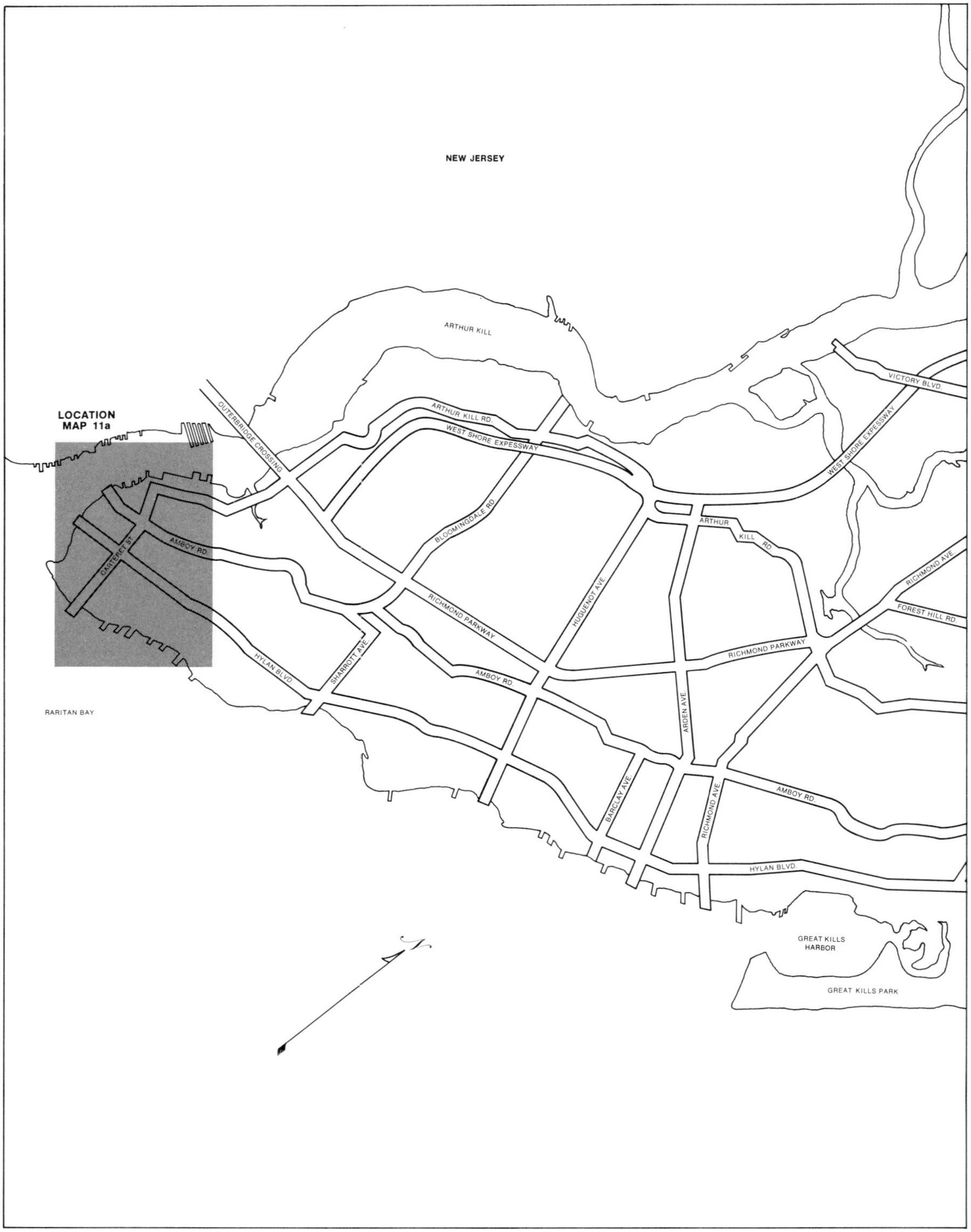
NEW JERSEY
ARTHUR KILL
LOCATION
MAP 11a
OUTERBRIDGE CROSSING
ARTHUR KILL RD.
WEST SHORE EXPESSWAY
VICTORY BLVD.
WEST SHORE EXPESSWAY
CARTERET ST.
AMBOY RD.
BLOOMINGDALE RD.
ARTHUR
KILL
RD.
RICHMOND AVE.
FOREST HILL RD.
RICHMOND PARKWAY
HUGUENOT AVE.
RICHMOND PARKWAY
HYLAN BLVD.
SHARROTT AVE.
AMBOY RD.
RARITAN BAY
ARDEN AVE.
AMBOY RD.
BARCLAY AVE.
RICHMOND AVE.
HYLAN BLVD.
GREAT KILLS
HARBOR
GREAT KILLS PARK

STATEN ISLAND (NORTH HALF)

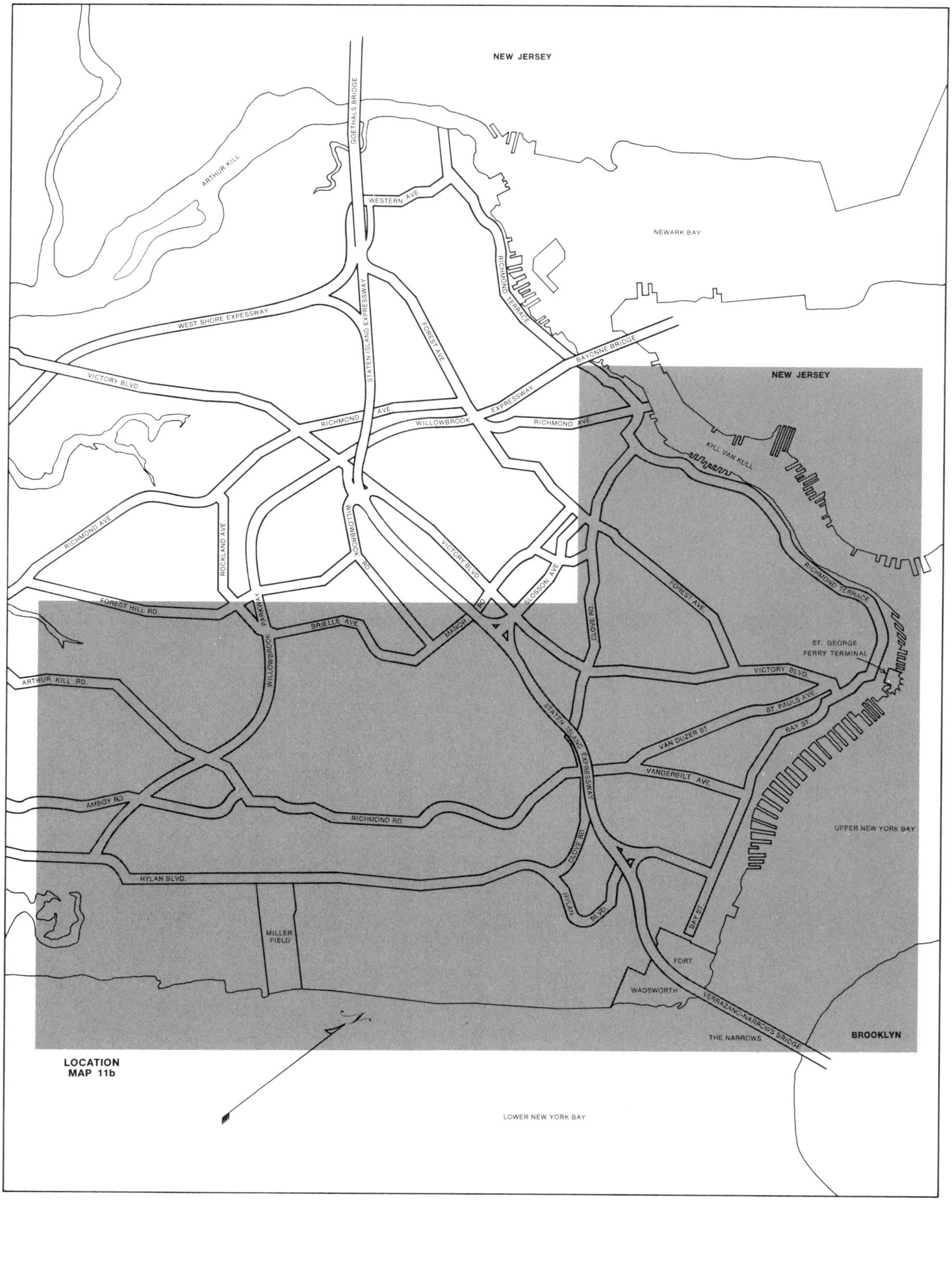

NEW JERSEY
GOETHALS BRIDGE
ARTHUR KILL
WESTERN AVE
NEWARK BAY
RICHMOND TERRACE
WEST SHORE EXPESSWAY
STATEN ISLAND EXPRESSWAY
FOREST AVE
BAYONNE BRIDGE
VICTORY BLVD
RICHMOND AVE
EXPRESSWAY
WILLOWBROOK
RICHMOND AVE
NEW JERSEY
KILL VAN KULL
RICHMOND AVE
ROCKLAND AVE
WILLOWBROOK RD
VICTORY BLVD
CLOVE RD
FOREST AVE
RICHMOND TERRACE
SLOSSON AVE
FOREST HILL RD
RD
WILLOWBROOK PARKWAY
BRIELLE AVE
MANOR
ST. GEORGE
FERRY TERMINAL
VICTORY BLVD
ARTHUR KILL RD
STATEN ISLAND EXPRESSWAY
ST PAULS AVE
BAY ST
VAN DUZER ST
VANDERBILT AVE
AMBOY RD
RICHMOND RD
UPPER NEW YORK BAY
CLOVE RD
HYLAN BLVD
HYLAN BLVD
BAY ST
MILLER FIELD
FORT
WADSWORTH
VERRAZANO-NARROWS BRIDGE
THE NARROWS
BROOKLYN
LOCATION
MAP 11b
LOWER NEW YORK BAY

164
Alice Austen House
2 Hylan Boulevard (Edgewater Street), Rosebank
Staten Island

"HERITAGE OF NEW YORK"
ALICE AUSTEN HOUSE
PORTIONS OF THIS STRUCTURE REPUTEDLY DATE FROM ABOUT 1700, BUT ADDITIONS IN GOTHIC REVIVAL STYLE WERE MADE AFTER ITS PURCHASE IN 1844 BY JOHN H. AUSTEN. HIS WIFE CALLED THE HOUSE "CLEAR COMFORT." HIS GRANDDAUGHTER, ELIZABETH ALICE AUSTEN (1866-1952), LIVED HERE FROM 1867 TO 1945 AND BECAME AN ACCOMPLISHED AMATEUR PHOTOGRAPHER. ACTIVE IN SOCIETY IN EARLY LIFE, HER LATER YEARS WERE CLOUDED BY CRIPPLING ARTHRITIS. THE STATEN ISLAND HISTORICAL SOCIETY POSSESSES A PRIZED COLLECTION OF HER NEGATIVES.
PLAQUE ERECTED 1968 BY
THE NEW YORK COMMUNITY TRUST

165
Biddle House
70 Satterlee Street (Shore Road), Tottenville
Staten Island

"HERITAGE OF NEW YORK"
BIDDLE HOUSE
DESIGNED IN THE GREEK REVIVAL STYLE, THIS HOUSE WAS BUILT ABOUT 1850 BY HENRY H. BIDDLE, A PROMINENT LANDOWNER. A NEARBY GROVE, FAVORED AS A SITE FOR TEMPERANCE AND REVIVAL MEETINGS, BORE HIS FAMILY NAME. A LARGE, SQUARE, GLASS-ENCLOSED CUPOLA ORIGINALLY SURMOUNTED THE ROOF. GEORGE T. BREWSTER, THE SCULPTOR, LIVED IN THE HOUSE AND USED A NEARBY BARN AS HIS STUDIO BETWEEN 1896 AND 1933.
PLAQUE ERECTED 1966 BY
THE NEW YORK COMMUNITY TRUST

166

Billopp House (Conference House)

Foot of Hylan Boulevard, Tottenville

Staten Island

LANDMARKS OF NEW YORK
BILLOPP HOUSE
BUILT BY AND FOR CHRISTOPHER BILLOPP ABOUT 1680, THIS HOUSE WAS LONG A CENTER OF COLONIAL HOSPITALITY. IT IS KNOWN ALSO AS "CONFERENCE HOUSE" BECAUSE BENJAMIN FRANKLIN, JOHN ADAMS AND EDWARD RUTLEDGE MET HERE WITH LORD HOWE AT HIS REQUEST ON SEPTEMBER 11, 1776, IN AN UNSUCCESSFUL EFFORT TO HALT THE AMERICAN REVOLUTION.
PLAQUE ERECTED 1958 BY
THE NEW YORK COMMUNITY TRUST

167

Cunard Hall

Wagner College, Grymes Hill

Staten Island

LANDMARKS OF NEW YORK
CUNARD HALL
SIR EDWARD CUNARD, SON OF THE FOUNDER OF THE STEAMSHIP LINE, BUILT THIS SPACIOUS ITALIAN VILLA STYLE MANSION SHORTLY AFTER 1850, SO SITUATED AS TO COMMAND A VIEW OF THE WATERS AROUND THE CITY. HE CALLED THE PROPERTY BELLEVUE. IT BECAME A PART OF THE CAMPUS OF WAGNER COLLEGE IN 1918.
PLAQUE ERECTED 1965 BY
THE NEW YORK COMMUNITY TRUST

168
Original Moravian Church
Moravian Cemetery, near Richmond Road and Otis Avenue, New Dorp
Staten Island

LANDMARKS OF NEW YORK
ORIGINAL MORAVIAN CHURCH
BUILT AS THE FIRST MORAVIAN CHURCH OF
STATEN ISLAND IN 1763, THIS STRUCTURE OF
DUTCH COLONIAL STYLE SERVED AS COMBINED
CHURCH AND PARSONAGE UNTIL 1845 WHEN
THE NEW CHURCH WAS CONSTRUCTED. IT HAS
SINCE BEEN USED AS A CHURCH SCHOOL AND
A CEMETERY OFFICE.
THE NEW YORK COMMUNITY TRUST

169

Reformed Protestant Dutch Church

54 Richmond Avenue (Richmond Terrace), Port Richmond
Staten Island

LANDMARKS OF NEW YORK
REFORMED PROTESTANT DUTCH CHURCH
BUILT IN 1845 IN GREEK REVIVAL STYLE, THIS IS THE THIRD CHURCH ON THE SITE. THE FIRST, A HEXAGONAL WOODEN BUILDING ERECTED IN 1714, WAS DESTROYED BY THE BRITISH DURING THE REVOLUTION. THE ORIGINAL LICENSE TO THE DUTCH CONGREGATION SIGNED BY GOVERNOR HUNTER IN 1714 IS PRESERVED.
PLAQUE ERECTED 1959 BY
THE NEW YORK COMMUNITY TRUST

170
St. John's Church (Episcopal)
1331 Bay Street (New Lane), Rosebank
Staten Island

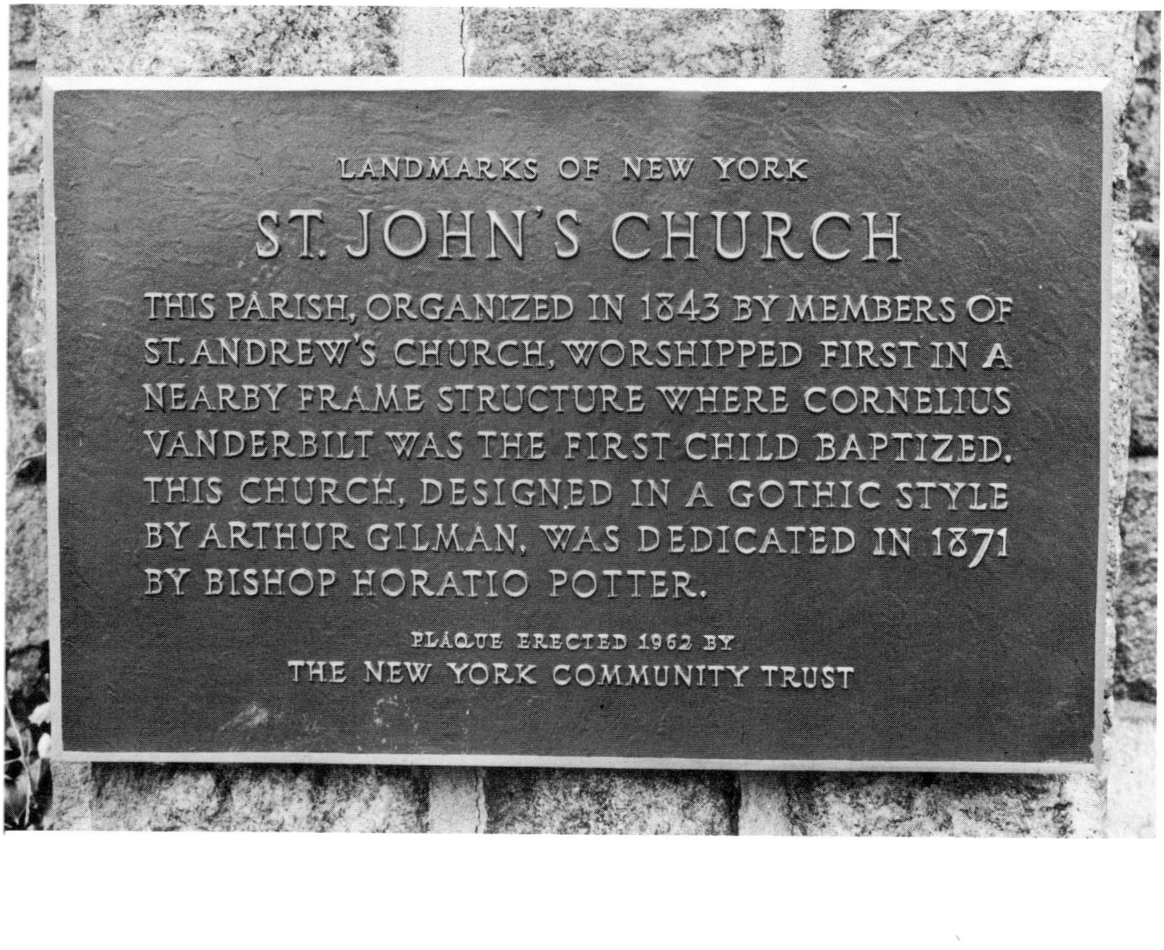
LANDMARKS OF NEW YORK
ST. JOHN'S CHURCH
THIS PARISH, ORGANIZED IN 1843 BY MEMBERS OF ST. ANDREW'S CHURCH, WORSHIPPED FIRST IN A NEARBY FRAME STRUCTURE WHERE CORNELIUS VANDERBILT WAS THE FIRST CHILD BAPTIZED. THIS CHURCH, DESIGNED IN A GOTHIC STYLE BY ARTHUR GILMAN, WAS DEDICATED IN 1871 BY BISHOP HORATIO POTTER.
PLAQUE ERECTED 1962 BY
THE NEW YORK COMMUNITY TRUST

171

St. Mary's Episcopal Church

Castleton and Davis Avenues, West New Brighton
Staten Island

"HERITAGE OF NEW YORK"
ST. MARY'S EPISCOPAL CHURCH
DESIGNED BY WILLS AND DUDLEY IN GOTHIC REVIVAL FORM, THIS STONE EDIFICE WAS CONSECRATED IN 1853, DESTROYED BY FIRE IN 1947, THEN RESTORED TO ITS ORIGINAL APPEARANCE.
PLAQUE ERECTED 1966 BY
THE NEW YORK COMMUNITY TRUST

172
St. Paul's Memorial Church (P.E.)
225 St. Paul's Avenue (Clinton Street), Stapleton
Staten Island

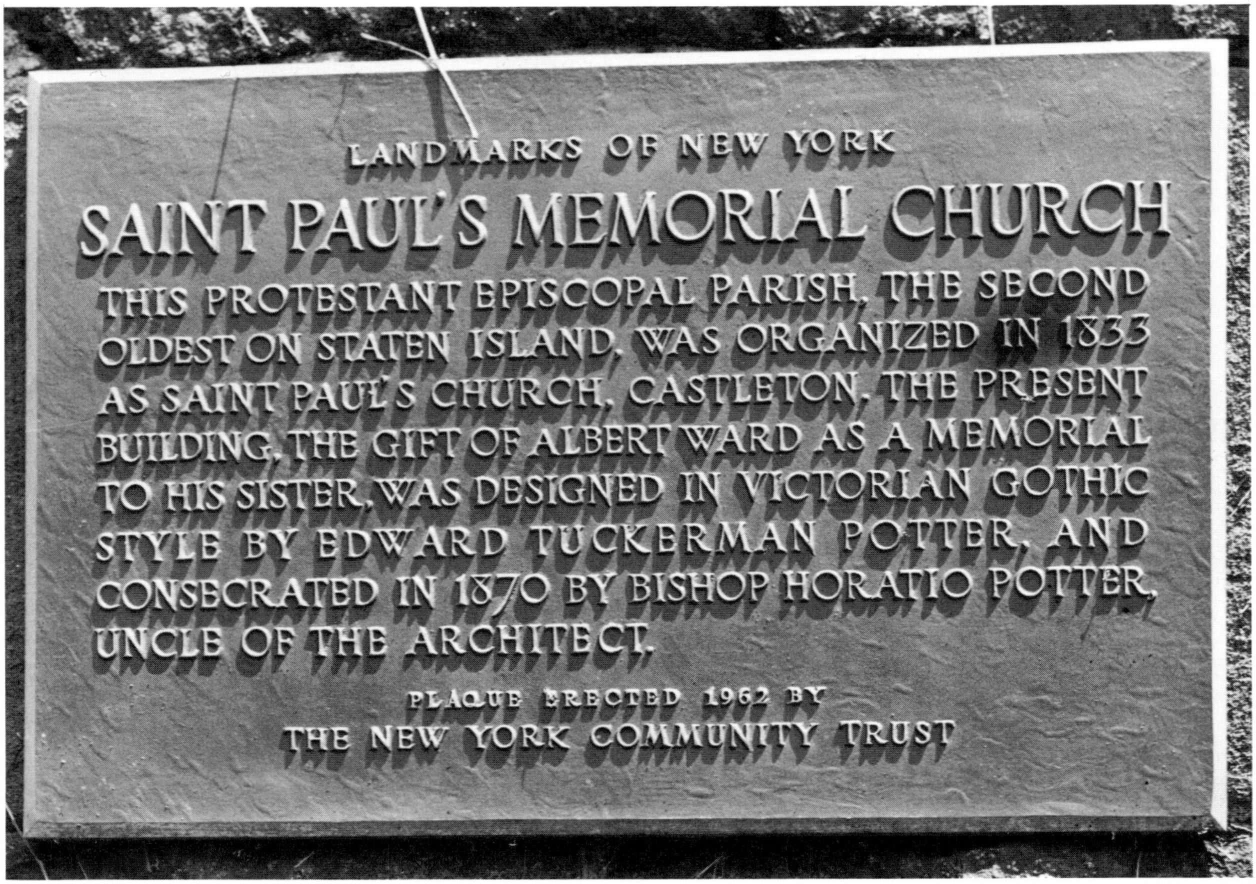
LANDMARKS OF NEW YORK
SAINT PAUL'S MEMORIAL CHURCH
THIS PROTESTANT EPISCOPAL PARISH, THE SECOND
OLDEST ON STATEN ISLAND, WAS ORGANIZED IN 1833
AS SAINT PAUL'S CHURCH, CASTLETON. THE PRESENT
BUILDING, THE GIFT OF ALBERT WARD AS A MEMORIAL
TO HIS SISTER, WAS DESIGNED IN VICTORIAN GOTHIC
STYLE BY EDWARD TUCKERMAN POTTER, AND
CONSECRATED IN 1870 BY BISHOP HORATIO POTTER,
UNCLE OF THE ARCHITECT.
PLAQUE ERECTED 1962 BY
THE NEW YORK COMMUNITY TRUST

173
Voorlezer's House
63 Arthur Kill Road (Richmond Road), Richmondtown
Staten Island

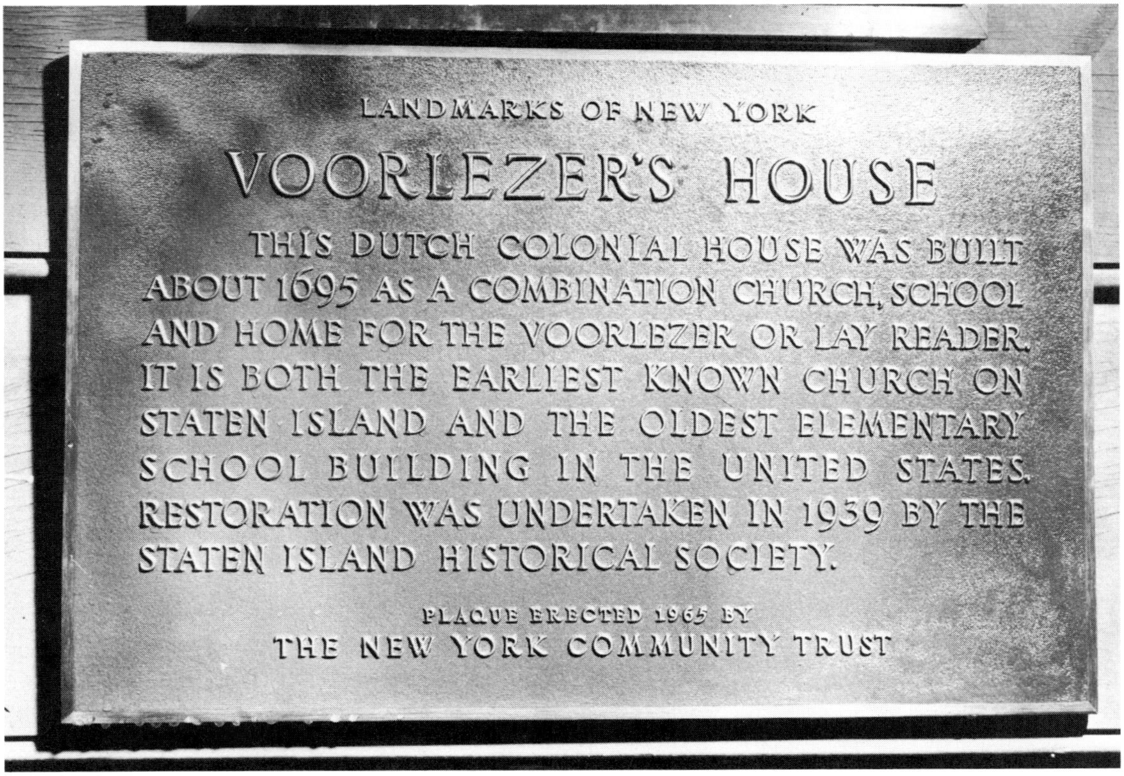
LANDMARKS OF NEW YORK
VOORLEZER'S HOUSE
THIS DUTCH COLONIAL HOUSE WAS BUILT ABOUT 1695 AS A COMBINATION CHURCH, SCHOOL AND HOME FOR THE VOORLEZER OR LAY READER. IT IS BOTH THE EARLIEST KNOWN CHURCH ON STATEN ISLAND AND THE OLDEST ELEMENTARY SCHOOL BUILDING IN THE UNITED STATES. RESTORATION WAS UNDERTAKEN IN 1939 BY THE STATEN ISLAND HISTORICAL SOCIETY.
PLAQUE ERECTED 1965 BY
THE NEW YORK COMMUNITY TRUST

QUEENS

THE BRONX
EAST RIVER
RIKERS ISLAND
MANHATTAN
NASSAU COUNTY
LITTLE NECK BAY
FLUSHING BAY
LA GUARDIA AIRPORT
LOCATION MAP 12a
LOCATION MAP 12b
LOCATION MAP 12c
BROOKLYN
JOHN F. KENNEDY INTERNATIONAL AIRPORT
JAMAICA BAY
ROCKAWAY INLET
ATLANTIC OCEAN
ROCKAWAY BEACH
TRIBOROUGH BRIDGE
BRONX-WHITESTONE BRIDGE
THROGS NECK BRIDGE
QUEENSBORO BRIDGE
QUEENS MIDTOWN TUNNEL
WELFARE ISLAND
DITMARS BLVD.
ASTORIA BLVD.
GRAND CENTRAL PKWY.
NORTHERN BLVD.
ROOSEVELT AVE.
QUEENS BLVD.
LONG ISLAND EXPWY.
BKLYN QUEENS EXPWY.
GRAND AVE.
METROPOLITAN AVE.
MYRTLE AVE.
JAMAICA AVE.
ATLANTIC AVE.
LIBERTY AVE.
ROCKAWAY BLVD.
SOUTHERN PKWY.
LINDEN BLVD.
HILLSIDE AVE.
UNION TPK.
BAYSIDE AVE.
CROSS ISLAND PKWY.
CLEARVIEW EXPWY.
FRANCIS LEWIS BLVD.
WHITESTONE PKWY.
VAN WYCK EXPWY.
MAIN ST.
164 ST.
188 ST.
UTOPIA PKWY.
108 ST.
94 ST.
21 ST.
STEINWAY ST.
BROADWAY
JUNCTION BLVD.
WOODHAVEN BLVD.
FRESH POND RD.
INTERBOROUGH PKWY.
LEFFERTS BLVD.
NEW YORK BLVD.
MERRICK BLVD.
HOLLIS AVE.
SPRINGFIELD BLVD.
LAURELTON PKWY.
FARMERS BLVD.
CROSS BAY BLVD.
CROSS BAY BRIDGE
CHANNEL BRIDGE
BEACH CHANNEL DR.
SEAGIRT BLVD.
MARINE PKWY. BR.
EAST RIVER

174
Bowne House
Bowne Street and 37th Avenue, Flushing
Queens

LANDMARKS OF NEW YORK
BOWNE HOUSE
THIS HOUSE, BELIEVED TO BE THE OLDEST IN THE CITY, WAS BUILT IN 1661 BY JOHN BOWNE, AN ENGLISHMAN WHO BECAME A QUAKER. FOR PERMITTING QUAKER MEETINGS IN THIS BUILDING HE WAS IMPRISONED IN 1662 AND SENT TO HOLLAND FOR TRIAL. HIS DEFENSE OF TOLERANCE WON A PARDON FOR HIM AND GREATER FREEDOM OF WORSHIP FOR NEW NETHERLAND. IN 1945 THE HOUSE WAS ACQUIRED BY THE BOWNE HOUSE HISTORICAL SOCIETY FOR PRESERVATION AS A SHRINE TO RELIGIOUS LIBERTY.
PLAQUE ERECTED 1963 BY
THE NEW YORK COMMUNITY TRUST

175
First Presbyterian Church in Jamaica
89-60 164th Street (Jamaica Avenue)
Queens

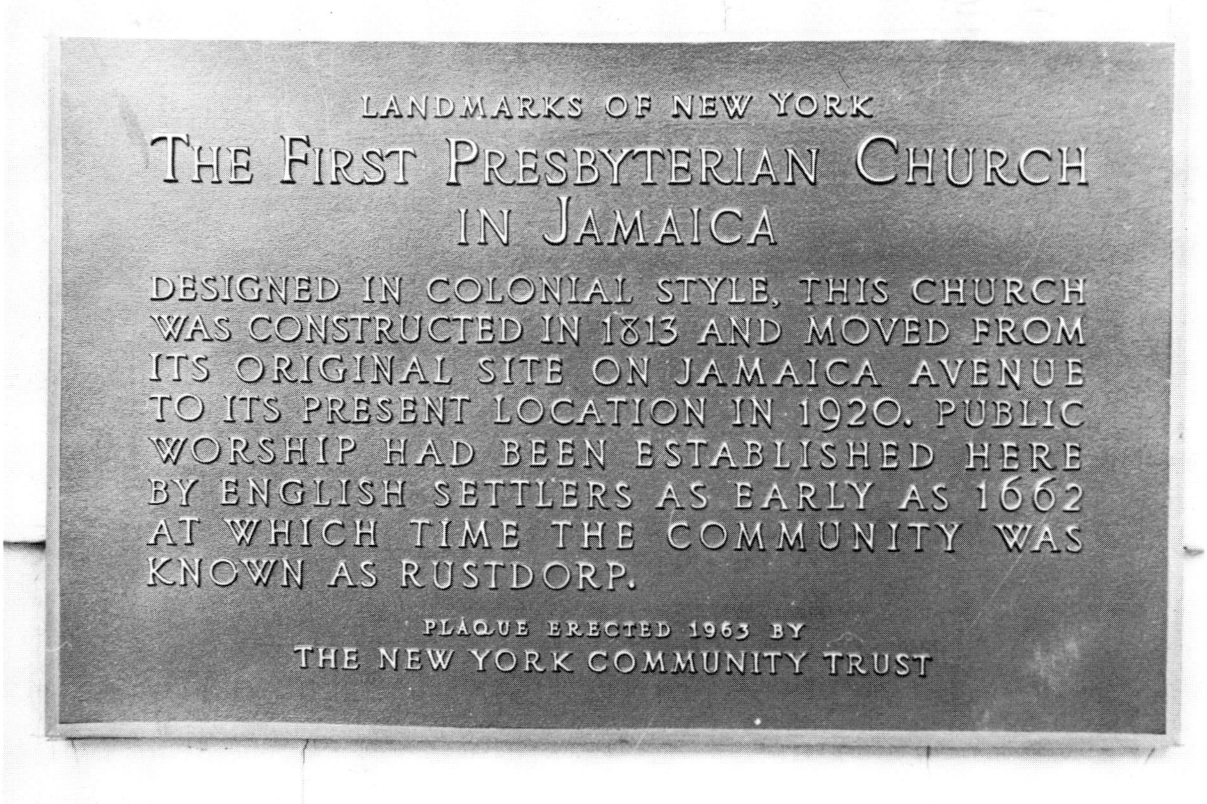
LANDMARKS OF NEW YORK
THE FIRST PRESBYTERIAN CHURCH
IN JAMAICA
DESIGNED IN COLONIAL STYLE, THIS CHURCH WAS CONSTRUCTED IN 1813 AND MOVED FROM ITS ORIGINAL SITE ON JAMAICA AVENUE TO ITS PRESENT LOCATION IN 1920. PUBLIC WORSHIP HAD BEEN ESTABLISHED HERE BY ENGLISH SETTLERS AS EARLY AS 1662 AT WHICH TIME THE COMMUNITY WAS KNOWN AS RUSTDORP.
PLAQUE ERECTED 1963 BY
THE NEW YORK COMMUNITY TRUST

176
Lent Homestead
7805 19th Road (78th Street), Steinway
Queens

LANDMARKS OF NEW YORK
LENT HOMESTEAD
THIS COLONIAL DUTCH FARMHOUSE, PROBABLY BUILT IN 1729 BY ABRAHAM LENT, GRANDSON OF ABRAHAM RIKER, IS ONE OF THE OLDEST IN NEW YORK CITY. IN 1797 IT BECAME THE PROPERTY OF THE RAPELYE FAMILY.
PLAQUE ERECTED 1960 BY
THE NEW YORK COMMUNITY TRUST

177

Old Quaker Meeting House

137-16 Northern Boulevard (Main Street), Flushing

Queens

LANDMARKS OF NEW YORK
OLD QUAKER MEETING HOUSE
ONE OF THE CITY'S FEW REMAINING HOUSES OF WORSHIP DATING FROM THE 17TH CENTURY, THIS BUILDING, ON LAND ACQUIRED IN 1676 AND 1692, WAS COMPLETED IN 1694 AND ENLARGED ABOUT 1716. EXCEPT WHEN OCCUPIED FOR A TIME BY BRITISH FORCES DURING THE REVOLUTIONARY WAR, THE STRUCTURE HAS BEEN CONTINUOUSLY USED AS A MEETING PLACE OF THE SOCIETY OF FRIENDS.
PLAQUE ERECTED 1959 BY
THE NEW YORK COMMUNITY TRUST

178

St. George's Church (Episcopal)

135-32 38th Avenue (Main Street), Flushing
Queens

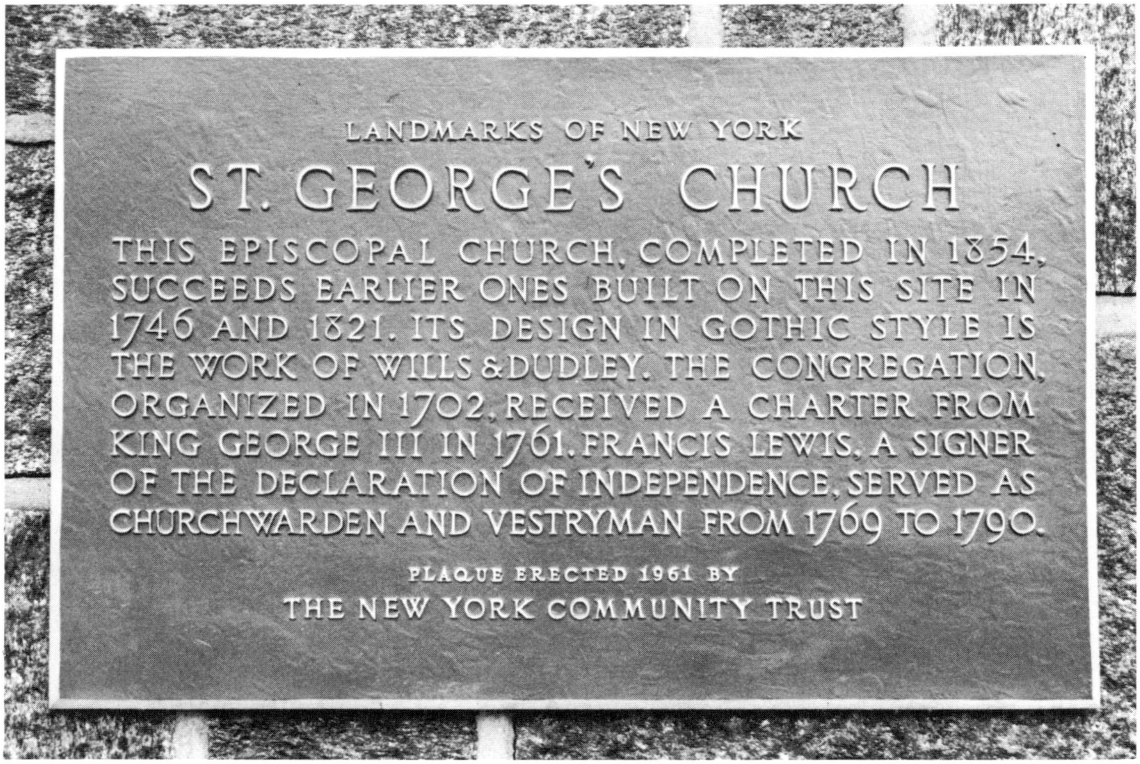
LANDMARKS OF NEW YORK
ST. GEORGE'S CHURCH
THIS EPISCOPAL CHURCH, COMPLETED IN 1854, SUCCEEDS EARLIER ONES BUILT ON THIS SITE IN 1746 AND 1821. ITS DESIGN IN GOTHIC STYLE IS THE WORK OF WILLS & DUDLEY. THE CONGREGATION, ORGANIZED IN 1702, RECEIVED A CHARTER FROM KING GEORGE III IN 1761. FRANCIS LEWIS, A SIGNER OF THE DECLARATION OF INDEPENDENCE, SERVED AS CHURCHWARDEN AND VESTRYMAN FROM 1769 TO 1790.
PLAQUE ERECTED 1961 BY
THE NEW YORK COMMUNITY TRUST

Appendix A / The Heritage Plaques

Code: Manhattan – M, Brooklyn – Bk, Bronx – Bx,
Queens – Q, Staten Island – SI
*Not illustrated; see Appendix B.
†Not illustrated; see Appendix C.

Location and year affixed

American Academy of Dramatic Arts, M (1), 1964
American Fine Arts Society, M (2), 1958
American Museum of Natural History, M (3), 1958
†American-Standard Building, M, 1962
†Apthorp Apartments, M, 1961
†The Arsenal, M, 1958
Assay Office Building Façade, M (4), 1965
Association of the Bar of the City of New York, M (5), 1960
Astor Library, M (6), 1967
Audubon House, M (7), 1964
Alice Austen House, SI (164), 1968
*Secretary of State Robert Bacon Residence, M, 1965
†Mott Bedell House, Bk, 1966
No. 70 Bedford Street, M (8), 1966
Bethesda Fountain and Terrace, M (9), 1965
Biddle House, SI (165), 1966
Billopp House, SI (166), 1958
Bowery Savings Bank, M (10), 1957
Bowling Green Fence, M (11), 1964
Bowne House, Q (174), 1963
No. 901 Broadway, M (12), 1963
Brooklyn Borough Hall, Bk (120), 1959
Brooklyn Botanic Garden, Administration Building, Bk (121), 1967
Brooklyn Children's Museum, Bk (122), 1966
Brooklyn Ethical Culture School, Bk (123), 1958
Brooklyn Municipal Building, Bk (124), 1967
Brooklyn Museum, Bk (125), 1966

William Cullen Bryant Residence, M (13), 1967
†Bush Terminal Building, M, 1963
Carnegie Hall, M (14), 1966
Carnegie House, M (15), 1957
Cartier Building, M (16), 1962
Cathedral Church of St. John the Divine, M (17), 1958
*Willa Cather Residence, M, 1967
Central Savings Bank, M (18), 1961
Central Synagogue, M (19), 1957
Chelsea Hotel, M (20), 1962
Christ Church, Bk (126), 1960
Christ Church, Bx (154), 1960
Church Missions House, M (21), 1960
Church of St. Bernard, M (22), 1963
Church of St. Ignatius Loyola, M (23), 1962
†Church of St. Paul the Apostle, M, 1957
Church of the Ascension, M (24), 1957
Church of the Heavenly Rest, M (25), 1964
Church of the Holy Apostles, M (26), 1961
Church of the Holy Communion, M (27), 1960
Church of the Holy Trinity, M (28), 1962
Church of the Incarnation, M (29), 1961
Church of the Sea and Land, M (30), 1959
Church of the Saviour, Bk (127), 1962
Church of the Transfiguration, M (31), 1958
*Vice-President George Clinton Residence, M, 1965
The Cloisters, M (32), 1966
*Secretary of State Bainbridge Colby Residence, *I,* M, 1965
*Secretary of State Bainbridge Colby Residence, *II,* M, 1965
*Secretary of State Bainbridge Colby Residence, *III,* M, 1965
Colonnade Row, M (33), 1963
†Consolidated Edison Building, M, 1963
*James Fenimore Cooper Residence, M, 1966
Cooper Union, M (34), 1959
Cunard Building, M (35), 1962
Cunard Hall, SI (167), 1965
Dakota Apartments, M (36), 1962
Dutch Reformed Church of Flatlands, Bk (128), 1959

Dyckman House, M (37), 1959
East River Savings Bank, M (38), 1961
East 23rd Street Bath House, M (39), 1965
†Emmanuel Baptist Church, Bk, 1960
Erasmus Hall, Bk (129), 1957
*Secretary of State William M. Evarts Residence, M, 1965
Evening Post Building, M (40), 1966
Federal Reserve Bank of New York, M (41), 1960
†Fifth Avenue Building, M, 1966
First National City Bank Building, M (42), 1958
First Presbyterian Church, M (43), 1963
First Presbyterian Church in Jamaica, Q (175), 1963
Flatiron Building, M (44), 1958
Fonthill Castle, Bx (155), 1965
Fordham University Church, Bx (156), 1966
General Theological Seminary, West Building, M (45), 1961
Grace Church, M (46), 1957
Gracie Mansion, M (47), 1960
Grand Central Terminal, M (48), 1957
*President Ulysses S. Grant Residence, M, 1965
*Horace Greeley Residence, M, 1967
Greenwich Savings Bank, M (49), 1960
Green-Wood Cemetery Gates, Bk (130), 1958
Nos. 4-10 Grove Street, M (50), 1966
Guaranty Trust Company Building, M (51), 1957
*Bret Harte Residence, M, 1967
The Harvard Club, M (52), 1959
Henry Street Settlement, M (53), 1965
No. 131 Hicks Street, Bk (131), 1966
*Home Term Court, M, 1961
President Herbert Hoover Residence, M (54), 1965
Hotel Margaret, Bk (132), 1962
*William Dean Howells Residence, M, 1967
*Chief Justice Charles Evans Hughes Residence, M, 1965
Institute of Fine Arts, M (55), 1959
Institute of Radio Engineers, M (56), 1960
Isaacs-Hendricks House, M (57), 1966
*Henry James Birthplace, M, 1967

Jefferson Market Courthouse, M (58), 1958
John Street Methodist Church, M (59), 1964
Judson Memorial Church, M (60), 1963
President John F. Kennedy Residence, Bx (157), 1965
Kings County Savings Bank, Bk (133), 1960
Knickerbocker Club, M (61), 1962
Lefferts Homestead, Bk (134), 1960
Lent Homestead, Q (176), 1960
Litchfield Mansion, Bk (135), 1958
*Secretary of State Edward Livingston Residence, M, 1965
Long Island Historical Society, Bk (136), 1966
Lotos Club, M (62), 1960
Lüchow's Restaurant, M (63), 1965
General Douglas MacArthur Residence, M (64), 1967
Manufacturers Hanover Trust Company, Bk (137), 1962
Metropolitan Club, M (65), 1966
Metropolitan Life Tower, M (66), 1957
Montauk Club, Bk (138), 1958
Morris-Jumel Mansion, M (67), 1959
*Vice-President Levi Parsons Morton Residence, M, 1965
Municipal Building, M (68), 1961
National Arts Club, M (69), 1962
New Utrecht Reformed Church, Bk (139), 1965
New York Academy of Medicine, M (70), 1967
New York Chamber of Commerce Building, M (71), 1967
New York County Court House, M (72), 1962
New York County Lawyers Association, M (73), 1961
New York Daily News Building, M (74), 1957
New York Life Building, M (75), 1961
New York Stock Exchange, M (76), 1957
New York Telephone Company Building, M (77), 1963
New York Yacht Club, M (78), 1966
Nine East 72nd Street, M (79), 1957
Old St. Patrick's Cathedral, M (80), 1963
Old St. Peter's Church, M (81), 1962
Old Quaker Meeting House, Q (177), 1959
Original Moravian Church, SI (168), 1958
Our Lady of Lebanon R. C. Church, Bk (140), 1965

Packer Collegiate Institute, Bk (141), 1958
Park Avenue Christian Church, M (82), 1960
The Players, M (83), 1962
Plaza Hotel, M (84), 1963
Plymouth Church of the Pilgrims, Bk (142), 1961
Poe Cottage, Bx (158), 1958
Prospect Park, Bk (143), 1965
Pulitzer Memorial Fountain, M (85), 1965
Reformed Protestant Dutch Church, SI (169), 1959
Regis High School, M (86), 1966
Riverdale Presbyterian Church, Bx (159), 1963
President Franklin D. Roosevelt Residence, M (87), 1965
Theodore Roosevelt Birthplace, M (88), 1962
*President Theodore Roosevelt Residence, M, 1965
*Secretary of State Elihu Root Residence, *I*, M, 1965
*Secretary of State Elihu Root Residence, *II*, M, 1965
*Secretary of State Elihu Root Residence, *III*, M, 1965
St. Ann's Church, Bk (144), 1963
St. Ann's Church of Morrisania, Bx (160), 1962
St. Augustine's Chapel, M (89), 1963
St. George's Church, Q (178), 1961
St. James' Church, M (90), 1962
St. James Church, Bx (161), 1965
St. John's Church, SI (170), 1962
St. John's Evangelical Lutheran Church, M (91), 1965
St. Joseph's Church, M (92), 1960
St. Luke's Chapel, M (93), 1960
St. Mary's Episcopal Church, SI (171), 1966
St. Nicholas Historic District, M (94), 1967
St. Paul's Chapel, M (95), 1957
St. Paul's Memorial Church, SI (172), 1962
St. Peter's Church, Bx (162), 1962
St. Peter's Episcopal Church, M (96), 1962
St. Regis Hotel, M (97), 1965
St. Thomas Church, M (98), 1967
St. Vincent Ferrer Church, M (99), 1962
Salmagundi Club, M (100), 1958
Schenck-Wyckoff House, Bk (145), 1961

Scribner Building, M (101), 1961
Serbian Cathedral Church of St. Sava, M (102), 1960
Seventh Regiment Armory, M (103), 1959
Spring Street Presbyterian Church, M (104), 1960
*Secretary of State Henry Lewis Stimson Residence, M, 1965
†Chief Justice Harlan Fiske Stone Residence, M, 1965
Temple Emanu-El, M (105), 1966
Tiffany and Company Stables, M (106), 1957
Times Tower, M (107), 1957
*Vice-President Daniel D. Tompkins Residence, M, 1965
Treadwell Farm Historic District, M (108), 1968
Trinity Church, M (109), 1959
United States Custom House, M (110), 1964
United States Post Office, Bk (146), 1963
University Club, M (111), 1957
Johannes Van Nuyse House, Bk (147), 1965
Joost Van Nuyse House, Bk (148), 1965
Villard Mansion, M (112), 1966
Vincent Office Building, M (113), 1963
Voorlezer's House, SI (173), 1965
Wall of New Amsterdam, M (114), 1965
No. 22, Washington Square North, M (115), 1965
Watson House, M (116), 1958
Wave Hill, Bx (163), 1963
West End Collegiate Church and Collegiate School, M (117), 1963
Robert White House, Bk (149), 1966
Williamsburg Savings Bank, Bk (150), 1960
Nos. 2-8 Willow Place, Bk (151), 1966
Nos. 155-157-159 Willow Street, Bk (152), 1963
The Willows, Bk (153), 1966
†Thomas Wolfe Residence, M, 1966
Woolworth Building, M (118), 1957
Yivo Institute for Jewish Research, M (119), 1960

Appendix B / Sites

Manhattan

Secretary of State Robert Bacon Residence
N.E. Corner Park Avenue and 34th Street
1897-1919

Willa Cather Residence
35 Fifth Avenue (11th Street), Greenwich Village
1927-1932

Vice-President George Clinton Residence
80 Pine Street (Pearl Street)
1784-1791

Secretary of State Bainbridge Colby Residence
41 East 64th Street (Madison Avenue)
1900-1906

(Idem)
55 East 66th Street (Madison Avenue)
1907-1923

(Idem)
1136 Fifth Avenue (95th Street)
1928-1935

James Fenimore Cooper Residence
6 St. Mark's Place (2nd Avenue)
1834-1836

Secretary of State William M. Evarts Residence
231 Second Avenue (14th Street)
1851-1901

President Ulysses S. Grant Residence
3 East 66th Street (5th Avenue)
1881-1885

Horace Greeley Residence
63 Barclay Street (West Broadway)
1842-1843

Bret Harte Residence
16 Fifth Avenue (8th Street), Greenwich Village
1871-1873

Home Term Court (former Old Police Headquarters)
300 Mulberry Street (East Houston Street)

William Dean Howells Residence
40 West 59th Street (Madison Avenue)
1899-1902

Chief Justice Charles Evans Hughes Residence
325 West End Avenue (75th Street)
1893-1905

Henry James Birthplace
21 Washington Place (Broadway), Washington Square
1843

Secretary of State Edward Livingston Residence
74 Wall Street (Pearl Street)
1784-1795

Vice-President Levi Parsons Morton Residence
85 Fifth Avenue (16th Street)
1886-1889

President Theodore Roosevelt Residence
689 Madison Avenue (62nd Street)
1895-1897

Secretary of State Elihu Root Residence
20 Irving Place (16th Street)
1871-1878

(Idem)
52 East 55th Street (Park Avenue)
1879-1885

(Idem)
25 East 69th Street (Madison Avenue)
1885-1906

Secretary of State Henry Lewis Stimson Residence
120 East 36th Street (Lexington Avenue)
1921-1927

Vice-President Daniel D. Tompkins Residence
6 Murray Street (Broadway)
1804-1808

Appendix C / Existing Locations Not Illustrated

Manhattan

American-Standard Building
40 West 40th Street (5th Avenue)

Apthorp Apartments
2201 Broadway (West 78th Street)

The Arsenal
Fifth Avenue and 64th Street, Central Park

Bush Terminal Building
130 West 42nd Street (Broadway)

Church of St. Paul the Apostle
West 60th Street and Columbus Avenue, Lincoln Square

Consolidated Edison Building
East 14th Street and Irving Place

Fifth Avenue Building
200 Fifth Avenue (23rd Street), Madison Square

Chief Justice Harlan Fiske Stone Residence
435 Riverside Drive (West 116th Street)

Thomas Wolfe Residence
27 West 15th Street (5th Avenue)

Brooklyn

Mott Bedell House
11 Cranberry Street (Columbia Heights), Brooklyn Heights

Emmanuel Baptist Church
279 Lafayette Avenue (St. James Place)

Appendix D / Location Maps

MANHATTAN

1

a

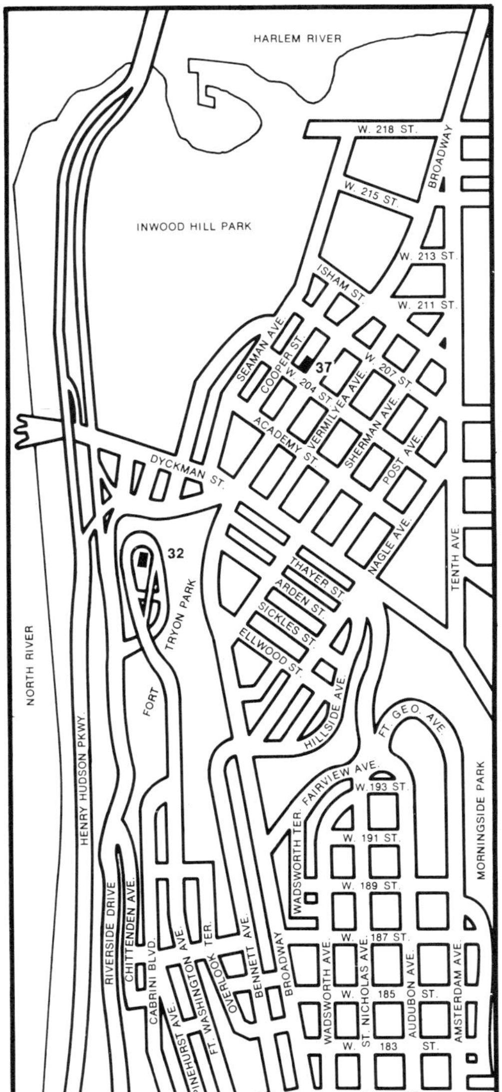
HARLEM RIVER
INWOOD HILL PARK
NORTH RIVER
HENRY HUDSON PKWY.
W. 218 ST.
BROADWAY
W. 215 ST.
W. 213 ST.
ISHAM ST.
W. 211 ST.
SEAMAN AVE.
COOPER ST.
W. 204 ST.
W. 207 ST.
37
VERMILYEA AVE.
SHERMAN AVE.
POST AVE.
ACADEMY ST.
DYCKMAN ST.
NAGLE AVE.
TENTH AVE.
32
THAYER ST.
ARDEN ST.
SICKLES ST.
ELLWOOD ST.
TRYON PARK
FORT
HILLSIDE AVE.
FT. GEO. AVE.
FAIRVIEW AVE.
W. 193 ST.
WADSWORTH TER.
W. 191 ST.
MORNINGSIDE PARK
W. 189 ST.
RIVERSIDE DRIVE
CHITTENDEN AVE.
CABRINI BLVD.
PINEHURST AVE.
FT. WASHINGTON AVE.
OVERLOOK TER.
BENNETT AVE.
BROADWAY
WADSWORTH AVE.
ST. NICHOLAS AVE.
AUDUBON AVE.
AMSTERDAM AVE.
W. 187 ST.
W. 185 ST.
W. 183 ST.
W. 181 ST.

b

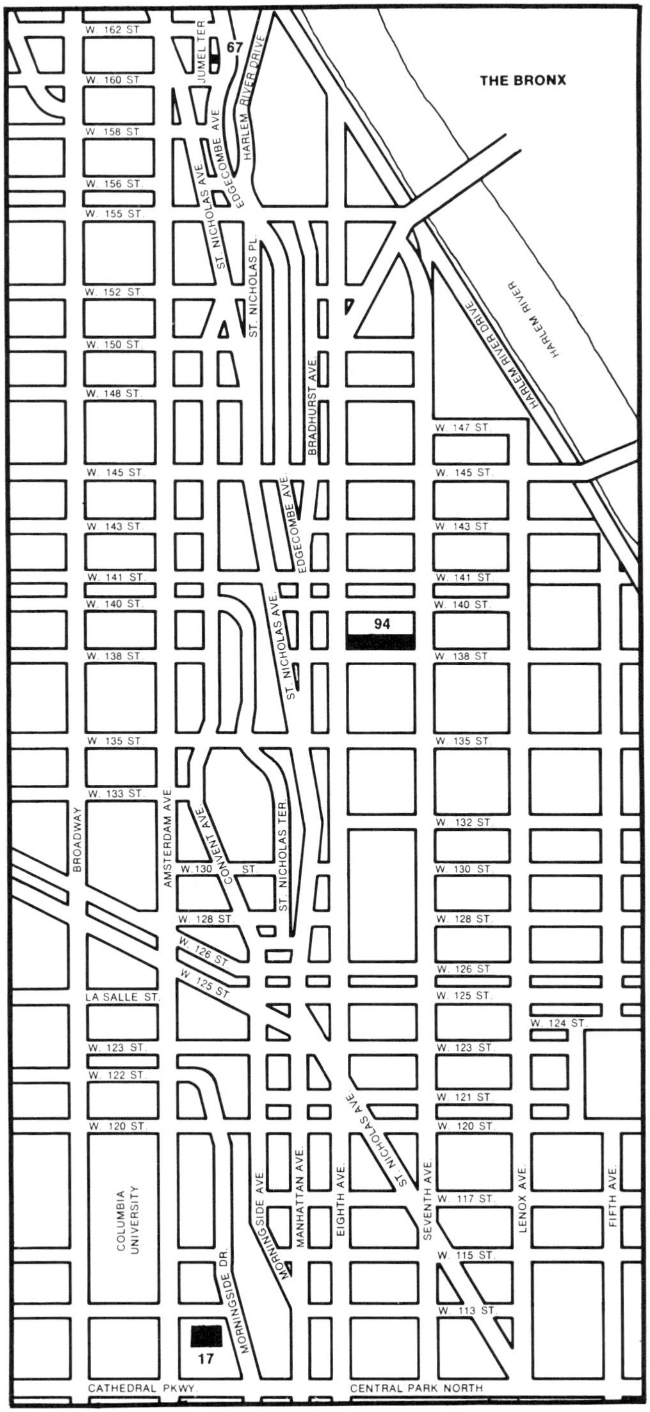
W. 162 ST.
JUMEL TER.
67
HARLEM RIVER DRIVE
THE BRONX
W. 160 ST.
W. 158 ST.
EDGECOMBE AVE.
W. 156 ST.
ST. NICHOLAS AVE.
W. 155 ST.
ST. NICHOLAS PL.
HARLEM RIVER
HARLEM RIVER DRIVE
W. 152 ST.
W. 150 ST.
BRADHURST AVE.
W. 148 ST.
W. 147 ST.
W. 145 ST.
W. 145 ST.
EDGECOMBE AVE.
W. 143 ST.
W. 143 ST.
W. 141 ST.
W. 141 ST.
W. 140 ST.
W. 140 ST.
94
ST. NICHOLAS AVE.
W. 138 ST.
W. 138 ST.
W. 135 ST.
W. 135 ST.
W. 133 ST.
BROADWAY
AMSTERDAM AVE.
CONVENT AVE.
ST. NICHOLAS TER.
W. 132 ST.
W. 130 ST.
W. 130 ST.
W. 128 ST.
W. 128 ST.
W. 126 ST.
W. 126 ST.
W. 125 ST.
LA SALLE ST.
W. 125 ST.
W. 124 ST.
W. 123 ST.
W. 123 ST.
W. 122 ST.
W. 121 ST.
ST. NICHOLAS AVE.
W. 120 ST.
W. 120 ST.
COLUMBIA UNIVERSITY
MORNINGSIDE AVE.
MANHATTAN AVE.
EIGHTH AVE.
SEVENTH AVE.
LENOX AVE.
FIFTH AVE.
W. 117 ST.
W. 115 ST.
MORNINGSIDE DR.
W. 113 ST.
17
CATHEDRAL PKWY.
CENTRAL PARK NORTH

17. Cathedral Church of St. John the Divine (Episcopal)
Amsterdam Avenue and Morningside Drive
(West 113th Street), Cathedral Heights

32. The Cloisters
Fort Tryon Park (200th Street), Inwood

37. Dyckman House
Broadway at 204th Street, Inwood

67. Morris-Jumel Mansion
West 106th Street and Jumel Terrace (Edgecombe Avenue)

94. St. Nicholas Historic District
West 138th and West 139th Streets between
Seventh and Eighth Avenues

2

MANHATTAN

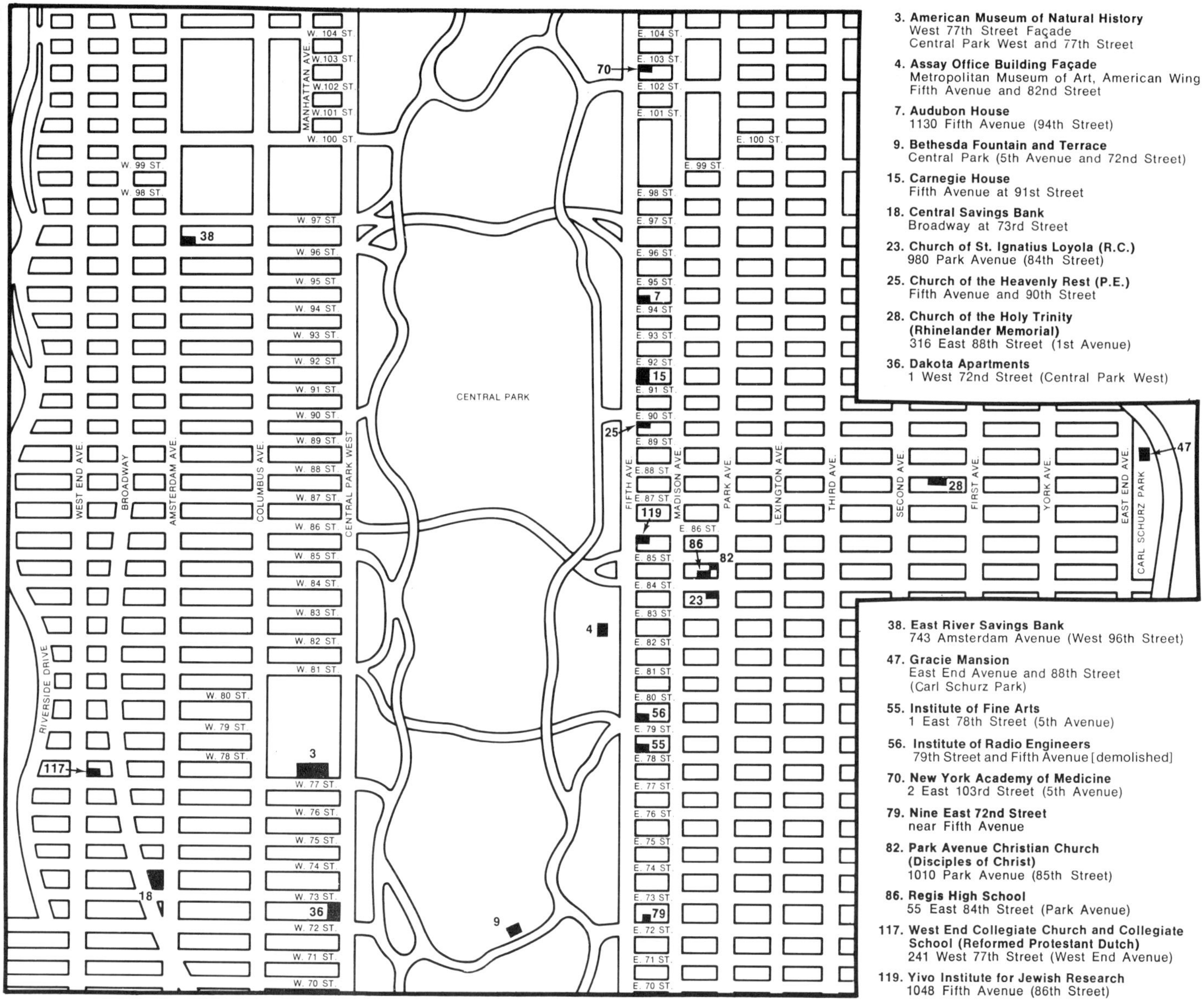
RIVERSIDE DRIVE
WEST END AVE.
BROADWAY
AMSTERDAM AVE.
COLUMBUS AVE.
MANHATTAN AVE.
CENTRAL PARK WEST
CENTRAL PARK
FIFTH AVE.
MADISON AVE.
PARK AVE.
LEXINGTON AVE.
THIRD AVE.
SECOND AVE.
FIRST AVE.
YORK AVE.
EAST END AVE.
CARL SCHURZ PARK
W. 104 ST.
W. 103 ST.
W. 102 ST.
W. 101 ST.
W. 100 ST.
W. 99 ST.
W. 98 ST.
W. 97 ST.
W. 96 ST.
W. 95 ST.
W. 94 ST.
W. 93 ST.
W. 92 ST.
W. 91 ST.
W. 90 ST.
W. 89 ST.
W. 88 ST.
W. 87 ST.
W. 86 ST.
W. 85 ST.
W. 84 ST.
W. 83 ST.
W. 82 ST.
W. 81 ST.
W. 80 ST.
W. 79 ST.
W. 78 ST.
W. 77 ST.
W. 76 ST.
W. 75 ST.
W. 74 ST.
W. 73 ST.
W. 72 ST.
W. 71 ST.
W. 70 ST.
E. 104 ST.
E. 103 ST.
E. 102 ST.
E. 101 ST.
E. 100 ST.
E. 99 ST.
E. 98 ST.
E. 97 ST.
E. 96 ST.
E. 95 ST.
E. 94 ST.
E. 93 ST.
E. 92 ST.
E. 91 ST.
E. 90 ST.
E. 89 ST.
E. 88 ST.
E. 87 ST.
E. 86 ST.
E. 85 ST.
E. 84 ST.
E. 83 ST.
E. 82 ST.
E. 81 ST.
E. 80 ST.
E. 79 ST.
E. 78 ST.
E. 77 ST.
E. 76 ST.
E. 75 ST.
E. 74 ST.
E. 73 ST.
E. 72 ST.
E. 71 ST.
E. 70 ST.
3
4
7
9
15
18
23
25
28
36
38
47
55
56
70
79
82
86
117
119

3. **American Museum of Natural History**
West 77th Street Façade
Central Park West and 77th Street

4. **Assay Office Building Façade**
Metropolitan Museum of Art, American Wing
Fifth Avenue and 82nd Street

7. **Audubon House**
1130 Fifth Avenue (94th Street)

9. **Bethesda Fountain and Terrace**
Central Park (5th Avenue and 72nd Street)

15. **Carnegie House**
Fifth Avenue at 91st Street

18. **Central Savings Bank**
Broadway at 73rd Street

23. **Church of St. Ignatius Loyola (R.C.)**
980 Park Avenue (84th Street)

25. **Church of the Heavenly Rest (P.E.)**
Fifth Avenue and 90th Street

28. **Church of the Holy Trinity (Rhinelander Memorial)**
316 East 88th Street (1st Avenue)

36. **Dakota Apartments**
1 West 72nd Street (Central Park West)

38. **East River Savings Bank**
743 Amsterdam Avenue (West 96th Street)

47. **Gracie Mansion**
East End Avenue and 88th Street
(Carl Schurz Park)

55. **Institute of Fine Arts**
1 East 78th Street (5th Avenue)

56. **Institute of Radio Engineers**
79th Street and Fifth Avenue [demolished]

70. **New York Academy of Medicine**
2 East 103rd Street (5th Avenue)

79. **Nine East 72nd Street**
near Fifth Avenue

82. **Park Avenue Christian Church (Disciples of Christ)**
1010 Park Avenue (85th Street)

86. **Regis High School**
55 East 84th Street (Park Avenue)

117. **West End Collegiate Church and Collegiate School (Reformed Protestant Dutch)**
241 West 77th Street (West End Avenue)

119. **Yivo Institute for Jewish Research**
1048 Fifth Avenue (86th Street)

MANHATTAN

3

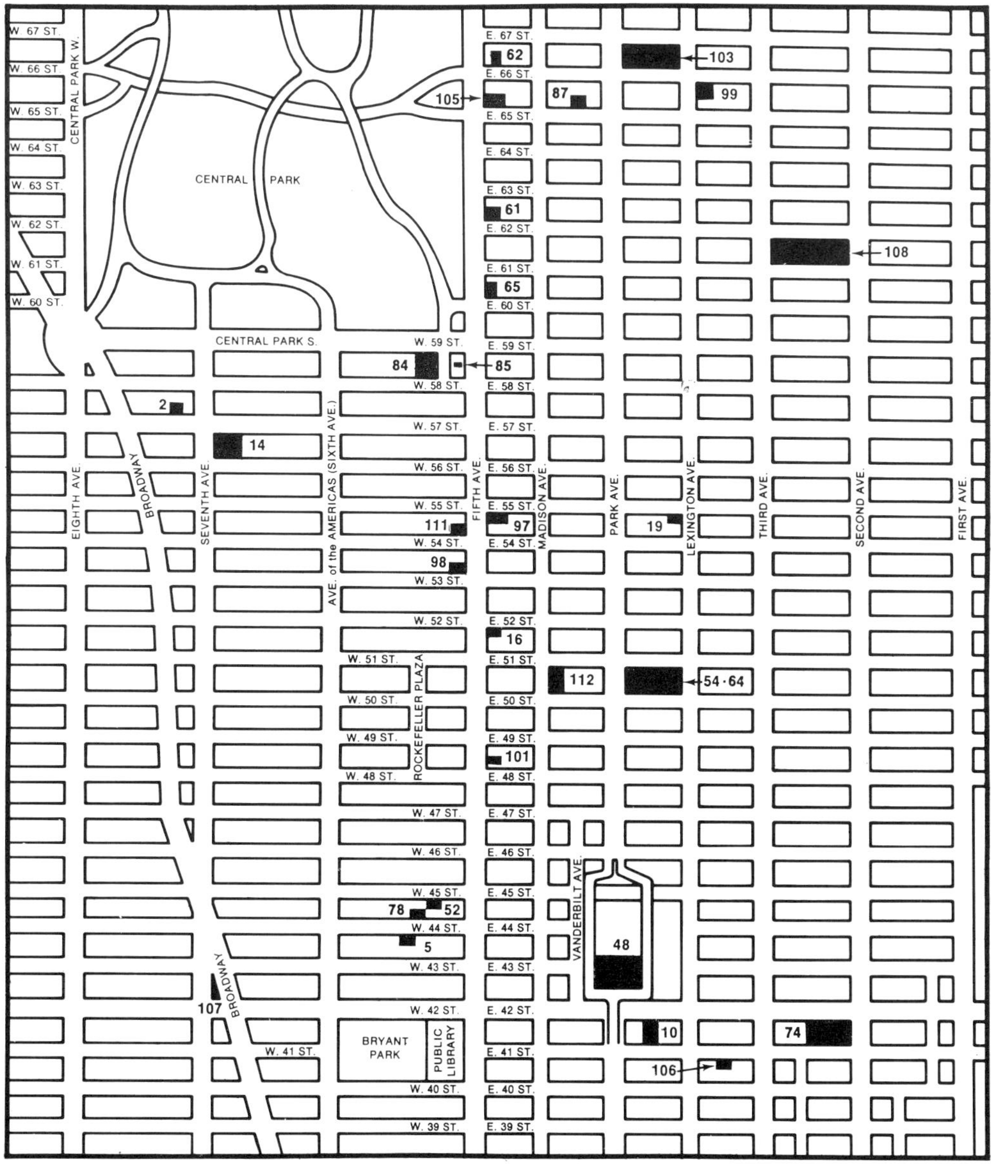

CENTRAL PARK
CENTRAL PARK W.
CENTRAL PARK S.
EIGHTH AVE.
BROADWAY
SEVENTH AVE.
AVE. of the AMERICAS (SIXTH AVE.)
ROCKEFELLER PLAZA
FIFTH AVE.
MADISON AVE.
VANDERBILT AVE.
PARK AVE.
LEXINGTON AVE.
THIRD AVE.
SECOND AVE.
FIRST AVE.
BRYANT PARK
PUBLIC LIBRARY
W. 67 ST.
W. 66 ST.
W. 65 ST.
W. 64 ST.
W. 63 ST.
W. 62 ST.
W. 61 ST.
W. 60 ST.
W. 59 ST.
W. 58 ST.
W. 57 ST.
W. 56 ST.
W. 55 ST.
W. 54 ST.
W. 53 ST.
W. 52 ST.
W. 51 ST.
W. 50 ST.
W. 49 ST.
W. 48 ST.
W. 47 ST.
W. 46 ST.
W. 45 ST.
W. 44 ST.
W. 43 ST.
W. 42 ST.
W. 41 ST.
W. 40 ST.
W. 39 ST.
E. 67 ST.
E. 66 ST.
E. 65 ST.
E. 64 ST.
E. 63 ST.
E. 62 ST.
E. 61 ST.
E. 60 ST.
E. 59 ST.
E. 58 ST.
E. 57 ST.
E. 56 ST.
E. 55 ST.
E. 54 ST.
E. 52 ST.
E. 51 ST.
E. 50 ST.
E. 49 ST.
E. 48 ST.
E. 47 ST.
E. 46 ST.
E. 45 ST.
E. 44 ST.
E. 43 ST.
E. 42 ST.
E. 41 ST.
E. 40 ST.
E. 39 ST.
62
103
105
87
99
61
108
65
84
85
2
14
111
97
19
98
16
112
54·64
101
78
52
5
48
107
10
74
106

2. **American Fine Arts Society**
215 West 57th Street (7th Avenue)

5. **Association of the Bar of the City of New York**
42 West 44th Street (5th Avenue)

10. **Bowery Savings Bank Building**
110 East 42nd Street (Park Avenue)

14. **Carnegie Hall**
154 West 57th Street (7th Avenue)

16. **Cartier Building**
653 Fifth Avenue (52nd Street)

19. **Central Synagogue**
Lexington Avenue at 55th Street

48. **Grand Central Terminal**
42nd Street and Park Avenue

52. **The Harvard Club**
32 West 45th Street (5th Avenue)

54. **President Herbert Hoover Residence**
Waldorf Towers, Park Avenue and 50th Street

61. **Knickerbocker Club**
807 Fifth Avenue (62nd Street)

62. **Lotos Club**
5 East 66th Street (5th Avenue)

64. **General Douglas MacArthur Residence**
Waldorf Towers, Park Avenue and 50th Street

65. **Metropolitan Club**
1 East 60th Street (5th Avenue)

74. **New York Daily News Building**
220 East 42nd Street (2nd Avenue)

78. **New York Yacht Club**
37 West 44th Street (5th Avenue)

84. **Plaza Hotel**
Fifth Avenue and 59th Street

85. **Pulitzer Memorial Fountain**
Fifth Avenue and 58th Street, Grand Army Plaza

87. **President Franklin D. Roosevelt Residence**
47 East 65th Street (Park Avenue)

97. **St. Regis Hotel**
Fifth Avenue and 55th Street

98. **St. Thomas Church (P.E.)**
Fifth Avenue and 53rd Street

99. **St. Vincent Ferrer Church (R.C.)**
Lexington Avenue and 66th Street

101. **Scribner Building**
597 Fifth Avenue (48th Street)

103. **Seventh Regiment Armory**
643 Park Avenue (66th Street)

105. **Temple Emanu-El (Reform)**
Fifth Avenue and 65th Street

106. **Tiffany and Company Stables**
140 East 41st St. (Lexington Ave.) [demolished]

107. **Times Tower (rebuilt as Allied Chemical Tower)**
Times Square and 42nd Street

108. **Treadwell Farm Historic District**
East 61st and East 62nd Streets between Second and Third Avenues

111. **University Club**
Fifth Avenue and 54th Street

112. **Villard Mansion**
Madison Avenue between 50th and 51st Streets

4

MANHATTAN

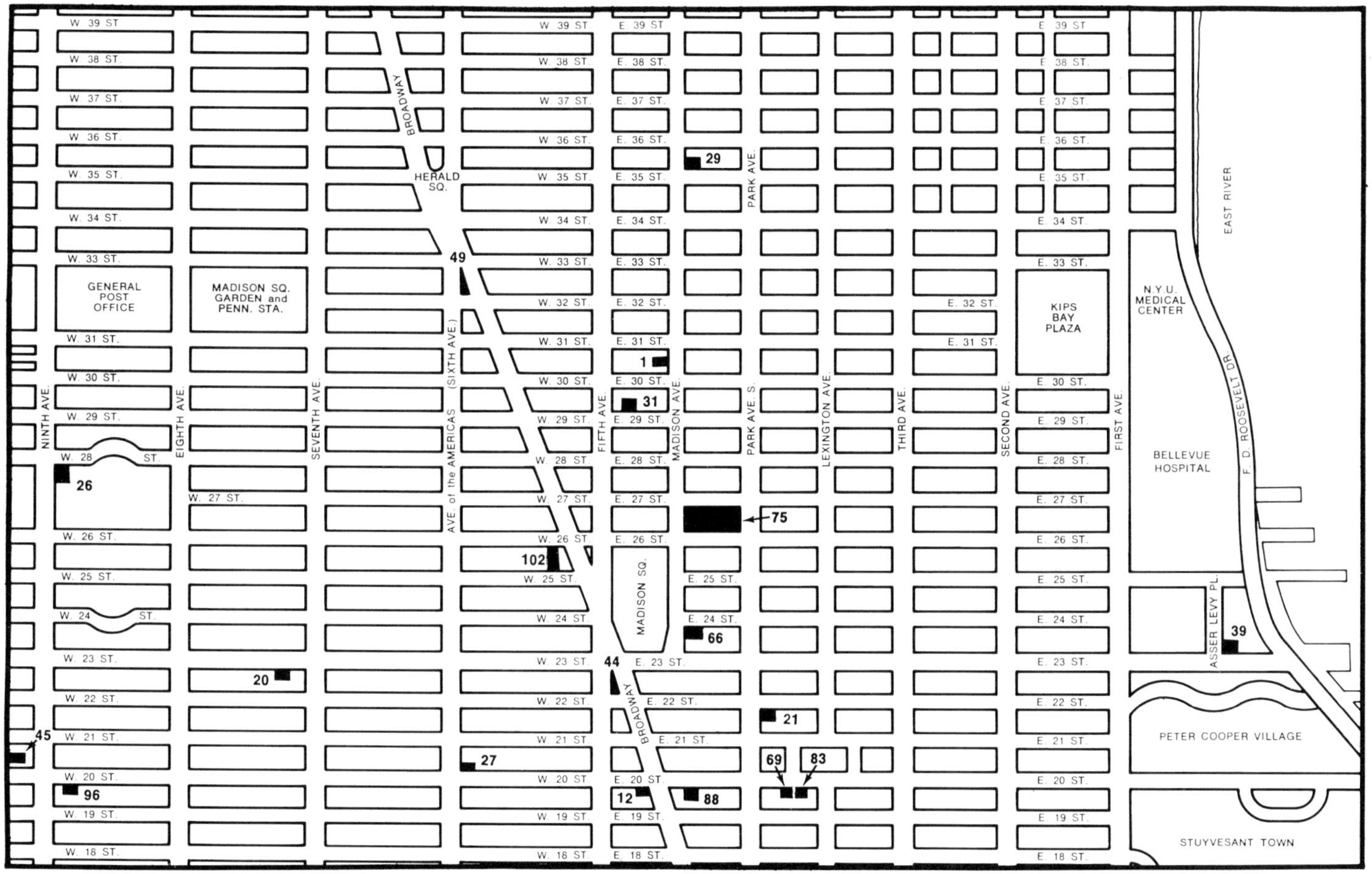

NINTH AVE.
EIGHTH AVE.
SEVENTH AVE.
AVE. of the AMERICAS (SIXTH AVE.)
FIFTH AVE.
MADISON AVE.
PARK AVE.
PARK AVE. S.
LEXINGTON AVE.
THIRD AVE.
SECOND AVE.
FIRST AVE.
BROADWAY
HERALD SQ.
GENERAL POST OFFICE
MADISON SQ. GARDEN and PENN. STA.
MADISON SQ.
KIPS BAY PLAZA
N.Y.U. MEDICAL CENTER
BELLEVUE HOSPITAL
F. D. ROOSEVELT DR.
EAST RIVER
ASSER LEVY PL.
PETER COOPER VILLAGE
STUYVESANT TOWN
1
12
20
21
26
27
29
31
39
44
45
49
66
69
75
83
88
96
102

1. **American Academy of Dramatic Arts**
   120 Madison Avenue (30th Street)
12. **No. 901 Broadway**
   Broadway and 20th Street
20. **Chelsea Hotel**
   222 West 23rd Street (7th Avenue)
21. **Church Missions House**
   281 Park Avenue South (22nd Street)
26. **Church of the Holy Apostles (P.E.)**
   360 West 28th Street (9th Avenue), Chelsea
27. **Church of the Holy Communion (Episcopal)**
   49 West 20th Street (6th Avenue)
29. **Church of the Incarnation (P.E.)**
   Madison Avenue and 35th Street
31. **Church of the Transfiguration—"Little Church Around the Corner" (P.E.)**
   29th Street near Fifth Avenue
39. **East 23rd Street Bath House**
   Asser Levy Place near F. D. Roosevelt (East River) Drive
44. **The Flatiron Building**
   Broadway, Fifth Avenue, and 23rd Street (Madison Square)
45. **General Theological Seminary, West Building**
   175 Ninth Avenue (20th Street), Chelsea
49. **Greenwich Savings Bank**
   Broadway, Sixth Avenue, and 33rd Street
66. **Metropolitan Life Tower**
   1 Madison Avenue (24th Street), Madison Square
69. **National Arts Club**
   15 Gramercy Park (20th Street)
75. **New York Life Building**
   51 Madison Avenue (26th Street), Madison Square
83. **The Players**
   16 Gramercy Park (20th Street)
88. **Theodore Roosevelt Birthplace**
   28 East 20th Street (Broadway)
96. **St. Peter's Episcopal Church**
   344 West 20th Street (9th Avenue)
102. **Serbian Cathedral Church of St. Sava (Orthodox)**
   16-20 West 26th Street (Broadway)

MANHATTAN

5

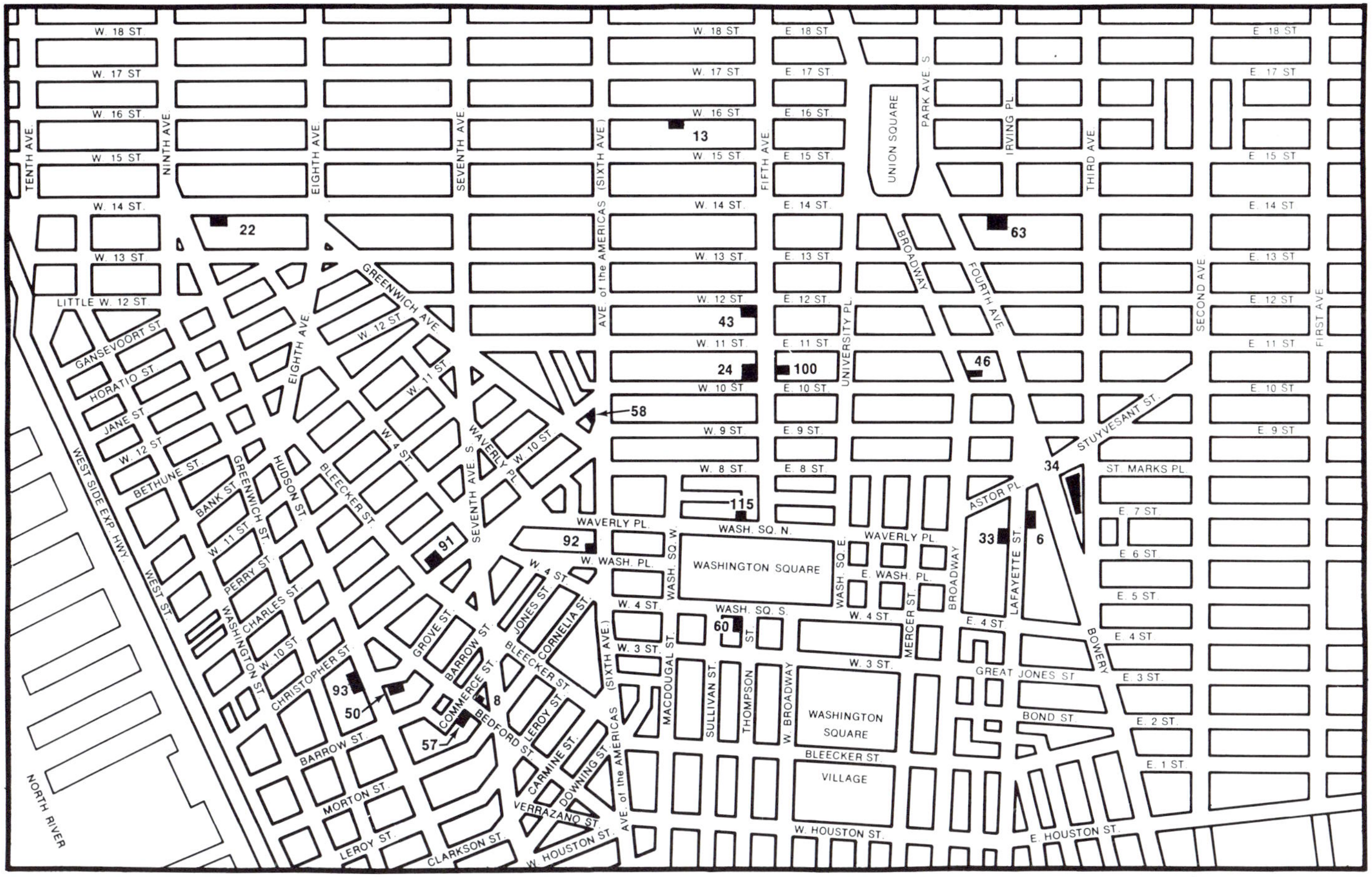

W. 18 ST
W. 17 ST
W. 16 ST
W. 15 ST
W. 14 ST.
W. 13 ST
W. 12 ST
W. 11 ST
W. 10 ST
W. 9 ST
W. 8 ST
E. 18 ST
E. 17 ST
E. 16 ST
E. 15 ST
E. 14 ST
E. 13 ST
E. 12 ST
E. 11 ST
E. 10 ST
E. 9 ST
E. 8 ST
E. 7 ST
E. 6 ST
E. 5 ST
E. 4 ST
E. 3 ST
E. 2 ST
E. 1 ST
LITTLE W. 12 ST
TENTH AVE.
NINTH AVE.
EIGHTH AVE.
SEVENTH AVE.
AVE. of the AMERICAS (SIXTH AVE.)
FIFTH AVE.
UNIVERSITY PL.
UNION SQUARE
PARK AVE S.
IRVING PL.
THIRD AVE.
SECOND AVE
FIRST AVE
BROADWAY
FOURTH AVE.
STUYVESANT ST.
ST. MARKS PL.
ASTOR PL.
LAFAYETTE ST.
BOWERY
GREAT JONES ST
BOND ST
E. HOUSTON ST.
GANSEVOORT ST
HORATIO ST.
JANE ST
BETHUNE ST.
BANK ST
GREENWICH ST.
HUDSON ST.
BLEECKER ST.
GREENWICH AVE.
W. 4 ST.
SEVENTH AVE. S
WAVERLY PL.
W. 10 ST.
WEST SIDE EXP. HWY
WEST ST.
PERRY ST.
CHARLES ST.
WASHINGTON ST.
CHRISTOPHER ST.
GROVE ST.
BARROW ST.
COMMERCE ST.
BEDFORD ST.
JONES ST.
CORNELIA ST.
LEROY ST.
CARMINE ST.
DOWNING ST.
VERRAZANO ST.
W. HOUSTON ST.
CLARKSON ST.
MORTON ST.
NORTH RIVER
W. WASH. PL.
WASH. SQ. N.
WASH. SQ. W.
WASH. SQ. E.
WASH. SQ. S.
WASHINGTON SQUARE
E. WASH. PL.
MERCER ST.
W. 3 ST.
MACDOUGAL ST.
SULLIVAN ST.
THOMPSON ST.
W. BROADWAY
BLEECKER ST.
VILLAGE
6
8
13
22
24
33
34
43
46
50
57
58
60
63
91
92
93
100
115

6. Astor Library
425 Lafayette Street (Astor Place)

8. No. 70 Bedford Street
near Commerce Street, Greenwich Village

13. William Cullen Bryant Residence
24 West 16th Street (6th Avenue), Chelsea

22. Church of St. Bernard (R.C.)
328 West 14th Street (Hudson Street), Greenwich Village

24. Church of the Ascension (Episcopal)
Fifth Avenue and 10th Street, Greenwich Village

33. Colonnade Row
432 Lafayette Street (Astor Place)

34. Cooper Union
Cooper Square and Astor Place, Greenwich Village

43. First Presbyterian Church
12 West 12th Street (5th Avenue), Greenwich Village

46. Grace Church (P.E.)
Broadway and 10th Street, Greenwich Village

50. Nos. 4-10 Grove Street
near Bedford Street, Greenwich Village

57. Isaacs-Hendricks House
77 Bedford Street (Commerce Street), Greenwich Village

58. Jefferson Market Courthouse
Sixth Avenue and 10th Street, Greenwich Village

60. Judson Memorial Church (Baptist)
55 Washington Square South (Thompson St.), Greenwich Village

63. Lüchow's Restaurant
110 East 14th Street (4th Avenue), Union Square

91. St. John's Evangelical Lutheran Church
81 Christopher Street (Bleecker Street), Greenwich Village

92. St. Joseph's Church (R.C.)
371 Sixth Avenue (Washington Place), Greenwich Village

93. St. Luke's Chapel (Episcopal)
487 Hudson Street (Christopher Street), Greenwich Village

100. Salmagundi Club
47 Fifth Avenue (10th Street), Greenwich Village

115. No. 22 Washington Square North
near Fifth Avenue, Greenwich Village

MANHATTAN

6

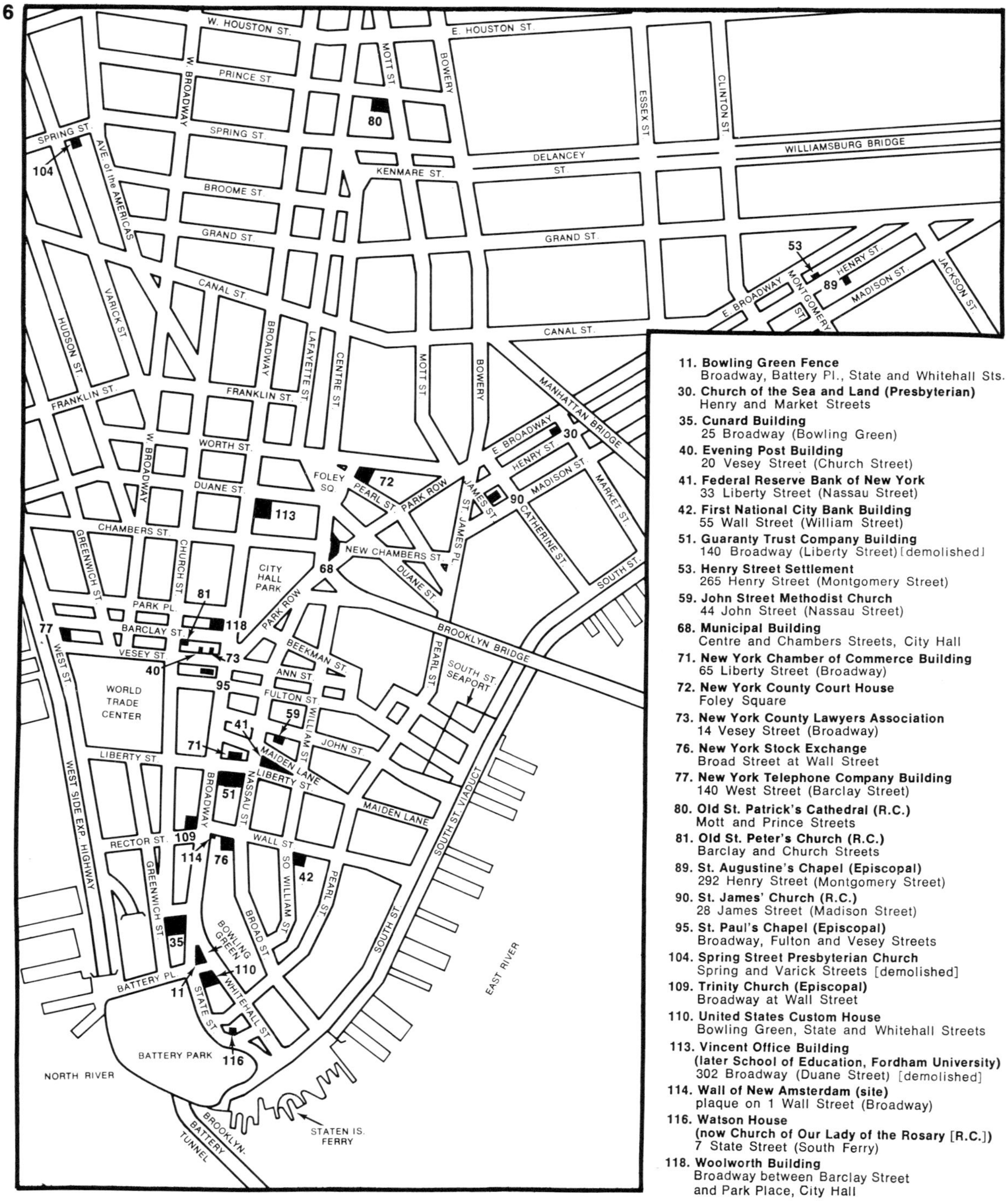
W. HOUSTON ST.
E. HOUSTON ST.
PRINCE ST.
W. BROADWAY
MOTT ST.
BOWERY
ESSEX ST.
CLINTON ST.
SPRING ST.
80
104
AVE. of the AMERICAS
KENMARE ST.
DELANCEY ST.
WILLIAMSBURG BRIDGE
BROOME ST.
GRAND ST.
53
HENRY ST.
89
MADISON ST.
JACKSON ST.
MONTGOMERY ST.
E. BROADWAY
CANAL ST.
HUDSON ST.
VARICK ST.
BROADWAY
LAFAYETTE ST.
CENTRE ST.
FRANKLIN ST.
MANHATTAN BRIDGE
WORTH ST.
30
FOLEY SQ.
72
PEARL ST.
PARK ROW
JAMES ST.
90
CATHERINE ST.
MARKET ST.
DUANE ST.
113
CHAMBERS ST.
GREENWICH ST.
CHURCH ST.
CITY HALL PARK
68
NEW CHAMBERS ST.
ST. JAMES PL.
SOUTH ST.
PARK PL.
81
77
BARCLAY ST.
118
VESEY ST.
73
40
BEEKMAN ST.
BROOKLYN BRIDGE
WEST ST.
WORLD TRADE CENTER
95
ANN ST.
FULTON ST.
SOUTH ST. SEAPORT
59
41
WILLIAM ST.
JOHN ST.
71
MAIDEN LANE
LIBERTY ST.
NASSAU ST.
51
WEST SIDE EXP. HIGHWAY
SOUTH ST. VIADUCT
RECTOR ST.
109
WALL ST.
114
76
SO. WILLIAM ST.
42
BOWLING GREEN
BROAD ST.
35
110
BATTERY PL.
11
STATE ST.
WHITEHALL ST.
EAST RIVER
BATTERY PARK
116
NORTH RIVER
BROOKLYN-BATTERY TUNNEL
STATEN IS. FERRY

11. Bowling Green Fence
Broadway, Battery Pl., State and Whitehall Sts.

30. Church of the Sea and Land (Presbyterian)
Henry and Market Streets

35. Cunard Building
25 Broadway (Bowling Green)

40. Evening Post Building
20 Vesey Street (Church Street)

41. Federal Reserve Bank of New York
33 Liberty Street (Nassau Street)

42. First National City Bank Building
55 Wall Street (William Street)

51. Guaranty Trust Company Building
140 Broadway (Liberty Street) [demolished]

53. Henry Street Settlement
265 Henry Street (Montgomery Street)

59. John Street Methodist Church
44 John Street (Nassau Street)

68. Municipal Building
Centre and Chambers Streets, City Hall

71. New York Chamber of Commerce Building
65 Liberty Street (Broadway)

72. New York County Court House
Foley Square

73. New York County Lawyers Association
14 Vesey Street (Broadway)

76. New York Stock Exchange
Broad Street at Wall Street

77. New York Telephone Company Building
140 West Street (Barclay Street)

80. Old St. Patrick's Cathedral (R.C.)
Mott and Prince Streets

81. Old St. Peter's Church (R.C.)
Barclay and Church Streets

89. St. Augustine's Chapel (Episcopal)
292 Henry Street (Montgomery Street)

90. St. James' Church (R.C.)
28 James Street (Madison Street)

95. St. Paul's Chapel (Episcopal)
Broadway, Fulton and Vesey Streets

104. Spring Street Presbyterian Church
Spring and Varick Streets [demolished]

109. Trinity Church (Episcopal)
Broadway at Wall Street

110. United States Custom House
Bowling Green, State and Whitehall Streets

113. Vincent Office Building
(later School of Education, Fordham University)
302 Broadway (Duane Street) [demolished]

114. Wall of New Amsterdam (site)
plaque on 1 Wall Street (Broadway)

116. Watson House
(now Church of Our Lady of the Rosary [R.C.])
7 State Street (South Ferry)

118. Woolworth Building
Broadway between Barclay Street
and Park Place, City Hall

BROOKLYN

120. **Brooklyn Borough Hall**
Fulton and Court Streets

124. **Brooklyn Municipal Building**
Fulton and Court Streets

126. **Christ Church (P.E.)**
Clinton and Kane Streets, Cobble Hill

127. **Church of the Saviour (First Unitarian Church)**
Pierrepont Street and Monroe Place, Brooklyn Heights

131. **No. 131 Hicks Street (Henry C. Bowen Residence)**
near Clark Street, Brooklyn Heights

132. **Hotel Margaret**
97 Columbia Heights (Orange Street), Brooklyn Heights

136. **Long Island Historical Society**
128 Pierrepont Street (Clinton Street)

137. **Manufacturers Hanover Trust Company**
177 Montague Street (Clinton Street)

140. **Our Lady of Lebanon R.C. Church (Maronite Rite)**
113 Remsen Street (Henry Street), Brooklyn Heights

141. **Packer Collegiate Institute**
170 Joralemon Street (Court Street), Brooklyn Heights

142. **Plymouth Church of the Pilgrims (Congregational)**
Orange and Hicks Streets, Brooklyn Heights

144. **St. Ann's Church (Episcopal)**
131 Clinton Street (Livingston Street), Brooklyn Heights

146. **United States Post Office (Brooklyn G.P.O.)**
271 Washington Street (Tillary Street)

149. **Robert White House**
57 Willow Street (Orange Street), Brooklyn Heights

151. **Nos. 2-8 Willow Place**
near Joralemon Street, Brooklyn Heights

152. **Nos. 155-157-159 Willow Street**
near Pierrepont Street, Brooklyn Heights

153. **The Willows**
37 Willow Street (Cranberry Street), Brooklyn Heights

7

EAST RIVER
BROOKLYN BRIDGE
MANHATTAN BRIDGE
WATER ST.
FRONT ST.
JOHN ST.
PLYMOUTH ST.
MAIN ST.
WASHINGTON ST.
ADAMS ST.
PEARL ST.
JAY ST.
FURMAN ST.
DOUGHTY ST.
YORK ST.
MIDDAGH ST.
CRANBERRY ST.
ORANGE ST.
BKLYN QUEENS EXPWY.
SANDS ST.
COLUMBIA HTS.
PINEAPPLE ST.
CLARK ST.
WILLOW ST.
FULTON ST.
NASSAU ST.
CONCORD ST.
DUFFIELD ST.
MONROE PL.
TILLARY ST.
PIERREPONT ST.
JOHNSON ST.
MONTAGUE ST.
REMSEN ST.
FLATBUSH AVE.
LAWRENCE ST.
BRIDGE ST.
COLUMBIA PL.
WILLOW PL.
HICKS ST.
GARDEN PL.
JORALEMON ST.
MYRTLE AVE.
STATE ST.
SIDNEY PL.
LIVINGSTON ST.
GOLD ST.
WILLOUGHBY ST.
SCHERMERHORN ST.
PEARL ST.
ATLANTIC AVE.
HENRY ST.
PACIFIC ST.
CLINTON ST.
AMITY ST.
CONGRESS ST.
COLUMBIA ST.
KANE ST.
VAN BRUNT ST.
WARREN ST.
BALTIC ST.
COURT ST.
BOERUM PL.
SMITH ST.
DEAN ST.
HOYT ST.
TIFFANY PL.
DEGRAW ST.
SACKETT ST.
UNION ST.
PRESIDENT ST.
CARROLL ST.
BKLYN. QUEENS EXPWY.
CHEEVER PL.
STRONG PL.
TOMPKINS PL.
BERGEN ST.
WYCKOFF ST.
BUTLER ST.
DOUGLASS ST.
BOND ST.
NEVINS ST.
120
124
126
127
131
132
136
137
140
141
142
144
146
149
151
152
153

BROOKLYN

121. **Brooklyn Botanic Garden, Administrative Building**
 1000 Washington Avenue (Crown Street), Prospect Park E.
122. **Brooklyn Children's Museum**
 Brooklyn Avenue and Park Place [demolished]
123. **Brooklyn Ethical Culture School**
 49-50 Prospect Park West (2nd Street), Park Slope
125. **Brooklyn Museum**
 Eastern Parkway and Washington Avenue, Prospect Park N.E.
129. **Erasmus Hall**
 Flatbush and Church Avenues
130. **Green-Wood Cemetery Gates**
 Fifth Avenue and 25th Street, Park Slope
134. **Lefferts Homestead**
 Prospect Park E. near Flatbush Avenue and Empire Boulevard
135. **Litchfield Mansion**
 Prospect Park near Prospect Park West and 5th Street
138. **Montauk Club**
 Eighth Avenue and Lincoln Place, Grand Army Plaza
139. **New Utrecht Reformed Church**
 18th Avenue and 83rd Street
143. **Prospect Park (Soldiers and Sailors Memorial Arch)**
 Grand Army Plaza

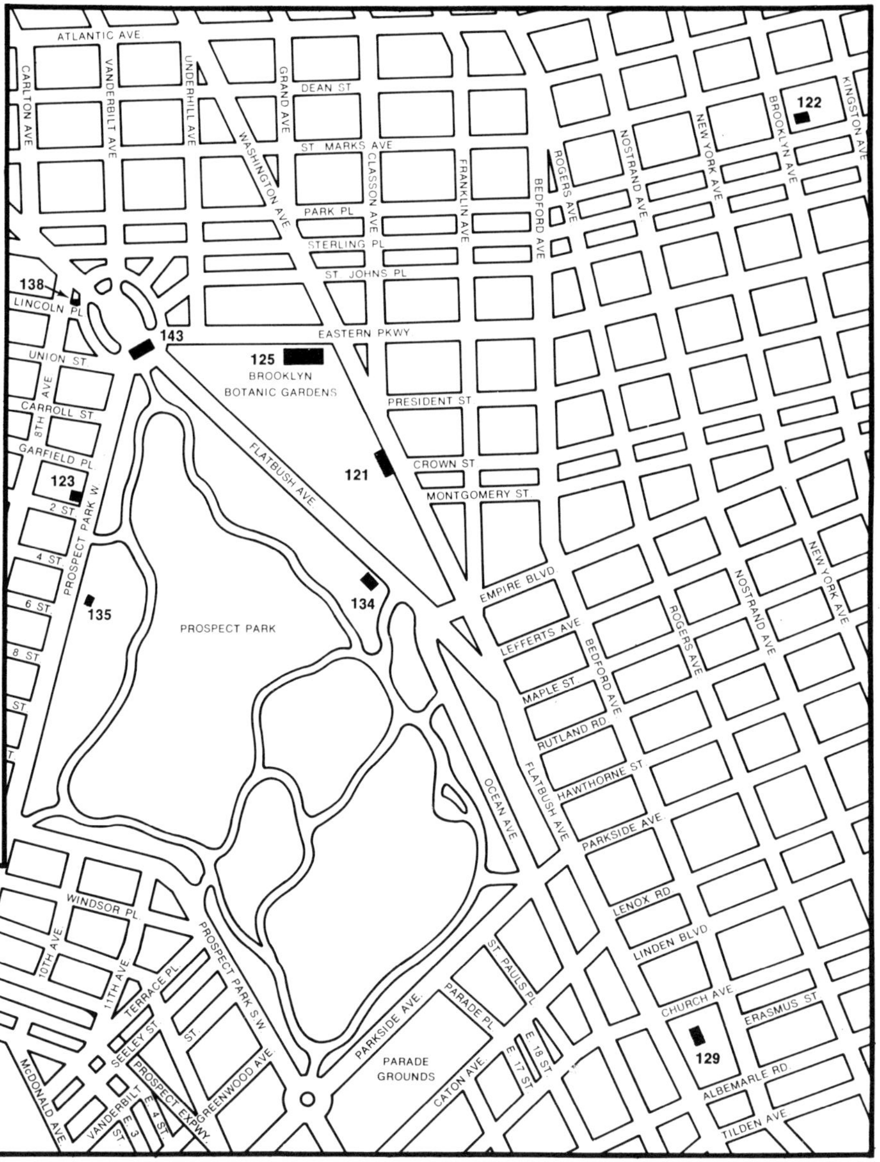

ATLANTIC AVE
CARLTON AVE
VANDERBILT AVE
UNDERHILL AVE
WASHINGTON AVE
GRAND AVE
DEAN ST
ST MARKS AVE
CLASSON AVE
PARK PL
STERLING PL
ST JOHNS PL
FRANKLIN AVE
BEDFORD AVE
ROGERS AVE
NOSTRAND AVE
NEW YORK AVE
BROOKLYN AVE
KINGSTON AVE
EASTERN PKWY
LINCOLN PL
UNION ST
CARROLL ST
GARFIELD PL
8TH AVE
2 ST
4 ST
6 ST
8 ST
PROSPECT PARK W
PRESIDENT ST
CROWN ST
MONTGOMERY ST
BROOKLYN BOTANIC GARDENS
FLATBUSH AVE
PROSPECT PARK
EMPIRE BLVD
LEFFERTS AVE
MAPLE ST
RUTLAND RD
HAWTHORNE ST
PARKSIDE AVE
LENOX RD
LINDEN BLVD
CHURCH AVE
ERASMUS ST
ALBEMARLE RD
TILDEN AVE
OCEAN AVE
ST PAULS PL
PARADE PL
E 18 ST
E 17 ST
CATON AVE
PARADE GROUNDS
PROSPECT PARK S W
GREENWOOD AVE
WINDSOR PL
PROSPECT AVE
TERRACE PL
SEELEY ST
VANDERBILT
PROSPECT EXPWY
McDONALD AVE
11TH AVE
10TH AVE
121
122
123
125
129
134
135
138
143

b

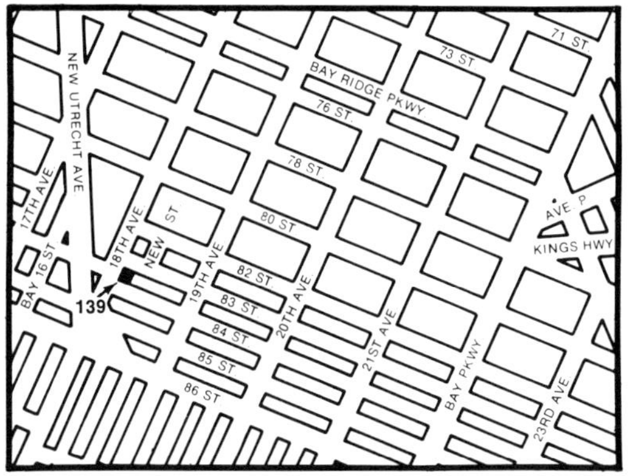

NEW UTRECHT AVE
17TH AVE
18TH AVE
NEW ST
19TH AVE
20TH AVE
21ST AVE
23RD AVE
BAY 16 ST
BAY RIDGE PKWY
BAY PKWY
KINGS HWY
AVE P
71 ST
73 ST
76 ST
78 ST
80 ST
82 ST
83 ST
84 ST
85 ST
86 ST
139

a

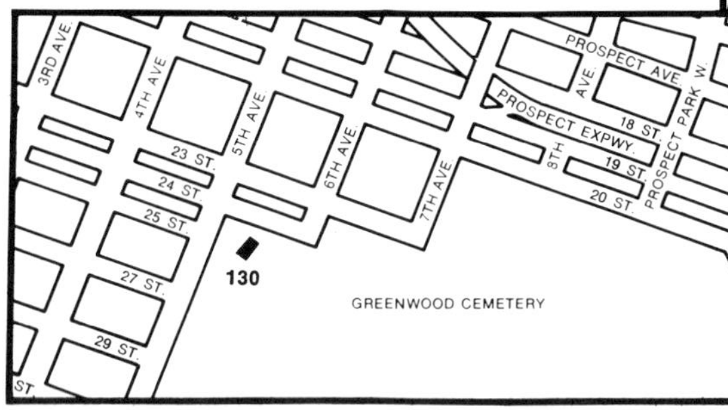

3RD AVE
4TH AVE
5TH AVE
6TH AVE
7TH AVE
8TH AVE
PROSPECT EXPWY
PROSPECT PARK W
18 ST
19 ST
20 ST
23 ST
24 ST
25 ST
27 ST
29 ST
GREENWOOD CEMETERY
130

BROOKLYN

9

a

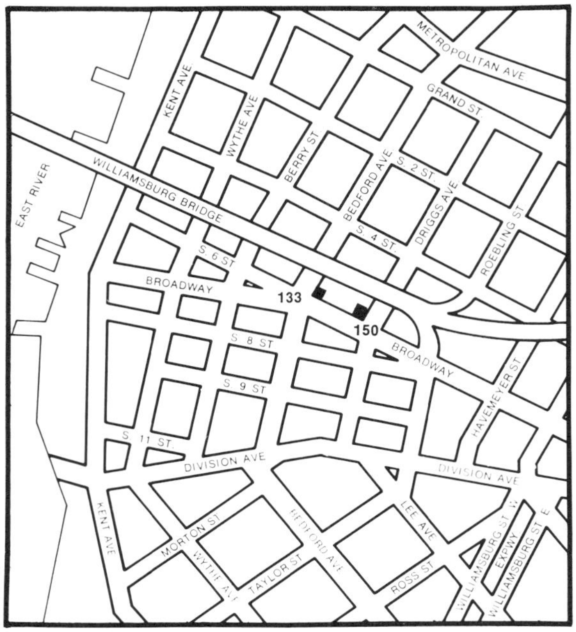

METROPOLITAN AVE
GRAND ST
KENT AVE
WYTHE AVE
BERRY ST
BEDFORD AVE
S 2 ST
DRIGGS AVE
ROEBLING ST
EAST RIVER
WILLIAMSBURG BRIDGE
S 4 ST
S 6 ST
BROADWAY
133
150
S 8 ST
BROADWAY
S 9 ST
HAVEMEYER ST
S 11 ST
DIVISION AVE
DIVISION AVE
KENT AVE
MORTON ST
BEDFORD AVE
LEE AVE
WYTHE AVE
TAYLOR ST
ROSS ST
WILLIAMSBURG ST W
EXPWY
WILLIAMSBURG ST E

b

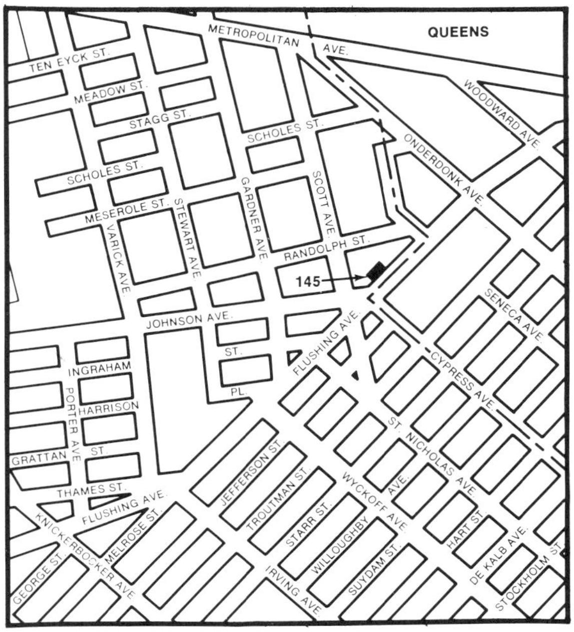

METROPOLITAN AVE
QUEENS
TEN EYCK ST
MEADOW ST
STAGG ST
WOODWARD AVE
SCHOLES ST
SCHOLES ST
ONDERDONK AVE
MESEROLE ST
STEWART AVE
GARDNER AVE
SCOTT AVE
VARICK AVE
RANDOLPH ST
145
SENECA AVE
JOHNSON AVE
FLUSHING AVE
ST.
INGRAHAM
PL.
CYPRESS AVE
PORTER AVE
HARRISON
ST. NICHOLAS AVE
GRATTAN
ST
JEFFERSON ST
TROUTMAN ST
THAMES ST.
FLUSHING AVE
WYCKOFF AVE
AVE.
KNICKERBOCKER AVE
MELROSE ST
STARR ST
HART ST
GEORGE ST
WILLOUGHBY
DE KALB AVE
IRVING AVE
SUYDAM ST
STOCKHOLM ST

c

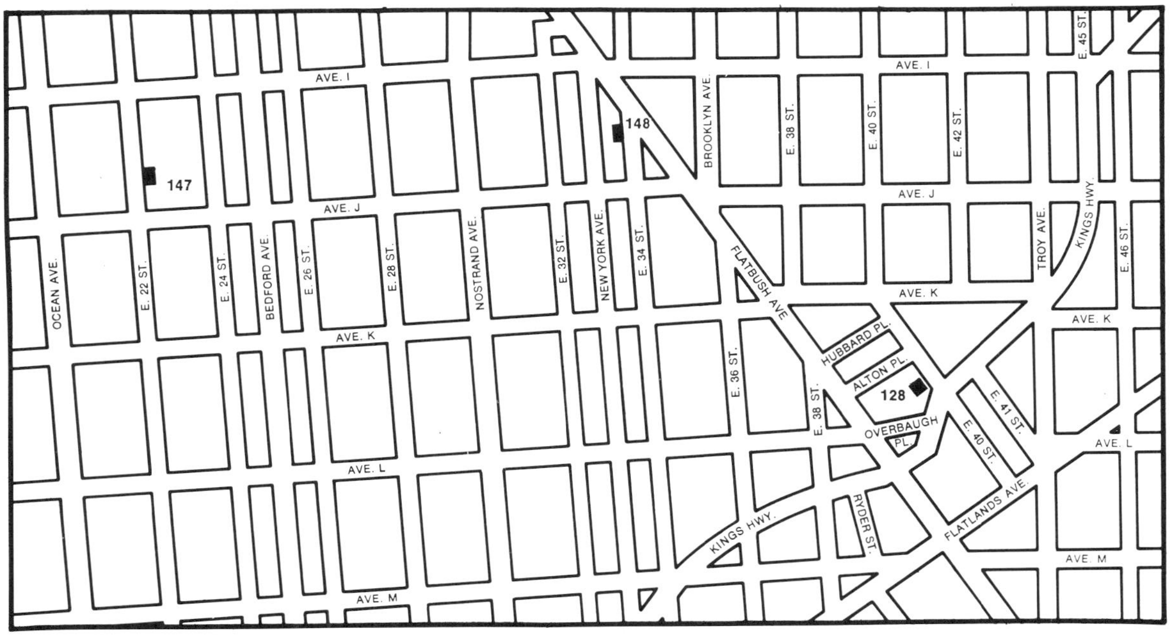

E. 45 ST.
AVE. I
AVE. I
148
BROOKLYN AVE.
E. 38 ST.
E. 40 ST.
E. 42 ST.
147
AVE. J
AVE. J
KINGS HWY.
OCEAN AVE.
E. 22 ST.
E. 24 ST.
BEDFORD AVE.
E. 26 ST.
E. 28 ST.
NOSTRAND AVE.
E. 32 ST.
NEW YORK AVE.
E. 34 ST.
FLATBUSH AVE
TROY AVE.
E. 46 ST.
AVE. K
AVE. K
AVE. K
HUBBARD PL.
E. 36 ST.
ALTON PL.
128
E. 38 ST.
E. 41 ST.
OVERBAUGH PL.
E. 40 ST.
AVE. L
AVE. L
FLATLANDS AVE.
RYDER ST.
KINGS HWY.
AVE. M
AVE. M

128. **Dutch Reformed Church of Flatlands**
Kings Highway and East 40th Street

133. **Kings County Savings Bank**
135 Broadway (Bedford Avenue), Williamsburg

145. **Schenck-Wyckoff House**
1325 Flushing Avenue (Johnson Avenue) [demolished]

147. **Johannes Van Nuyse House**
1041 East 22nd Street (Avenue J), Flatbush

148. **Joost Van Nuyse House**
1128-30 East 34th Street (Flatbush Avenue), Flatbush

150. **Williamsburg Savings Bank**
175 Broadway (Driggs Avenue), Williamsburg

THE BRONX

10
a
YONKERS
155
W. 263 ST.
W. 262 ST.
W. 261 ST.
W. 261 ST.
W. 260 ST.
W. 259 ST.
W. 256 ST.
W. 255 ST.
W. 254 ST.
W. 252 ST.
W. 250 ST.
W. 249 ST.
W. 248 ST.
W. 247 ST.
W. 246 ST.
W. 246 ST.
SIGMA AVE
RIVERDALE AVE
DELAFIELD AVE
LIEBIG AVE
TYNDALL AVE
FIELDSTONE RD
MOSHOLU AVE
FARADAY AVE
NETHERLAND AVE
NORTH RIVER
PALISADE AVE
SYCAMORE AVE
RIVERDALE PARK
163
157
154
159
INDEPENDENCE AVE
BLACKSTONE AVE
ARLINGTON AVE
HENRY HUDSON PKWY WEST
HENRY HUDSON PKWY EAST
HENRY HUDSON PKWY
DELAFIELD AVE
GROSVENOR AVE
FIELDSTONE RD
DOUGLAS AVE
HADLEY AVE
b
E. KINGSBRIDGE RD
VALENTINE AVE
E. 193 ST
E. 194 ST
156
FORDHAM UNIVERSITY
W. 192 ST
JEROME AVE
CRESTON AVE
GRAND CONCOURSE
158
BAINBRIDGE AVE
MARION AVE
DECATUR AVE
WEBSTER AVE
161
W. 190 ST
MORRIS AVE
E. FORDHAM RD
E. FORDHAM RD
E. 189 ST
WASHINGTON AVE
E. 188 ST
E. 188 ST
E. 187 ST
E. 187 ST
VALENTINE AVE
MARION AVE
WEBSTER AVE
BATHGATE AVE
THIRD AVE
E. 184 ST
c
WATERS AVE
HALPERIN AVE
BLONDEL AVE
E. TREMONT AVE
HUTCHINSON RIVER PKWY
WESTCHESTER CREEK
SACKETT AVE
WILLIAMSBRIDGE RD
SILVER ST
LANE AVE
BENSON ST
FRISBY AVE
TRATMAN AVE
WESTCHESTER AVE
COMMERCE AVE
SEABURY AVE
E. TREMONT AVE
ST. PETERS AVE
162
MUNN AVE
SEDDON ST
MACLAY AVE
ST. RAYMOND AVE
ROWLAND ST
HERSCHELL ST
WATERBURY AVE
COMMERCE AVE
CASTLE HILL AVE
ZEREGA AVE
ZEREGA AVE
ELLIS AVE
PURDY ST
d
THIRD AVE
E. 145 ST
E. 143 ST
ST. MARY'S ST
SOUTHERN BLVD
160
E. 141 ST
E. 140 ST
E. 139 ST
E. 138 ST
E. 137 ST
ALEXANDER AVE
WILLIS AVE
BROOK AVE
ST. ANN'S AVE
CYPRESS AVE
JACKSON AVE
BRUCKNER EXPWY
BROWN PL
E. 135 ST
MAJOR DEEGAN EXPWY
BRUCKNER BLVD
E. 133 ST
WILLOW AVE
E. 132 ST

154. Christ Church (Episcopal)
Henry Hudson Parkway East at West 252nd Street, Riverdale

155. Fonthill Castle
Elizabeth Seton Library, College of Mt. St. Vincent-on Hudson

156. Fordham University Church (R.C.)
Rose Hill Campus, near E. Fordham Road and Webster Avenue

157. President John F. Kennedy Residence
5040 Independence Avenue (West 252nd Street), Riverdale

158. Poe Cottage
Grand Concourse and Kingsbridge Road, Fordham

159. Riverdale Presbyterian Church (Episcopal)
4765 Henry Hudson Parkway West (West 247th Street)

160. St. Ann's Church of Morrisania
295 St. Ann's Avenue (East 140th Street)

161. St. James Church (P.E.)
Jerome Avenue and 190th Street, Fordham

162. St. Peter's Church, Westchester (P.E.)
2500 Westchester Avenue (St. Peter's Avenue), Westchester Square

163. Wave Hill
645 West 252nd Street (Independence Avenue), Riverdale

STATEN ISLAND

164. Alice Austen House
2 Hylan Boulevard (Edgewater Street), Rosebank

165. Biddle House
70 Satterlee Street (Shore Road), Tottenville

166. Billopp House (Conference House)
Foot of Hylan Boulevard, Tottenville

167. Cunard Hall
Wagner College, Grymes Hill

168. Original Moravian Church
Moravian Cemetery, near Richmond Road and Otis Avenue, New Dorp

169. Reformed Protestant Dutch Church
54 Richmond Avenue (Richmond Terrace), Port Richmond

170. St. John's Church (Episcopal)
1331 Bay Street (New Lane), Rosebank

171. St. Mary's Episcopal Church
Castleton and Davis Avenues, West New Brighton

172. St. Paul's Memorial Church (P.E.)
225 St. Paul's Avenue (Clinton Street), Stapleton

173. Voorlezer's House
63 Arthur Kill Road (Richmond Road), Richmondtown

a

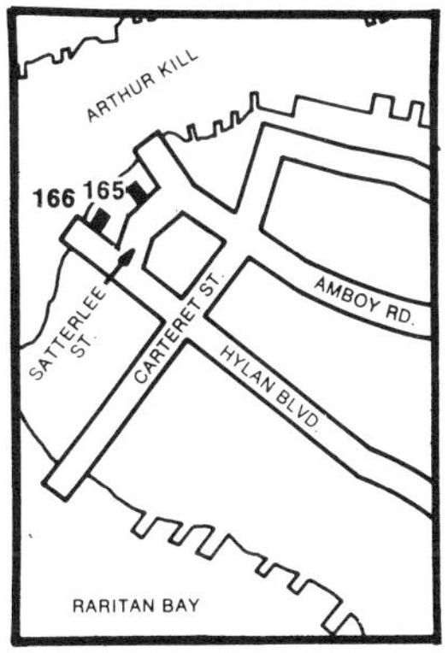

ARTHUR KILL
166
165
SATTERLEE ST.
CARTERET ST.
AMBOY RD.
HYLAN BLVD.
RARITAN BAY

11
b

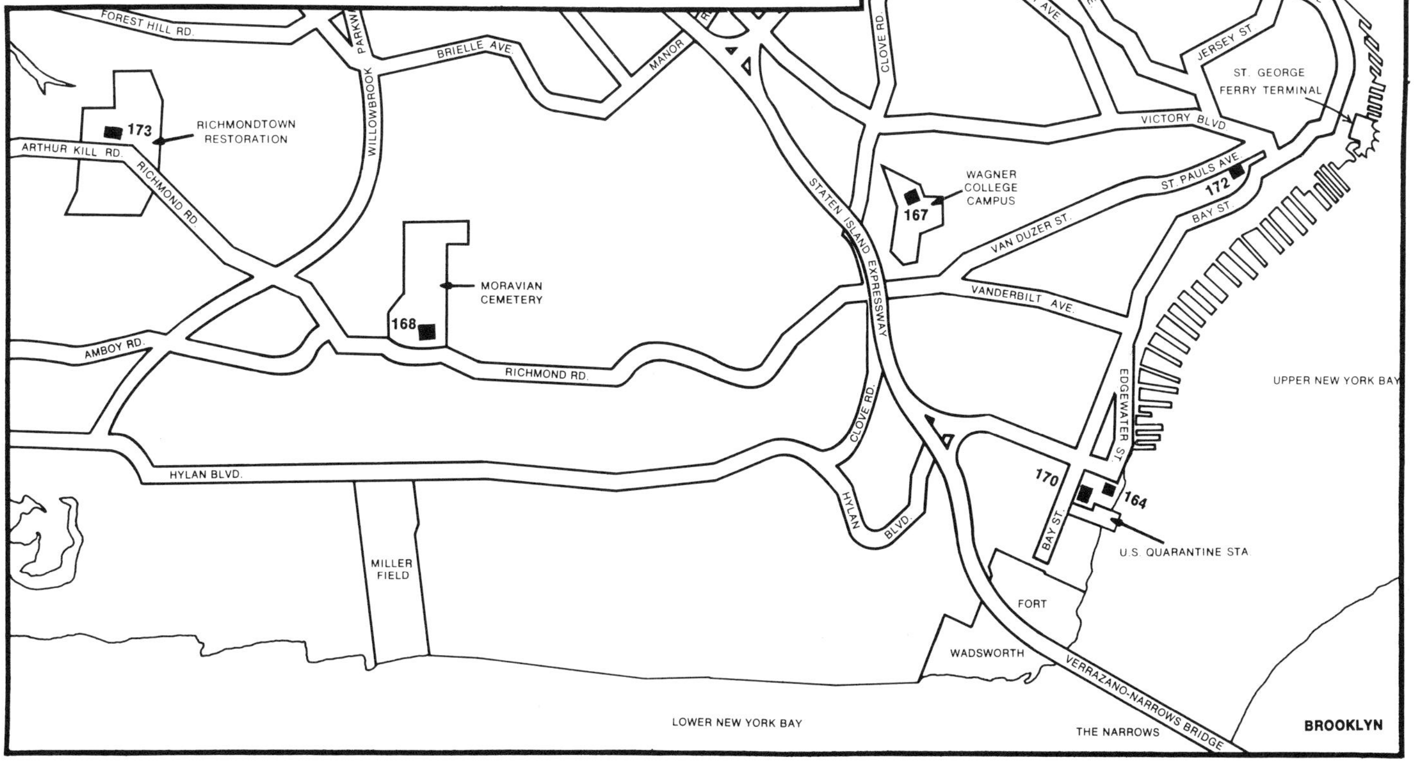

NEW JERSEY
169
RICHMOND AVE
KILL VAN KULL
171
DAVIS AVE.
CASTLETON AVE.
FOREST AVE.
RICHMOND TERRACE
JERSEY ST.
ST. GEORGE
FERRY TERMINAL
VICTORY BLVD.
CLOVE RD.
ST. PAULS AVE.
172
BAY ST.
WAGNER
COLLEGE
CAMPUS
167
VAN DUZER ST.
VANDERBILT AVE.
STATEN ISLAND EXPRESSWAY
EDGEWATER ST.
UPPER NEW YORK BAY
170
164
U.S. QUARANTINE STA.
FORT
WADSWORTH
VERRAZANO-NARROWS BRIDGE
THE NARROWS
BROOKLYN
LOWER NEW YORK BAY
FOREST HILL RD.
BRIELLE AVE.
MANOR
WILLOWBROOK
173
RICHMONDTOWN
RESTORATION
ARTHUR KILL RD.
RICHMOND RD.
MORAVIAN
CEMETERY
168
AMBOY RD.
RICHMOND RD.
HYLAN BLVD.
HYLAN
BLVD.
MILLER
FIELD

QUEENS

12

a

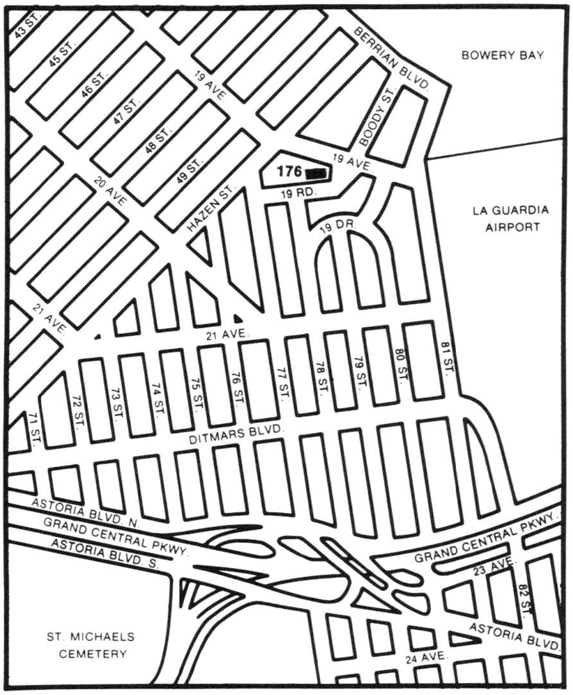

43 ST.
45 ST.
46 ST.
47 ST.
48 ST.
49 ST.
19 AVE.
20 AVE.
21 AVE.
BERRIAN BLVD.
BOWERY BAY
BOODY ST.
176
19 AVE.
19 RD.
19 DR.
HAZEN ST.
LA GUARDIA AIRPORT
21 AVE.
71 ST.
72 ST.
73 ST.
74 ST.
75 ST.
76 ST.
77 ST.
78 ST.
79 ST.
80 ST.
81 ST.
DITMARS BLVD.
ASTORIA BLVD. N.
GRAND CENTRAL PKWY.
ASTORIA BLVD. S.
GRAND CENTRAL PKWY.
23 AVE.
82 ST.
ASTORIA BLVD.
24 AVE.
ST. MICHAELS CEMETERY

b

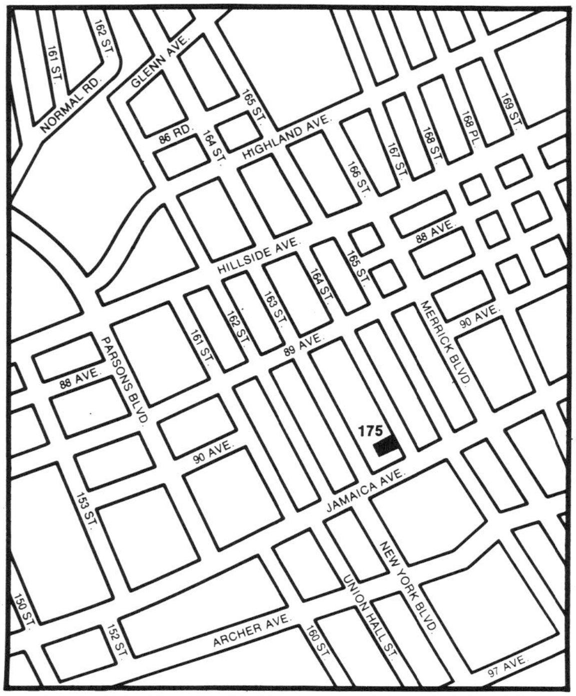

161 ST.
162 ST.
NORMAL RD.
GLENN AVE.
86 RD.
164 ST.
165 ST.
HIGHLAND AVE.
166 ST.
167 ST.
168 ST.
168 PL.
169 ST.
HILLSIDE AVE.
88 AVE.
165 ST.
164 ST.
163 ST.
162 ST.
161 ST.
89 AVE.
MERRICK BLVD.
90 AVE.
88 AVE.
PARSONS BLVD.
175
90 AVE.
153 ST.
JAMAICA AVE.
NEW YORK BLVD.
UNION HALL ST.
150 ST.
152 ST.
ARCHER AVE.
160 ST.
97 AVE.

c

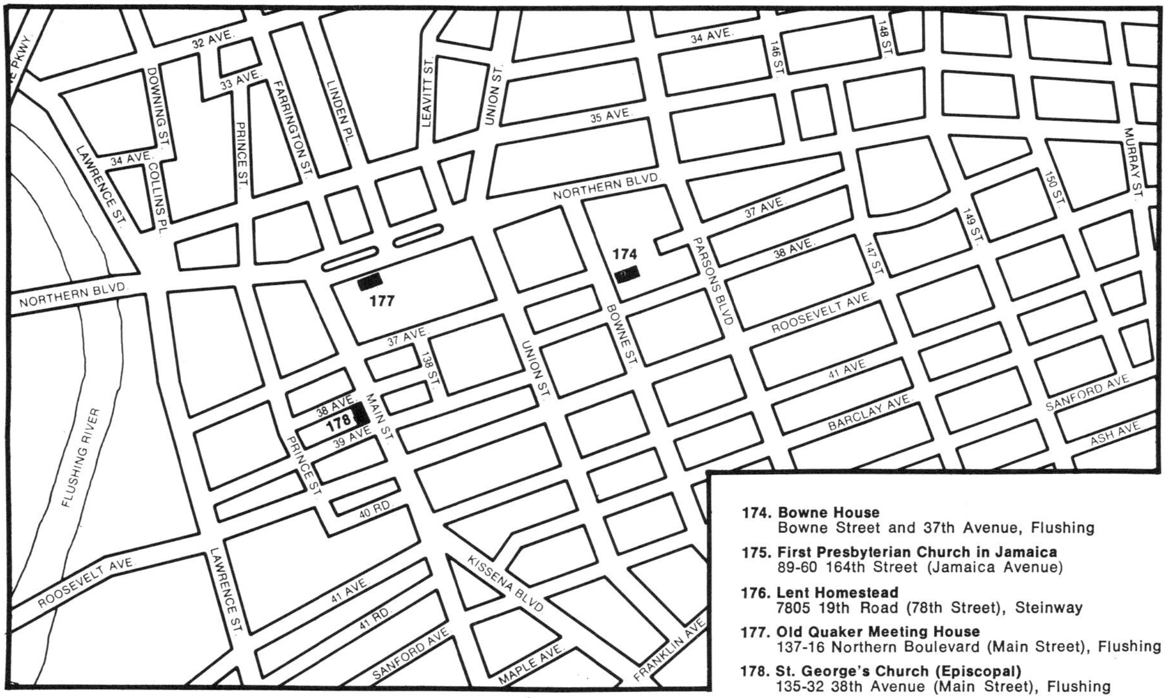

PKWY
32 AVE.
33 AVE.
DOWNING ST.
PRINCE ST.
FARRINGTON ST.
LINDEN PL.
LEAVITT ST.
UNION ST.
34 AVE.
146 ST.
148 ST.
35 AVE.
LAWRENCE ST.
34 AVE.
COLLINS PL.
MURRAY ST.
150 ST.
NORTHERN BLVD.
37 AVE.
149 ST.
174
38 AVE.
147 ST.
PARSONS BLVD.
NORTHERN BLVD.
177
BOWNE ST.
ROOSEVELT AVE.
37 AVE.
138 ST.
UNION ST.
41 AVE.
SANFORD AVE.
38 AVE.
178
MAIN ST.
39 AVE.
BARCLAY AVE.
ASH AVE.
PRINCE ST.
FLUSHING RIVER
40 RD.
KISSENA BLVD.
ROOSEVELT AVE.
LAWRENCE ST.
41 AVE.
41 RD.
SANFORD AVE.
MAPLE AVE.
FRANKLIN AVE.

174. Bowne House
Bowne Street and 37th Avenue, Flushing

175. First Presbyterian Church in Jamaica
89-60 164th Street (Jamaica Avenue)

176. Lent Homestead
7805 19th Road (78th Street), Steinway

177. Old Quaker Meeting House
137-16 Northern Boulevard (Main Street), Flushing

178. St. George's Church (Episcopal)
135-32 38th Avenue (Main Street), Flushing

Appendix E / Picture Credits

Numbers refer to pages

Camera Associates 5, 11, 13, 15, 17, 19, 21 (bottom), 25 (bottom), 27, 29, 31, 33, 35, 37, 39, 41, 43, 45, 47, 49, 53, 55, 57, 59, 61, 63, 67, 69, 71, 73, 75, 79, 81, 83, 85, 89, 91, 93, 97, 101, 103, 107, 109, 111, 113, 115, 117, 119, 121, 123, 125, 127, 129, 131, 133, 139, 141, 143, 145, 147, 149, 153, 157, 159, 163, 165, 167, 169, 171, 173, 175, 177, 179, 181, 183, 185 (bottom), 187, 189, 191 (bottom), 193, 195, 197, 201, 203, 205, 207, 209, 211, 213, 223, 227, 229, 233, 237, 239, 241, 245, 247, 249, 253, 255, 257, 259, 267, 269, 271, 273, 277, 279, 281, 283, 285, 287, 289, 291, 293, 295, 297, 299, 301, 303, 305, 307, 311, 315, 317, 319, 321, 323, 325, 327, 329, 331, 333, 339, 343, 347, 349, 351, 353, 355, 359, 361, 363, 365, 367.

Historic American Building Survey (by Jack E. Boucher) 337.

Constance M. Jacobs 7, 9, 23, 51, 65, 77, 87, 95, 99, 105, 135, 137, 151, 155, 161, 199, 215, 217, 221, 225, 235, 251, 261, 263, 265, 275, 341, 345.

Landmarks Preservation Commission of the City of New York 191 (top), 219.

Museum of the City of New York 21 (top), 25 (middle), 231 (bottom).

New-York Historical Society 25 (top).

New York Public Library 231 (top).

New York World-Telegram & Sun (by Roger Higgins) 309.

Index

Illustrations are designated by numbers in brackets; the other reference numbers are to pages.

Academy of Medicine, *see* New York Academy of Medicine
Adams, Herbert, 122
Adams, James Truslow, 248
Adams, John, 340
Adams, William Newton, 248
Adams House (William Newton Adams), *see* Brooklyn Children's Museum
Adler, Dankmar, 30
Aiken, Martin, 80
Aldrich, C. H., *see* Delano and Aldrich
All Saints Church, *see* St. Augustine's Chapel
Allied Chemical Tower, *see* Times Tower
American Academy of Dramatic Arts, 4 [1], 369
American Fine Arts Society, 6 [2], 369
American Institute of Architects, 104
American Museum of Natural History, 8 [3], 369
American Revolution, *see* Revolutionary War
American Society of Composers, Authors, and Publishers, 128
American-Standard Building, 369, 377
"America's Cup," 158
"Annabel Lee" (Poe), 322
Anne, Queen (England), 330
Apartment house, early type, 310
Appleton, Thomas H., 332
Apthorp Apartments, 369, 377
Arbuckle, Charles, 268
Architectural League of New York, 6
Architecture, styles of, *see* Styles, architectural
Armory, *see* Seventh Regiment Armory
Arsenal, The, 369, 377
"Art Nouveau," 82
Art Students' League, 6
"Ascension, The" (mural by La Farge), 50
Assay Office Building Façade, 10 [4], 369
Association of the Bar of the City of New York, 12 [5], 369
Astor, John Jacob, 14, 68, 196, 228
Astor, Vincent, 196
Astor Library, 14 [6], 369
Audubon House, 16 [7], 369
Austen, Elizabeth Alice, 336
Austen, John H., 336
Austen House (Alice Austen), 336 [164], 369
Babb, Cook, & Willard, 32
Babcock, Charles, 54
Bacon Residence (Secretary of State Robert Bacon), 369, 375
Baker, James Barnes, 144
Bank of the United States, New York Branch of, 10
Bar Association, *see* Association of the Bar of the City of New York
Barnard, George Grey, 66
Barnard Collection of Romanesque and Gothic sculpture, Metropolitan Museum of Art (The Cloisters), 66
Barney, J. Stewart, 58
Barnum, P. T., 152
Baroque style, 48
Bartlett, Paul W., 154
Bath House, East 23rd Street, 80 [39]
Baum, Dwight James, 324
Beaux Arts style, 222
Bedell House (Mott Bedell), 369, 377
Bedford Street, No. 70, 18 [8], 369
Beecher, Henry Ward, 288
Bell, Mifflin E., 296
"Bellevue," *see* Cunard Hall
"Bells, The" (Poe), 322
Beth-el Chapel, Temple Emanu-El, 212
Bethesda Fountain and Terrace, 20 [9], 369
Biddle, Henry H., 338
Biddle House, 338 [165], 369
Billopp, Christopher, 340
Billopp House (Conference House), 340 [166], 369
Bitter, Karl, 172
Bolton, William Jay, 54
Booth, Edwin, 168
Borglum, Gutzon, 82
Borough Hall, Brooklyn, *see* Brooklyn Borough Hall
Bosworth, William Welles, 34
Botanic Garden, Administrative Building (Brooklyn), *see* Brooklyn Botanic Garden
Bowen Residence (Henry C. Bowen), *see* Hicks Street, No. 131
Bowery Savings Bank Building, 22 [10], 369

Bowling Green Fence, 24 [11], 369
Bowne, John, 358
Bowne House, 358 [174], 369
Bowne House Historical Society, 358
Brewster, George T., 338
Brick: Flemish-bond, 302, 308; Harvard, 106
Brides' Altar, *see* Church of the Transfiguration
British Ambassador to United Nations, residence of, 332
British-Hessian forces, 136
Broadway, No. 901, 26 [12], 369
Brokaw, Isaac V., 114
Brokaw Residence (Isaac Vail Brokaw), *see* Institute of Radio Engineers
Brooklyn Borough Hall, 244 [120], 369
Brooklyn Botanic Garden, Administration Building, 246 [121], 369
Brooklyn Children's Museum (former "Spanish Adams House"), 248 [122], 369
Brooklyn City Hall, *see* Brooklyn Borough Hall
Brooklyn Ethical Culture Society (former Henry C. Hulbert Residence), 250 [123], 369
Brooklyn Female Academy site, *see* Packer Collegiate Institute
Brooklyn General Post Office, *see* United States Post Office
Brooklyn Heights, 258, 266, 268, 276, 278, 284, 286, 288, 292, 302, 306, 308, 310
Brooklyn Municipal Building, 252 [124], 369
Brooklyn Museum, 254 [125], 369
Brooklyn Park Headquarters, *see* Litchfield Mansion
Brooklyn Post Office, *see* United States Post Office
Brooklyn Trust Company, *see* Manufacturers Hanover Trust Company
Brown, James Lord, 190
Brownstone, Belleville, 264
Brunner, Arnold W., 80
Bryant Residence (William Cullen Bryant), 28 [13], 370
Burnham, D. H., & Company, 90
Burr, Aaron, 262
Burrows, Lieutenant, 102
Burrows Street, *see* Grove Street
Bush Terminal Building, 370, 377
Butler, Charles, 212

Ca' d'Oro, Venice, 280
Cady, J. C., 8
Cady, J. C., and Company, 8
Canarsie House, 254
Carl Schurz Park, 96
Carnegie, Andrew, 30, 32
Carnegie Foundation, 142
Carnegie Hall, 30 [14], 370
Carnegie House, 32 [15], 370
Carrère, John Merven, *see* Carrère & Hastings
Carrère & Hastings, 160, 172, 240
Cartier Building, 34 [16], 370
Casson, *see* Irving & Casson
Castleton, 352
Cathedral Church of St. John the Divine (Episcopal), 36 [17], 370
Cather Residence (Willa Cather), 370, 375
Central Park, 28, 140, 290; *see also* Arsenal, The; Bethesda Fountain and Terrace
Central Savings Bank, 38 [18], 370
Central Synagogue, 40 [19], 370
Chamber of Commerce Building, *see* New York Chamber of Commerce Building
Chancery Office of the Roman Catholic Archdiocese of New York, *see* Villard Mansion
Chapel of the Beloved Disciple, *see* Church of the Heavenly Rest
Chelsea, 28, 42, 54, 92, 194
Chelsea Hotel, 42 [20]
Chenonceaux, Chateau of (France), 114
Children's Museum, Brooklyn, *see* Brooklyn Children's Museum
Christ Church (Episcopal, Bronx), 314 [154], 370
Christ Church (P. E., Brooklyn), 256 [126], 370
Church, *see* churches by name; *see also* Cathedral Church
Church Missions House, 44 [21], 370
Church of Our Lady, Mediatrix of All Graces, *see* Fordham University Church
Church of Our Lady of the Rosary (R. C.), *see* Watson House
Church of St. Bernard (R. C.), 46 [22], 370
Church of St. Ignatius Loyola (R. C.), 48 [23], 370
Church of St. Paul the Apostle, 370, 377
Church of St. Saviour (Bath, England), 88
Church of the Ascension (Episcopal), 50 [24], 370
Church of the Beloved Disciple, *see* Church of the Heavenly Rest
Church of the Heavenly Rest (P. E.), 52 [25], 370
Church of the Holy Apostles (P. E.), 54 [26], 370
Church of the Holy Communion (Episcopal), 56 [27], 370
Church of the Holy Trinity (Rhinelander Memorial), 58 [28], 370
Church of the Holy Trinity in the Parish of St. James, *see* Church of the Holy Trinity (Rhinelander Memorial)
Church of the Incarnation (P. E.), 60 [29], 370
Church of the People, Methodist and Presbyterian, at Sea and Land, *see* Church of the Sea and Land
Church of the Pilgrims, *see* Our Lady of Lebanon R. C. Church; Plymouth Church of the Pilgrims

Church of the Saviour (First Unitarian Church) 258 [127], 370
Church of the Sea and Land (Presbyterian), 62 [30], 370
Church of the Transfiguration—"Little Church Around the Corner" (P. E.), 64 [31], 370
City Hall, Brooklyn, *see* Brooklyn Borough Hall
"Civic Fame" (statue by Weinman), 138
Civil War, postwar architecture, 26
Clark, Edward, 74
Clark, Colonel Emmons, 208
Classical style, 12, 276; Classic Eclectic, 158, 174; Classic Revival, 108; Corinthian Classical, 100; Roman Classical, 80; *see also* Greek style
Cleveland, President Grover, 144
Clinton, Charles W., 208
Clinton Residence (Vice-President George Clinton), 370, 375
Clock (Villard Mansion), 226
Cloisters, The, 66 [32], 370
Cobble Hill, 256
Coe, Ditmas, 300
Colby Residences (Secretary of State Bainbridge Colby), 370, 375
Colgate, Robert, 324
College of Mount St. Vincent-on Hudson, *see* Fonthill Castle
Collegiate Reformed Protestant Dutch Church, *see* West End Collegiate Church and Collegiate School
Collegiate School, *see* West End Collegiate Church and Collegiate School
Collens, Charles, 66
Colonial style, 360
  Dutch Colonial, 294, 298, 344, 354, 362
    Late Dutch, 272
  Georgian Colonial, 136
Colonnade Row, 68 [33], 370
Colony Club, 4
Columbia Street, *see* Grove Street
Common Council, 24
Community House, Temple Emanu-El, 212
Concert Garden site, *see* New York Life Building
Conference House, *see* Billopp House
Congregation Ahawath Chesed Shaar Hashomayim, *see* Central Synagogue
Congregational Church of the Pilgrims, *see* Our Lady of Lebanon R. C. Church; Plymouth Church of the Pilgrims
Consolidated Edison Building, 370, 377
Constitution (U. S.), 326
Cook, Walter, *see* Babb, Cook, & Willard
Cooper, Peter, 70
Cooper Residence (James Fenimore Cooper), 370, 375
Cooper Union, 70 [34], 370
Cornell, J. B. & J. M., 42
Corrigan, Michael Augustine (Archbishop of New York), 48
County Court House, *see* New York County Court House
Coutan, Jules, 98
Cowes, England, 158
Cozine Street, *see* Grove Street
Cram, Ralph Adams, *see* Cram and Ferguson; Cram, Goodhue, & Ferguson
Cram and Ferguson, 36
Cram, Goodhue, & Ferguson, 166, 198
Cunard, Sir Edward, 342
Cunard Building, 72 [35], 370
Cunard Hall (Wagner College), 342 [167], 370
Cunard Steamship Line, 72, 342

Daily News Building, *see* New York Daily News Building
Dakota Apartments, 74 [36], 370
Daughters of the American Revolution, Fort Greene Chapter, 272
Davies, Arthur B., 42
Davis, Alexander Jackson, 274
Dean, Bashford, 332
Declaration of Independence, 326, 366
Delafield, Joseph, 324
Delano and Aldrich, 16, 124
Delmonico's Hotel site, *see* Cunard Building
De Wolfe, Elsie, 4
Ditmars, Isaac E., *see* Ditmars and Schickel
Ditmars and Schickel, 48
Dodge, William E., Jr., 324
Domestic and Foreign Missionary Society of the Protestant Episcopal Church, 44
Dominicans, 200
Dudley, *see* Wills and Dudley
Duke, Miss Doris, 112
Duke, Mr. & Mrs. James B., 112
Duke Mansion, *see* Institute of Fine Arts
Duplexes, 306
Dutch Colonial style, *see* Colonial style
Dutch Reformed Church of Flatlands, 260 [128], 370
Dyckman, William, 76
Dyckman House, 76 [37], 371

East River Savings Bank, 78 [38], 371
East 72nd Street, *see* Nine East 72nd Street
East 61st and East 62nd Streets between Second and Third Avenues, *see* Treadwell Farm Historic District
East 23rd Street Bath House, *see* Bath House
Eclectic style, 276; Classic Eclectic, 158, 174; Georgian Eclectic, 190; Roman Eclectic Modified, 252
École des Beaux Arts, 204
Eidlitz, Cyrus L. W., 12; *see also* Eidlitz and McKenzie
Eidlitz, Leopold, 330
Eidlitz, Marc, 60; *see also* Eidlitz, Marc & Son

Eidlitz, Marc, & Son, 84, 100, 104, 142, 196
Eidlitz and McKenzie, 216
Eighth Presbyterian Church, *see* St. John's Evangelical Lutheran Church
Elementary school building (oldest in U.S.), *see* Voorlezer's House
Elizabeth, Queen Mother (England), 332
Elizabeth Seton Library, *see* Fonthill Castle
Embury, Philip, 120
Emmanuel Baptist Church, 371, 377
Empire style, *see* Second Empire style
Erasmus Hall, 262 [129], 371
Erasmus Hall High School, *see* Erasmus Hall
Ethical Culture Society, Brooklyn, *see* Brooklyn Ethical Culture Society
"Eureka" (Poe), 322
Evarts Residence (Secretary of State William M. Evarts), 371, 375
Evening Post, 28, 82
Evening Post Building, 82 [40], 371

Farmhouses: Brooklyn, 294; Fordham, 322; Manhattan, 76; Queens, 362
Farragut, Admiral David G., 60
Farrell, James T., 42
Federal Reserve Bank of New York, 84 [41], 371
Federal style, 18, 116, 234, 298, 308; Late, 260; Modified, 184; Simplified, 302
Fence, *see* Bowling Green Fence
Ferguson, F. W., *see* Cram and Ferguson; Cram, Goodhue, & Ferguson
Fernbach, Henry, 40
Fifth Avenue Building, 371, 377
Fire, *see* Great Fire of 1776
First Chinese Presbyterian Church, *see* Church of the Sea and Land
First National City Bank Building, 86 [42], 371
First Presbyterian Church, Greenwich Village, 88 [43], 371
First Presbyterian Church in Jamaica, 360 [175], 371
First Unitarian Church, Brooklyn, *see* Church of the Saviour
Flagg, Ernest, 204
Flaherty, Robert, 42
Flatbush, 260, 262, 298, 300
Flatiron Building, The, 90 [44], 371
Flatlands house, 254
Flatlands Plain, 298
Flemish style, 236; brickwork, 302, 308
Flushing, 358, 364, 366
Fonthill Abbey (England), 316
Fonthill Castle, 316 [155], 371
Fordham, 318, 322, 328
Fordham, manor of, 318, 322, 328
Fordham University Church (R. C.), 318 [156], 371
Forrest, Edwin, 316
Fort Amsterdam, 222
Fort Tryon Park, 66
"Four Periods of Publicity" statues, 82
Francis I style, 6
Franklin, Benjamin, 340
Fraunces Tavern, 144
Freeman, Mr. and Mrs. Edward Woolsey, 332
Freeman, Frank, 268
French, Daniel Chester, 60, 222, 254
Freret, William E., 296
Friends Meeting House, *see* Old Quaker Meeting House
Fuller Building, *see* Flatiron Building

Gardner, Julia, 50
Gary, Judge Elbert H., 16
Geer, Seth, 68
General Theological Seminary, West Building, 92 [45], 371
George III (King of England), 330, 366; statue of, 24
Georgian style, 16, 32, 148, 192; Georgian Colonial, 136; Georgian Eclectic, 190; Georgian 18th century, 190; Georgian Gothic, 62
Gibbs, James, 192
Gibson, Robert W., 34, 44, 236
Gilbert, Cass, 148, 152, 222, 238
Giles, James H., 26
Gillette, Leon N., *see* Walker & Gillette
Gilman, Arthur, 348
Glass façades, 204
Gmelin, Paul, *see* McKenzie, Voorhees, and Gmelin
Goodhue, Bertram G., 200; *see also* Cram, Goodhue, & Ferguson
Gothic style, 36, 40, 52, 94, 166, 194, 198, 238, 316, 318, 326, 330, 348, 366
  early 14th century, 64
  English, 50, 56, 200, 206, 256, 324
  French, 58
  Georgian, 62
  Gothic Revival, 60, 92, 220, 258, 264, 266, 306, 328, 336, 350
    Early Gothic Revival, 282
  Rural Gothic, 314
  Victorian Gothic, 118, 286, 292, 352
Gould family, 170
Government House, 222
Grace Church (P. E.), 94 [46], 371
Gracie, Archibald, 96
Gracie Mansion, 96 [47], 371
Grand Central Terminal, 98 [48], 371
Granite, 138, 278, 316; Maine, 252; New England, 104
Grant, President Ulysses S., 8, 371, 375
Grant Residence (President Ulysses S. Grant), 371, 375
Great Fire of 1776, 220
Greco-Romanesque style, 122

Greek style, 78, 174; Greek Revival, 102, 116, 164, 182, 186, 210, 232, 338, 346; *see also* Classical style; Greco-Romanesque style
Greeley Residence (Horace Greeley), 371, 375
Greenwich Savings Bank, 100 [49], 371
Greenwich Village, 18, 46, 50, 70, 88, 94, 102, 116, 118, 122, 184, 186, 188, 202, 232
Green-Wood Cemetery Gates, 264 [130], 371
Grove Street, Nos. 4-10, 102 [50], 371
Guaranty Trust Company Building, 104 [51], 371
Guthrie, J. Gordon, 52

Hamilton, Alexander, 262
Handel, G. F., 134
Hanover Bank, *see* Manufacturers Hanover Trust Company
Hardenbergh, Henry J., 6, 74, 170
Harlem, 190
Harriman family, 170
Harte Residence (Bret Harte), 371, 376
Hartley, Jonathan Scott, 202
Harvard Club, The, 106 [52], 371
Hastings, Thomas, 72; *see also* Carrère & Hastings
Hayes, President Rutherford B., 8
Hebrew Sheltering and Immigrant Aid Society, *see* Astor Library
Heck, Barbara, 120
Heins, George L., *see* Heins and La Farge
Heins and La Farge, 36
Hendricks, Harmon, 116
Hendricks House, *see* Isaacs-Hendricks House
Henry, O. (William Sydney Porter), 42
Henry Street Settlement, 108 [53], 371
Herbert, Victor, 128
Hicks Street, No. 131 (Henry C. Bowen Residence), 266 [131], 371
Hippodrome (P. T. Barnum's) site, *see* New York Life Building
Hobart, Bishop John Henry, 180
Hogan, J. H., 52
Holy Rood, St. Vincent Ferrer Church, 200
Home Term Court, 371, 376
Hood, Raymond, 150
Hoover Residence (President Herbert Hoover), 110 [54], 371
Hotel Labottière (Bordeaux, France), 112
Hotel Margaret, 268 [132], 371
Howe, Lord (General Sir William Howe, Viscount Howe), 340
Howells, John Mead, 150
Howells Residence (William Dean Howells), 371, 376
Hubert & Pirsson, 42
Hughes, Bishop John, 164
Hughes Residence (Chief Justice Charles Evans Hughes), 371, 376
Hulbert, Henry C., 250
Hulbert Residence (Henry C. Hulbert), *see* Brooklyn Ethical Culture Society
Hunt, Richard Howland, 126
Hunter, Governor Robert, 346
Huxley, Thomas, 332

Independence Hall, Philadelphia, 148
Institute of Fine Arts (former Duke Mansion), 112 [55], 371
Institute of Radio Engineers (former Isaac Vail Brokaw Residence), 114 [56], 371
Inwood, 66, 76
Irving, Washington, 68
Irving & Casson, 198
Isaacs, Joshua, 116
Isaacs-Hendricks House, 116 [57], 371
Italian villa style, 274, 342

Jamaica, 360
James Birthplace (Henry James), 371, 376
Jansen, Aucke, 300
Jay, John, 262
Jefferson Market Courthouse, 118 [58], 372
Jesuits, *see* Society of Jesus
John Street Methodist Church, 120 [59], 372
Judson, Adoniram, 122
Judson, Edward, 122
Judson Memorial Church (Baptist), 122 [60], 372
Jumel, Stephen, 136
Jumel Mansion, *see* Morris-Jumel Mansion

Kennedy, President John Fitzgerald, 320
Kennedy, Joseph B., 226
Kennedy Residence (President John F. Kennedy), 320 [157], 372
Kimball, Francis H., 280
King, D. H., Jr., 190
King, Gamaliel, 244
Kings County Savings Bank, 270 [133], 372
Knickerbocker Club, 124 [61], 372
Kohn, Estelle Rumbold, 82
Kohn, Robert D., 82, 212

Labottière Hotel, *see* Hotel Labottière
La Farge, C. G., *see* Heins and La Farge
La Farge, John, 50, 60, 122
Lafayette, Marquis de, 68
Lafever, Minard, 54, 182, 258, 286
La Grange Terrace, *see* Colonnade Row
Lawrie, Lee, 198, 200
Le Brun & Sons, 134
Lefferts, Lieutenant Peter, 272
Lefferts Homestead, 272 [134], 372
Lenox Library, 14
Lent, Abraham, 362
Lent Homestead, 362 [176], 372
Lewis, Francis, 366
Liberty Pole, 282
Libraries, *see* Association of the Bar of the City of New York; Astor Library; Fonthill Castle; Jefferson Market Courthouse; New York Public Library; Vincent Office Building

Limestone, 148, 212, 278; Indiana limestone, 12, 84, 106, 252
Lincoln, President Abraham, 70, 288
Litchfield, Edwin C., 274
Litchfield Mansion, 274 [135], 372
Littell, E. T., 60
"Little Church Around the Corner," *see* Church of the Transfiguration
Livingston, G., *see* Trowbridge & Livingston
Livingston Residence (Secretary of State Edward Livingston), 372, 376
Lombardy chapel architecture, 246
Long Island, Battle of, 272
Long Island Historical Society, 276 [136], 372
Lord and Taylor Store, *see* Broadway, No. 901
Lotos Club, 126 [62], 372
Louis XIII period (French), 240
Lowell, Guy, 146
Luce, Clarence S., 190
Lüchow, August, 128
Lüchow's Restaurant, 128 [63], 372

MacArthur Residence (General Douglas MacArthur), 130 [64], 372
McBean, Thomas, 192
McCloskey, John Cardinal, 162, 186
McComb, John, 234
MacDougal Street, 232
McKenzie, A., *see* Eidlitz and McKenzie
McKenzie, Voorhees, and Gmelin, 156, 252
McKim, Charles F., *see* McKim, Mead, & White
McKim, Mead, & White, 86, 106, 122, 132, 138, 190, 214, 224, 226, 246, 254
Madison Square Garden site, *see* New York Life Building
Magaw, Robert, 300
Magdalen College, Oxford, 88
Maginnis and Walsh, 174
Mangin, Joseph F., 162
Manufacturers Hanover Trust Company, 278 [137], 372
Manufacturers Trust Company, *see* Manufacturers Hanover Trust Company
Marble, 12, 94, 144; Hauteville, 104; Tennessee, 252; Tuckahoe, 10; Vermont, 148, 252
Margaret Hotel, *see* Hotel Margaret
Marlborough, Duchess of, 132
Mayor of New York, official residence of, *see* Gracie Mansion
Mazzini, Giuseppe, 28
Mead, William R., *see* McKim, Mead, & White
Megapolensis, Rev. Johannes, 260
Meiere, Hildreth, 212
Merchants Exchange Building, *see* First National City Bank Building
Metropolitan Club, 132 [65], 372
Metropolitan Life Tower, 134 [66], 372
Metropolitan Museum of Art, 66; American Wing, 10; The Cloisters, 66
Miller, William Starr, 240
Miller Residence (William Starr Miller), *see* Yivo Institute for Jewish Research
Mission of Our Lady of the Rosary, *see* Watson House
Moffitt, John M., 264
Montauk Club, 280 [138], 372
Montauk Indians, 280
Moore, Clement Clarke, 92, 188, 194
Moorish Revival style, 40
Moorish-Romanesque style, 212
Moravian Cemetery Office, *see* Original Moravian Church
Moravian Church, *see* Original Moravian Church
Moravian Church School, *see* Original Moravian Church
Morgan, J. Pierpont, 132, 158
Morris, Benjamin W., 72
Morris, Gouverneur, I, 326
Morris, Gouverneur, II, 326
Morris, Lewis, 326
Morris, Montrose W., 250
Morris, Roger, 136
Morris, William Lewis, 332
Morrisania, 326
Morris-Jumel Mansion, 136 [67], 372
Morton Residence (Vice-President Levi Parsons Morton), 372, 376
Mosaics, Temple Emanu-El, 212
Mother Seton Shrine, *see* Watson House
Mott, John, 324
Mould, Jacob Wrey, 20
Mount St. Vincent-on Hudson College, *see* Fonthill Castle
Muhlenberg, Dr. William A., 56
Municipal Art Society, 22, 32, 78, 142, 150, 160, 202, 250, 270
Municipal Building, Brooklyn, *see* Brooklyn Municipal Building
Municipal Building, Manhattan, 138 [68], 372
Mural, Church of the Incarnation (La Farge), 60
Museum of the City of New York, 96
Music Hall, *see* Carnegie Hall

Napier Hotel, 38
National Arts Club, 140 [69], 372
National Audubon Society, 16
Neo-classical style, 146, 254
New Amsterdam, 300; *see also* Wall of New Amsterdam
New Dorp, 344
New Netherland, 358
New Utrecht Reformed Church, 282 [139], 372
New York Academy of Medicine, 142 [70], 372
New York Chamber of Commerce Building, 144 [71], 372
New York City Hall, *see* Municipal Building, Manhattan
New York County Court House, 146 [72], 372

New York County Lawyers Association, 148 [73], 372
New York Daily News Building, 150 [74], 372
New York *Evening Post*, see *Evening Post*
New York Life Building, 152 [75], 372
New York Life Insurance Company, 152
New York, New Haven and Hartford Railroad Depot site, *see* New York Life Building
New York Public Library, 14
New York State Regents, 262
New York Stock Exchange, 154 [76], 372
New York Telephone Company Building, 156 [77], 372
New York University Faculty Club, *see* Washington Square North, No. 22; *see also* Institute of Fine Arts
New York Yacht Club, 158 [78], 372
Nine East 72nd Street (former Stillman Residence), 160 [79], 372
Nineteenth Century style (Late), 298; *see also* Gothic, Victorian; Victorian style
Norman style, 316
Norris, A. F., 310

Ochs, Adolph S., 216
Old Assay Office Building Façade, *see* Assay Office Building Façade
Old Quaker Meeting House, 364 [177], 372
Old St. Patrick's Cathedral (R. C.), 162 [80], 372
Old St. Peter's Church (R. C.), 164 [81], 372
Olmsted, Frederick Law, 20, 290
Onderdonk, Bishop Benjamin T., 194
Original Moravian Church, 344 [168], 372
O'Toole, Lawrence (Saint), 48
Our Lady of Lebanon R. C. Church (Maronite Rite), 284 [140], 372

Packer, William S., 286
Packer Collegiate Institute, 286 [141], 373
Paderewski, Ignace, 30
Palazzo della Cancelleria, Rome, 226
Palladian style, 214
Park Avenue Christian Church (Disciples of Christ), 166 [82], 373
Pennell, Joseph, 268
Perkins, George W., 332
Peterson, Frederick A., 70
Phillip, Hardie, 52
Pirsson, James W., *see* Hubert & Pirsson
Plant, Morton F., 34
Players, The, 168 [83], 373
Plaza Hotel, 170 [84], 373
Plymouth Church of the Pilgrims (Congregational), 284, 288 [142], 373
Plymouth Rock fragment, 288
Poe, Edgar Allan, 322
Poe, Virginia, 322
Poe Cottage, 322 [158], 373
Port Richmond, 346
Post, George B., 154, 228, 276, 304
Post Office, Brooklyn, *see* United States Post Office
Potter, Edward Tuckerman, 352
Potter, Bishop Horatio, 348, 352
Presbyterian Church of the Sea and Land, *see* Church of the Sea and Land
Price, Bruce, 190
Prospect Park, 274; Prospect Park East, 246; Soldiers and Sailors Memorial Arch, 290 [143], 373
Provincial Assembly of 1693, 330
Public Baths, *see* Bath House
Pulitzer, Joseph, 172
Pulitzer Memorial Fountain, 172 [85], 373

Quaker Meeting House, *see* Old Quaker Meeting House
Queen Anne style, 310

Randolph, Ann Carey, 326
Random House, 226
Rapelye family, 362
Reed & Stem, 98
Reformed Protestant Dutch Church, 346 [169], 373
Regis High School, 174 [86], 373
Reid, Whitelaw, 226
Religious liberty, shrine to, 358
Renaissance style, 174, 250, 304
  Florentine, 84
  French, 6, 114, 126, 144, 170
    Late French, 160
  German (Late), 128
  Italian, 14, 30, 38, 72, 132, 134, 190
    Modified Italian, 246, 278
    Palace architecture, 224
Renwick, James, 324
Renwick, James, Jr., 94, 292
Residence, British Ambassador to United Nations, 332
Revolutionary War, 76, 294, 340, 346, 364
Rhinelander, Serena, 58
Rhinelander Memorial Church, *see* Church of the Holy Trinity
Ricci and Zari, 22
Richmondtown, 354
"Ridgewood," *see* Litchfield Mansion
Riker, Abraham, 362
Riverdale, 314, 320, 324, 332
Riverdale Country School, 320
Riverdale Presbyterian Church, 324 [159], 373
Rockefeller, John D., Jr., 66
Rogers, Isaiah, 86, 164
Rogers, Mrs. John, 56
Roman style, 72, 104, 174; Roman Classical, 80; Roman Eclectic Modified, 252
Romanesque style, 22, 36, 44, 142, 268, 276; Early Romanesque Revival, 284; Romanesque Revival, 228, 296; *see also* Greco-Romanesque; Moorish-Romanesque

Roome, John P., 18
Roosevelt, Elbert, 116
Roosevelt, President Theodore, 144, 178, 332
Roosevelt Birthplace (President Theodore Roosevelt), 178 [88], 373
Roosevelt Residence (President Franklin D. Roosevelt), 176 [87], 373
Roosevelt Residence (President Theodore Roosevelt), 373, 376
Root Residence (Secretary of State Elihu Root), 373, 376
Rorimer, James J., 66
Rose & Stone, 114
Rosebank, 336, 348
"Row, The," *see* Washington Square North, No. 22
Row house architecture, 266, 308
Rustdorp, 360
Rutgers, Colonel Henry, 62
Rutledge, Edward, 340

Saeltzer, Alexander, 14
St. Andrew's Church, 348
St. Ann's Church (Episcopal, Brooklyn), 292 [144], 373
St. Ann's Church of Morrisania (Episcopal), 326 [160], 373
St. Augustine's Chapel (Episcopal), 180 [89], 373
Sainte Chapelle (Paris), 166
St. Faith Window, *see* Church of the Transfiguration
Saint-Gaudens, Augustus, 122, 226
St. George's Church (Episcopal), 366 [178], 373
St. James Church (P. E., Bronx), 328 [161], 373
St. James' Church, Manhattan, *see* Church of the Holy Trinity (Rhinelander Memorial)
St. James' Church (R. C.), 182 [90], 373
St. John's Church (Episcopal), 348 [170], 373
St. John the Divine, *see* Cathedral Church of St. John the Divine
St. John's Evangelical Lutheran Church, 184 [91], 373
St. Joseph's Church (R. C.), 186 [92], 373
St. Luke's Chapel (Episcopal), 188 [93], 373
St. Luke's Church, 188
St. Luke's Hospital, 56
St. Martin-in-the-Fields (London), 192
St. Mary's Chapel, *see* Church of the Transfiguration
St. Mary's Episcopal Church, 350 [171], 373
St. Matthew's Protestant Episcopal Church, *see* St. John's Evangelical Lutheran Church
St. Nicholas Historic District, 190 [94], 373
St. Patrick's Cathedral, 318, 324; *see also* Old St. Patrick's Cathedral
St. Paul's Chapel (Episcopal), 192 [95], 373
St. Paul's Church, Castleton, *see* St. Paul's Memorial Church
St. Paul's Memorial Church (P. E.), 352 [172], 373
St. Peter's Church (R. C.), *see* Old St. Peter's Church
St. Peter's Church, Westchester (P. E.), 330 [162], 373
St. Peter's Episcopal Church, Chelsea, 194 [96], 373
St. Regis Hotel, 196 [97], 373
St. Thomas Church (P. E.), 198 [98], 373
St. Vincent de Paul, Sisters of Charity of, 316
St. Vincent Ferrer Church (R. C.), 200 [99], 373
Salmagundi Club, 202 [100], 373
Sandstone, Ohio, 84
Sargent, Franklin Haven, 4
Sawyer, Philip, *see* York and Sawyer
Schenck, Jan Martense, 254
Schenck, Nicholas, 254
Schenck, Peter, 294
Schenck-Wyckoff House, 294 [145], 373
Schickel, *see* Ditmars and Schickel
Schieffelin, William Jay, 126
Schiff, Jacob H., 108
School of Education, Fordham University, *see* Vincent Office Building
Schurz Park, *see* Carl Schurz Park
Scribner Building, 204 [101], 374
Second Empire style, 26
Serbian Cathedral Church of St. Sava (Orthodox), 206 [102], 374
Seton Library, *see* Fonthill Castle
Seton Shrine, *see* Watson House
Seventh Regiment Armory, 208 [103], 374
Shrine of Blessed Elizabeth Seton, *see* Watson House
Singer Building, 204
Singer Sewing Machine Company, 74
Sisters of Charity of St. Vincent de Paul, 316
Sloan, John, 42
Sloane Residence (Henry T. Sloane), *see* Nine East 72nd Street
Smith, Governor Alfred E., 182
Smith, James W., 194
Smith, Lillian, 268
Smith, Thomas L., 316
Society of American Artists, The, 6
Society of Architectural Historians, 22, 32, 142, 150, 160, 202, 250
Society of Friends, *see* Old Quaker Meeting House
Society of Jesus, 48, 174, 318
Soldiers and Sailors Memorial Arch, *see* Prospect Park
South Reformed Church, *see* Park Avenue Christian Church
"Spanish Adams House," *see* Brooklyn Children's Museum
Spellman, Francis Cardinal, 318
Spencer, Herbert, 332
Spring Street Presbyterian Church, 210 [104], 374

Stables: post-Civil War, 308; Tiffany and Company, 214
Stapleton, 352
Staten Island Historical Society, 336, 354
Stebbins, Emma, 20
Stein, Clarence S., 212
Steinway, 362
Stem, Allen H., *see* Reed & Stem
Stent, Thomas, 14
Stevens House, 72
Stillman Residence (James Stillman), *see* Nine East 72nd Street
Stimson Residence (Secretary of State Henry Lewis Stimson), 374, 376
Stone, *see* Rose & Stone
Stone (material), 206, 350; Dorchester stone, 270; tooled stone, 302
Stone Residence (Chief Justice Harlan Fiske Stone), 374, 377
Stoothoff, Wilhemus, 300
Straight Residence (Willard Straight), *see* Audubon House
Styles, architectural: *see* "Art Nouveau"; Baroque; Beaux Arts; Classical; Colonial; Eclectic; Federal; Georgian; Gothic; Greco-Romanesque; Greek; Italian Villa; Lombardy chapel; Louis XIII period; Moorish-Romanesque; Neo-classical; Nineteenth Century (Late); Norman; Palladian; Queen Anne; Renaissance; Roman; Romanesque; Row house; Second Empire; Tudor; Tuscan; Victorian

Tchaikovsky, Peter, 30
Temple Emanu-El (Reform), 212 [105], 374
Thackeray, William M., 332
Thomas, Dylan, 42
Thomas, Griffith, 14
Thompson, Martin E., 10
Thorne, Stephen, Jr., 218
Tiffany, Louis C., 60, 208, 256, 258
Tiffany and Company Stables, 214 [106], 374
Tilden, Samuel J., 140
Tilden Trust, 14
Times Tower (rebuilt as Allied Chemical Tower), 216 [107], 374
Tompkins Residence (Vice-President Daniel D. Tompkins), 374, 376
Tontine Coffee House, 218
Toscanini, Arturo, 332
Tottenville, 338, 340
Treadwell, Adam, 218
Treadwell Farm Historic District, 218 [108], 374
Trinity Chapel, *see* St. Augustine's Chapel; Serbian Cathedral Church of St. Sava
Trinity Church (Episcopal), 156, 180, 220 [109], 374; parish of, 188, 206
Trowbridge & Livingston, 196
Trumbauer, Horace, 112
Tudor arched doorway style, 266
Tuscan style, 54
Tuthill, William Burnet, 30
Twain, Mark, 332
"'Twas the night before Christmas," see *Visit from St. Nicholas, A*
Tyler, President John, 50
Tyndall, John, 332

"Ulalume" (Poe), 322
Undset, Sigrid, 268
United Nations, residence of British Ambassador to, 332
United States Custom House, 222 [110], 374; *see also* First National City Bank Building
United States Post Office (Brooklyn G.P.O.), 296 [146], 374
University Club, 224 [111], 374
University Place, 232
Upjohn, Richard, 50, 56, 206, 220, 256, 284
Upjohn, Richard M., 264
Upjohn, Richard, and Company, 54, 314

Vanderbilt, Commodore Cornelius, 98, 348
Vanderbilt, Mrs. Cornelius, 240
Vanderbilt family, 170
Vanderbilt home (Mrs. Cornelius Vanderbilt), *see* Yivo Institute for Jewish Research
Van Nuyse, Johannes, 298
Van Nuyse, Joost, 300
Van Nuyse House (Johannes Van Nuyse), 298 [147], 374
Van Nuyse House (Joost Van Nuyse), 300 [148], 374
Van Zandt, Peter, 218
Vaux, Calvert, 20, 140, 290; *see also* Vaux & Withers
Vaux & Withers, 118
Venice, 280
Victorian style, 270; *see also* Gothic, Victorian; Nineteenth Century style
Villard, Henry, 226
Villard Mansion (Henry Villard), 226 [112], 374
Vincent de Paul, Sisters of Charity of St., 316
Vincent Office Building (later, School of Education, Fordham University), 228 [113], 374
Visit from St. Nicholas, A (Moore), 194
Voorhees, Stephen F., *see* McKenzie, Voorhees, and Gmelin
Voorlezer's House, 354 [173], 374

Wagner College, *see* Cunard Hall
Wailes, William, 314
Wald, Lillian D., 108
Waldorf Towers, 110, 130
Walker, Ralph, 156
Walker & Gillette, 78
Wall of New Amsterdam (site), 230 [114], 374
Wall Street: Bank of the United States, 10; *see also* First National City Bank Building;

New York Stock Exchange; Trinity Church; Wall of New Amsterdam
Walsh, Timothy F., *see* Maginnis and Walsh
War of 1812, 102
Ward, Albert, 352
Ward, J. Q. A., 154
Warren & Wetmore, 98, 158
Washington, President George, 136, 192
Washington Square North, No. 22, 232 [115], 374
Watson House (now Church of Our Lady of the Rosary [R. C.]), 234 [116], 374
Wave Hill, 332 [163], 374
Weinman, Adolph Alexander, 138
Wells, Joseph C., 88, 288
Wesley Chapel, 59
West End Collegiate Church and Collegiate School (Reformed Protestant Dutch), 236 [117], 374
West New Brighton, 350
West 138th and West 139th Streets between Seventh and Eighth Avenues, *see* St. Nicholas Historic District
Westchester, 330
Wetmore, Charles D., *see* Warren & Wetmore
Wheeler, John, 322
White, Robert, 302
White, Stanford, 4, 50, 152, 168, 226; *see also* McKim, Mead, & White
White House (Robert White), 302 [149], 374
Whitefriars of London, 198
Willard, *see* Babb, Cook, & Willard
Willcox, William H., 270
William III (King of England), 220
Williams, Mrs. Harrison, 16
Williamsburg (Brooklyn), 270, 304
Williamsburg Savings Bank, 304 [150], 374
Willow Place, Nos. 2-8, 306 [151], 374
Willow Street, Nos. 155-157-159, 308 [152], 374
Willows, The, 310 [153], 374
Wills, C. T., 214
Wills and Dudley, 350, 366
Withers, *see* Vaux & Withers
Wolfe, Thomas, 42, 374, 377
Wolfe Residence (Thomas Wolfe), 374, 377
Women's Court, *see* Jefferson Market Courthouse
Woolworth, Frank W., 238
Woolworth Building, 238 [118], 374
Wyckoff, Nicholas, 294
Wyckoff House, *see* Schenck-Wyckoff House

Yellin, Samuel, 84
Yivo Institute for Jewish Research (former William Starr Miller Residence), 240 [119], 374
York, Edward P., *see* York and Sawyer
York and Sawyer, 22, 38, 84, 100, 104, 142, 278

Zari, *see* Ricci and Zari

The Heritage of New York
is set in Linofilm by Wrightson Typographers
and printed by Halliday Lithograph Corporation
on Mohawk Superfine paper.
Editing by Harry George Fletcher III.
Production by Burton L. Stratton.
Design by Gretchen Rosengren.
Cartography by Bli Graphics Incorporated.
Index by Lisa McGaw.

Fordham University Press, New York